Steven Holzner

MW00837879

XPath

Navigating XML with XPath 1.0 and 2.0

KICK START

800 East 96th Street, Indianapolis, Indiana 46240

XPath Kick Start

International Standard Book Number: 0-672-32411-3

Library of Congress Catalog Card Number: 2002100933

Printed in the United States of America

First Printing: December 2003

06   05   04   03   4   3   2   1

Trademarks

All terms mentioned in this book that are known to be trademarks or service marks have been appropriately capitalized. Sams Publishing cannot attest to the accuracy of this information. Use of a term in this book should not be regarded as affecting the validity of any trademark or service mark.

Warning and Disclaimer

Every effort has been made to make this book as complete and as accurate as possible, but no warranty or fitness is implied. The information provided is on an "as is" basis. The author and the publisher shall have neither liability nor responsibility to any person or entity with respect to any loss or damages arising from the information contained in this book.

Bulk Sales

Sams Publishing offers excellent discounts on this book when ordered in quantity for bulk purchases or special sales. For more information, please contact

> **U.S. Corporate and Government Sales**
> 1-800-382-3419
> corpsales@pearsontechgroup.com

For sales outside of the U.S., please contact:

> **International Sales**
> 1-317-428-3341
> international@pearsontechgroup.com

Associate Publisher
Michael Stephens

Acquisitions Editor
Todd Green

Development Editor
Songlin Qiu

Managing Editor
Charlotte Clapp

Project Editor
Elizabeth Finney

Copy Editor
Margaret Berson

Indexer
Ken Johnson

Proofreader
Linda Seifert

Expert Reviewers
Mary Fernandez
Ashok Malhotra
Jim Melton

Technical Editor
Alaric B. Snell

Publishing Coordinator
Cindy Teeters

Multimedia Developer
Dan Scherf

Interior Designer
Gary Adair

Cover Designer
Gary Adair

Page Layout
Kelly Maish

Contents at a Glance

Table of Contents

About the Author

Steven Holzner has been writing about XML topics like XPath as long as XML has been around. He's written several XML bestsellers, and his books have been translated into 16 languages around the world. He's been on the faculty of both Cornell University and MIT, and teaches corporate programming classes around the country. Dr. Holzner has written over 80 computer books and has been a contributing editor of *PC Magazine*.

Dedication

To Nancy

Acknowledgments

Thanks very much to my sweetie, Nancy, who put up with the long hours involved in writing this book. Thank you, honey!

Thanks to Alaric Snell, Mary Fernandez, Ashok Malhotra, and Jim Melton, for making the time to review the manuscript.

And thanks to everyone at Sams: Todd Green, Songlin Qiu, Elizabeth Finney, Margaret Berson, and all the other editors who worked on this book.

We Want to Hear from You!

As the reader of this book, *you* are our most important critic and commentator. We value your opinion and want to know what we're doing right, what we could do better, what areas you'd like to see us publish in, and any other words of wisdom you're willing to pass our way.

As an associate publisher for Sams Publishing, I welcome your comments. You can email or write me directly to let me know what you did or didn't like about this book—as well as what we can do to make our books better.

Please note that I cannot help you with technical problems related to the topic of this book. We do have a User Services group, however, where I will forward specific technical questions related to the book.

When you write, please be sure to include this book's title and author as well as your name, email address, and phone number. I will carefully review your comments and share them with the author and editors who worked on the book.

Email: feedback@samspublishing.com

Mail: Michael Stephens
         Associate Publisher
         Sams Publishing
         800 East 96th Street
         Indianapolis, IN 46240 USA

For more information about this book or another Sams Publishing title, visit our Web site at www.samspublishing.com. Type the ISBN (excluding hyphens) or the title of a book in the Search field to find the page you're looking for.

Foreword

XPath 1.0 is the World Wide Web Consortium (W3C) recommended language for accessing information in XML documents. XPath provides the core functionality necessary to access XML documents: path navigation of an XML document to identify XML values of interest; selection of XML values that satisfy predicates; and extraction of the selected XML values. Given the breadth of these requirements, it is surprising that developers of XML applications do not have numerous languages to choose from. Luckily, XPath 1.0 meets all these requirements with a concise, intuitive syntax that makes it easy to use and to incorporate into other XML technologies. XPath 1.0 is most commonly used as an embedded language in XSLT 1.0, the extensible stylesheet language used to transform XML into HTML, and it is also used in XML Schema 1.0, XLink, and XPointer.

In *XPath Kick Start*, Steven Holzner provides a thorough introduction to XPath 1.0 and its many uses in other XML technologies. The first five chapters flow from a gentle introduction for readers entirely new to XML and XPath to a hands-on guide to using XPath 1.0 in XSLT 1.0. By the end of Chapter 5, the reader will be able to write non-trivial XPath expressions and understand how to apply them effectively to write useful XSLT stylesheets.

In Chapters 6 through 8, Steven introduces XPath 2.0, which at the time of this writing, is a W3C Last Call Working Draft—just two short steps from Recommendation status. For current XPath 1.0 users, the most significant addition in XPath 2.0 is support for XML Schema. XPath 2.0 recognizes and respects the strong type information of schema-validated documents—for example, XPath 2.0 can distinguish dates from inventory numbers from currency values—but preserves much of XPath 1.0's flexible support for schema-less, well-formed documents. Like XPath 1.0, XPath 2.0 is already a significant part of other XML technologies. XQuery 1.0, the W3C query language for XML that is also a Last Call Working Draft, contains all of XPath 2.0 as a proper sub-language. XPath 2.0 is such a large part of XQuery 1.0 that by the end of *XPath Kick Start*, the reader will have learned yet another important XML technology.

Given XPath's already significant and growing impact in numerous XML technologies, getting a kick start on XPath is a valuable investment for any XML-application developer.

Mary Fernandez
Principal Technical Staff Member
AT&T Labs Research

Co-editor of the W3C working drafts: XQuery 1.0 and XPath 2.0 Data Model, XPath 2.0, XQuery 1.0, and the XQuery 1.0 Formal Semantics

Introduction

Welcome to XPath, the XML-related specification that lets you locate data in XML documents. XPath is becoming more and more important as XML develops, and there's more need to work with the data in XML documents in detailed ways.

In this book, we're going to examine both XPath 1.0 and 2.0 to see what makes them tick, and we're going to emphasize seeing everything at work in dozens of examples.

What's in This Book?

This book is intended to cover all of XPath 1.0 and the current working draft of XPath 2.0. XPath 1.0 is an established recommendation from the World Wide Web Consortium (W3C), and as of this writing, XPath 2.0 is in W3C working draft form. We're going to work from the most basic to the fairly advanced in both these specifications.

The first half of this book is dedicated to XPath 1.0, and the second to XPath 2.0. You won't need any programming skills to work with XPath in this book—you will, however, need a basic knowledge of HTML and XML.

Here's an overview of some of the topics we'll see in this book:

- ▶ How XPath fits in with XML
- ▶ The XPath 1.0 and 2.0 syntax
- ▶ Using XPath and XSLT to transform XML
- ▶ Using XPath in XSLT match patterns
- ▶ XML Schemas and the XML Information Set
- ▶ Nodes
- ▶ Expressions
- ▶ Literals
- ▶ Variables
- ▶ Parenthesized expressions
- ▶ Function calls
- ▶ Comments

- ▶ Paths
- ▶ Axes
- ▶ Axis steps
- ▶ Node tests
- ▶ General steps
- ▶ Step qualifiers
- ▶ Predicates
- ▶ Unabbreviated and abbreviated XPath syntax
- ▶ Handling node-sets in code
- ▶ XPath operators
- ▶ Node-set functions
- ▶ String functions
- ▶ Boolean functions
- ▶ Number functions
- ▶ Using XLink and XPointer
- ▶ Creating simple and complex links
- ▶ Using XPath inside XQuery
- ▶ Differences between XPath 2.0 and XPath 1.0
- ▶ Sequences
- ▶ Working with data types
- ▶ Logical expressions
- ▶ For expressions
- ▶ Conditional expressions
- ▶ Quantified expressions
- ▶ Constructors, functions, and operators on numbers
- ▶ Constructors
- ▶ The many new XPath 2.0 functions

As you can see, we've got a great deal of XPath coverage planned for this book—both XPath 1.0 and 2.0.

Who This Book Is For

This book is for anyone who wants to learn XPath and how it's used today. We'll assume you've had experience with XML and HTML, but that's all we'll assume. We will be using the (free and downloadable) Java language when we discuss XPath 2.0 in order to run the (also free and downloadable) Saxon processor (the only one that handles XPath 2.0 at this point), but you'll get all the details on how to get that working.

We're going to be as platform-independent as we can be in this book. XPath is not the province of any one particular operating system, so we're not going to lean one way or the other on that issue. On the other hand, it's a fact of life that a great deal of XML-oriented software these days is targeted at Windows. And among the standard browsers, the Internet Explorer has many times more XPath 1.0 support than any other browser does. This book doesn't have any special pro- or anti-Microsoft bias, but to cover what's available for XPath these days, we're going to find ourselves in Microsoft territory sometimes; there's no getting around it.

Conventions Used in This Book

This book uses some conventions that you should know about, for instance:

▶ When we've added some new lines of XPath code and are discussing it, it'll appear shaded, and when there's more code to come, you'll see three vertical dots. Here's what that looks like:

```
<?xml version="1.0" encoding="UTF-8"?>
<xsl:stylesheet version="1.0" xmlns:xsl="http://www.w3.org/1999/XSL/Transform">

    <xsl:template match="planets">
        <HTML>
            <xsl:apply-templates/>
        </HTML>
    </xsl:template>
        .
        .
        .
```

▶ You'll see notes and tips throughout the book, which are meant to give you something more, a little more insight or a pointer to some new technique.

▶ You'll see special "Shop Talk" sections designed to bring you behind-the-scenes discussions of what's going on in XPath.

▶ Program code appears in a special `monospace` font.

▶ New terms appear in *italic*.

Source Code

The associated code files described in this book are available on the Sams Web site at `http://www.samspublishing.com`. Enter this book's ISBN (without the hyphens) in the Search box and click Search. When the book's title is displayed, click the title to go to a page where you can download the code.

Essential XPath

Why XPath?

The main purpose of XPath is to make it easy to work with the data in an XML document. XPath lets you address specific parts of XML documents.

Let's begin with an example to demonstrate the reason to use XPath. Say, for example, that you have an XML document, ch01_01.xml, that stores information about various planets in three <planet> elements, as you see in Listing 1.1.

LISTING 1.1   A Sample XML Document (ch01_01.xml)

```xml
<?xml version="1.0" encoding="UTF-8"?>
<?xml-stylesheet type="text/xsl" href="ch01_02.xsl"?>
<planets>

    <planet>
        <name>Mercury</name>
        <mass units="(Earth = 1)">.0553</mass>
        <day units="days">58.65</day>
        <radius units="miles">1516</radius>
        <density units="(Earth = 1)">.983</density>
        <distance units="million miles">43.4</distance><!--At perihelion-->
    </planet>

    <planet>
        <name>Venus</name>
        <mass units="(Earth = 1)">.815</mass>
        <day units="days">116.75</day>
        <radius units="miles">3716</radius>
        <density units="(Earth = 1)">.943</density>
        <distance units="million miles">66.8</distance><!--At perihelion-->
    </planet>

    <planet>
        <name>Earth</name>
        <mass units="(Earth = 1)">1</mass>
        <day units="days">1</day>
        <radius units="miles">2107</radius>
        <density units="(Earth = 1)">1</density>
        <distance units="million miles">128.4</distance><!--At perihelion-->
    </planet>

</planets>
```

Now say that you want to extract the names of the three planets here—Mercury, Venus, and Earth—from this XML document. Each of these names is buried deep in the document, stored as text in the <name> elements. How can you access them?

This is where XPath comes in. To do what it does, XPath uses a non-XML syntax that the creators of XPath, the World Wide Web Consortium (W3C), call "compact." As we'll see, if you don't know XPath, that syntax can be more than compact—it can be impenetrable. But when you know XPath, you'll be able to access any part of any XML document.

XPath doesn't work by itself—it was meant to be embedded in other languages and applications. XPath was originally developed for use with Extensible Stylesheet Language Transformations (XSLT), and in fact, XSLT can do the work we want—recovering the data we're after—using XPath. XPath points out the data to use, and XSLT actually grabs and uses that data, so they're natural to use together.

Because XPath is used so often with XSLT, we'll get an introduction to XSLT later in this chapter, and we'll see a more in-depth treatment of XSLT with XPath in Chapter 5. For now, what's important to know is that the way you select the data you want in an XML document is by using an XPath *expression*, and that you can put such expressions to work in XSLT *stylesheets*. Using an XSLT processor, you can apply XSLT stylesheets to XML documents and so access the data you want.

To get to the data we want in ch01_01.xml, we'll start by accessing the <planets> element in the XSLT stylesheet, matching that element with the XPath expression planets. Then we'll match each <planet> element inside the <planets> element with the XPath expression planet, and finally, we'll extract the name of each planet from each <planet> element's <name> element, using the XPath expression name. You can see what it looks like in the XSLT stylesheet in Listing 1.2 (don't worry about the XSLT details at this point; we'll see how to construct XSLT stylesheets like this one later in the chapter and in depth in Chapter 5) .

LISTING 1.2   A Sample XSLT Document (ch01_02.xsl)

```
<?xml version="1.0" encoding="UTF-8"?>
<xsl:stylesheet version="1.0" xmlns:xsl="http://www.w3.org/1999/XSL/Transform">

    <xsl:template match="planets">
        <HTML>
            <xsl:apply-templates/>
        </HTML>
    </xsl:template>

    <xsl:template match="planet">
        <P>
            <xsl:value-of select="name"/>
        </P>
    </xsl:template>

</xsl:stylesheet>
```

Open this example—that is, navigate to ch01_01.xml—in Microsoft Internet Explorer to see it at work. You can see the results in Figure 1.1.

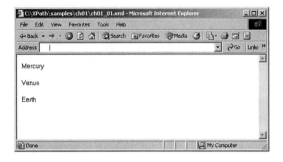

FIGURE 1.1 Performing an XSL transformation in Internet Explorer.

As you see in the figure, the XSLT processor in Internet Explorer has used our XSLT stylesheet—which uses XPath—to retrieve the data we wanted from our XML document: the names of the three planets. Even though the details may not be clear yet, you can begin to see in this example the part that XPath plays in letting you access specific parts of XML documents. As you see, XPath is central to XSLT, because it gives you the ability to select the data you want in an XML document.

This example has given us a quick look at the kind of thing that XPath can do for you. Now it's time to get more systematic and take a look at the whole XPath picture in overview.

XPath in Overview

XPath was created by the World Wide Web Consortium, W3C (www.w3.org), the same group that created XML and standardized HTML. W3C has three main levels for their specifications:

- Working drafts, which are works in progress and still subject to much change

- Candidate recommendations, which are the step before a specification becomes a recommendation

- Recommendations, which are the final versions of specifications

XPath 1.0 is in recommendation status, and XPath 2.0 is in working draft status as of this writing. You can find the official XPath 1.0 Web page at http://www.w3.org/TR/xpath. Here's what W3C has to say about XPath 1.0:

> XPath is the result of an effort to provide a common syntax and semantics for functionality shared between XSL Transformations (XSLT) and XPointer. The primary purpose of XPath is to address parts of an XML document. In support of this primary purpose, it also provides basic facilities for manipulation of strings, numbers and booleans. XPath uses a compact, non-XML syntax to facilitate use of XPath within URIs and XML attribute values. XPath operates on the abstract, logical structure of an XML document, rather than its surface syntax. XPath gets its name from its use of a path notation as in URLs for navigating through the hierarchical structure of an XML document.

> In addition to its use for addressing, XPath is also designed so that it has a natural subset that can be used for matching (testing whether or not a node matches a pattern); this use of XPath is described in [the XSLT specification] .

The whole XPath story began with XSLT. XSLT itself was the result of trying to fill a long-standing need—letting people format and work with the data in general markup documents. W3C's efforts here stretch back quite a way, back to its original Document Style Semantics and Specification Language (DSSSL) specification. DSSSL was originally intended to work with Standardized General Markup Language (SGML), the ancestor of both HTML and XML, and to let you style SGML documents for presentation. However, SGML never became very popular, although its descendants like HTML and XML did.

In the XML branch of the family, W3C concentrated on its Extensible Stylesheet Language (XSL) to let users format XML in a general way, much as a word processor might. However, XSL by itself was so complex that it never really caught on either—today, software giants like Microsoft use Cascading Style Sheets (CSS) to format XML (Microsoft has said publicly that it considers the future of XSL in question).

However, one part of XSL did actually catch on—Extensible Stylesheet Language Transformations (XSLT). XSLT doesn't worry so much about formatting XML as giving you easy access to the data in an XML document and transforming it into another kind of document—HTML is the most common, where you display the data in an XML document in HTML format. But you can also use XSLT to transform XML documents into other XML documents that might have different organization (reorganizing an XML database's records from storing purchase data by customer to using records organized by product ID, for example) or additional data (such as computing the average score for each of a set of student's records). You can also use XSLT to transform XML into plain text, or even rich text format (RTF) files or JavaScript files—in fact, just about any kind of files you want.

In this way, XSLT presents an extraordinarily powerful way of handling your XML data without resorting to a lot of programming involving XML parsers and Java or C++. All you have to do, as we've already seen, is to create an XSLT stylesheet and let an XSLT processor (like the one in Internet Explorer) do the rest. For that reason, XSLT became popular, and eventually split off from the XSL specification. And when W3C started creating XSLT 1.0, they quickly realized that giving people access to the data in XML documents using simple path expressions was such a great idea that XPath 1.0 was born.

XPath 1.0

XPath 1.0 is the version that's most supported today, and we're going to spend the first half of the book on it. XPath 1.0 was central to XSLT 1.0—in fact, the two specifications became W3C recommendations on the same day (November 16, 1999). Originally a part of the XSLT specification, XPath broke out and became its own specification when W3C realized that many XML specifications needed a way to access the parts of XML documents.

As its own specification, however, XPath 1.0 could be used by many XML-related specifications, not confined to use with XSLT alone (if you've worked with XML, you know that many of the specifications are related). That's how XPath was intended to be used—in a host language or specification of some sort, not simply on its own (although we'll see some tools later in this chapter that do use XPath by itself).

Today, XPath is essential to other XML-related specifications, such as XPointer, which lets you select and refer to fragments of XML documents as well as XQuery, which is all about addressing the data, treating that data as you would a standard database. We'll take a look at those two specifications and how XPath works with them, in this book.

XPath 2.0

The new version of XPath is version 2.0, and you can see the W3C specification for it at http://www.w3.org/TR/xpath20/. There's not a lot of software support for XPath 2.0 yet. This new version is considerably more involved than XPath 1.0—and that growth is an indication of the importance of XPath. We'll be covering XPath 2.0 in the second half of this book.

XPath 2.0 is tied not just to XSLT (which is now also in version 2.0), but the new XQuery specification (XQuery is all about treating XML documents as you would treat a database file)—the XSLT and XQuery groups at W3C are jointly responsible for XPath 2.0, and W3C says that XPath 2.0 and XQuery 1.0 are "generated from a common source." (In fact, XQuery 1.0 is an extension of XPath 2.0.)

That gives us the historical background—now it's time to get some of the basic details about XPath itself, giving us the foundation we'll need in the coming chapters.

XPath Basics

XPath's primary purpose is to address parts of an XML document. To do that, XPath uses its own, non-XML, syntax. XPath operates on the abstract, logical structure of an XML document, and this logical structure is known as the *data model*, as we'll see in the next chapter. XPath reduces an XML document to a tree of XML *nodes*, as we're going to see in detail in Chapter 2, and that's what it actually works with. A node is an individual data item in an XML document—elements can be nodes, XML processing instructions can be nodes, element attributes can be nodes, the text in an element is a text node, XML comments are comment nodes, and so on. The *root node* is the very beginning of the document, before anything else (before any XML elements, processing instructions, or anything else).

To work with the nodes in an XML document, you use XPath *expressions*, which are the primary construct in XPath. An XPath expression is a term or group of terms that XPath can evaluate to produce a result.

Probably the most important type of XPath expression is the *location path*, and for many people, this is what XPath is all about, because you use a location path to select a set of nodes (which may contain just a single node). Using a location path, you can tell XPath exactly what data you want to extract from an XML document.

Introducing Location Paths

How do location paths work? As we're going to see in Chapter 3, location paths are much like the standard file directory paths that you're already familiar with. For example, you might store data on stocks for April 2004 in a directory with this path if you're using Windows:

```
\2004\april\stocks\data
```

or this path if you're using Unix:

```
/2004/april/stocks/data
```

That's much how a location path works. A location path consists of one or more *location steps*, separated by / or //. You use successive steps—separated by /—to get to the data you want, just as you use successive directories in a file path to narrow down the location of a file. Starting the whole location path with a / means that you're starting from the root node (the very beginning of the document, before anything else), and working from that point.

As we're going to see in Chapter 3, a location step, in turn, is made up of an *axis*, a *node test*, and zero or more *predicates*.

Here's an example. In the location step `child::planet[position() = 5]`, child is the name of the axis (which you follow with `::`), `planet` is the node test, and `[position() = 5]` is a predicate. In this case, the `child` axis selects child nodes of the node you start from. The node test, `planet`, will match `<planet>` elements. And the predicate consists of an XPath function, `position`, that must return a value of 5 to make the predicate true. Putting all that together, then, this location step selects the fifth `<planet>` child element.

You create location paths with one or more location steps, such as `/child::planet[position() = 5]/child::name`, which starts at the root node and selects all the `<name>` elements that are children of the fifth `<planet>` child element in the document.

The evaluation of each location step in a location path starts at its *context node*. The idea of a context node is an important one, because as you navigate deep into an XML document, each successive location step starts from a different location, which XPath calls the location step's context node. In the present example, / makes the context node the document's root node for the next location step, which is `child::planet[position() = 5]`. That location step in turn makes the context node the fifth `<planet>` child element for the next location step, which is `child::name`. The thing to remember is that the evaluation of each location step starts from its context node.

Here are a number of location path examples to get us started—we're going to see how to create these in detail over the next three chapters, so don't try to memorize any of these now. But it's worth taking a look at these examples in overview:

- `child::planet` returns the `<planet>` element children of the context node.

- `child::*` returns all element children (* only matches elements) of the context node.

- `child::text()` returns all text node children of the context node.

- `child::node()` returns all the children of the context node, no matter what their node type is.

- `attribute::units` returns the units attribute of the context node.

- `child::name/descendant::planet` returns the `<planet>` element descendants of the child `<name>` elements of the context node.

- `child::*/child::planet` returns all `<planet>` grandchildren of the context node.

- `/` returns the root node (that is, the parent of the document element).

- `child::planet[position() = 3]` returns the third `<planet>` child of the context node.

- `child::planet[position() = last()]` returns the last `<planet>` child of the context node.

As you can see, some of this syntax is pretty involved, and a little lengthy to type. However, there is an abbreviated form of XPath syntax, as we're going to see in Chapter 3.

XPath at Work

We've already put XPath to work in Internet Explorer in an example at the beginning of this chapter. That example used XSLT to extract the names of the three planets in `ch01_01.xml`, as you saw in Figure 1.1. XSLT is a big use of XPath (and we're going to take a look at some basic XSLT next so that we can use it with XPath throughout the book), but some software packages let you use XPath directly.

The XPath Visualiser

The XPath Visualiser by Dimitre Novachev is a great tool that lets you see which nodes an XPath expression would select in an XML document. You can get the XPath Visualiser for free at `http://www.vbxml.com/xpathvisualizer/`.

After unzipping the download file, you use Internet Explorer to navigate to `XPathMain.htm`, opening this XPath tool as you see in Figure 1.2. You can use the Browse button in this tool to load an XML document, and enter the XPath expression you want to test into the "XPath Expression" box. In this example, we'll use our XML document `ch01_01.xml` that holds information about various planets, and test out the XPath expression `//planet`, which should find all the `<planet>` elements in this document. As you can see when you click the Select Nodes button, XPath Visualiser does indeed find all `<planet>` elements, as shown in Figure 1.2.

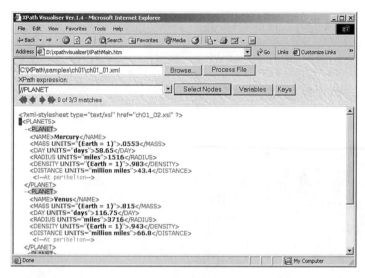

FIGURE 1.2   Using XPath Visualiser to apply an XPath expression.

XPath Visualiser is a great tool that we'll see throughout our discussion of XPath 1.0.

The Interactive Expression Builder

The Interactive Expression Builder is an online tool that lets you test your XPath expressions, and you'll find it at `http://www.develop.com/books/essentialxml/samples/xpath-builder/default.htm`. You can see this tool at work in Figure 1.3.

As with the XPath Visualiser, you can enter the XPath expression you want to test into the Interactive Expression Builder. The problem here is that you can't use the Interactive Expression Builder to load any but the sample document you see in Figure 1.3 (there is a text field for loading other documents at the very bottom of this page, but it only generates JavaScript errors).

Still, if you're comfortable using the sample XML document that comes loaded into the Interactive Expression Builder, you can test your XPath expressions using that document, as you see in Figure 1.3, where we're selecting all `<LineItem>` elements.

XPath and .NET

The Microsoft .NET initiative uses a great deal of XML behind the scenes, and there's some XPath support built into .NET. You can see a few XPath .NET examples online at `http://samples.gotdotnet.com/quickstart/howto`. The current URL for the XPath examples is `http://samples.gotdotnet.com/quickstart/howto/doc/xml/overviewofxml.aspx` (if that URL has been changed by the time you read this, go to `http://samples.gotdotnet.com/quickstart/howto` and search for XML examples).

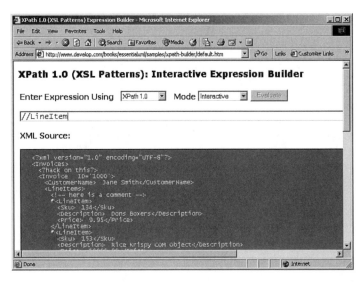

FIGURE 1.3   Using the Interactive Expression Builder.

There are two .NET XPath examples at this site, and they both use this XML file, books.xml:

```
<?xml version="1.0" ?>
<!--  This file represents a fragment of a book store inventory database -->
<bookstore>
    <book genre="autobiography" publicationdate="1981" ISBN="1-861003-11-0">
        <title>The Autobiography of Benjamin Franklin</title>
        <author>
            <first-name>Benjamin</first-name>
            <last-name>Franklin</last-name>
        </author>
        <price>8.99</price>
    </book>
    <book genre="novel" publicationdate="1967" ISBN="0-201-63361-2">
        <title>The Confidence Man</title>
        <author>
            <first-name>Herman</first-name>
            <last-name>Melville</last-name>
        </author>
        <price>11.99</price>
    </book>
    <book genre="philosophy" publicationdate="1991" ISBN="1-861001-57-6">
        <title>The Gorgias</title>
        <author>
```

```
                <name>Plato</name>
            </author>
            <price>9.99</price>
        </book>
</bookstore>
```

To run the examples, click the "Query XML with an XPath Expression" and "Navigate with XPathNavigator" links under the heading "XPath and XSL Transformations" on the left of the page at http://samples.gotdotnet.com/quickstart/howto/doc/xml/overviewofxml. aspx. You can see the first example, which queries books.xml with XPath, at work in Figure 1.4 (its full URL is http://samples.gotdotnet.com/quickstart/howto/samples/ Xml/QueryXmlDocumentXPath/VB/QueryXmlDocumentXPath.aspx).

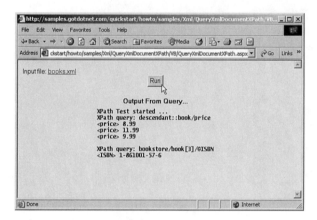

FIGURE 1.4   Using XPath in .NET.

When you click the Run button, the example applies various XPath expressions to books.xml, as you can see in the results in Figure 1.4.

The XPath Explorer

Besides .NET, a number of XPath tools are available that are Java-based. To use these tools, you'll need to have Java installed; the current version as of this writing is 1.4, which you can download for free from http://java.sun.com/j2se/1.4/download.html. You'll also find installation instructions in the download.

A useful Java XPath tool is the XPath Explorer, XPE, from Purple Technologies. You can get this tool for free from http://sourceforge.net/project/showfiles.php?group_ id=54719&release_id=98894. XPE comes as a Java Archive (JAR) file, and you start it at the command prompt as follows. (This example assumes that the Java program java.exe, which is in the Java installation's bin directory, is in your system's path and that xpe.jar is in the current directory). Here we'll use the command-line prompt % to stand for either the Windows command-line prompt in a DOS window or the Unix command-line prompt:

```
%java -jar xpe.jar
```

You can enter the URL of the XML file to work with in XPE, as you see in Figure 1.5. For example, to load our ch01_01.xml file into XPE, you'd use a file URL something like file:/c:/xpath/samples/ch01/ch01_01.xml in Windows.

FIGURE 1.5 Using the XPath Explorer.

Now you can enter the XPath expression you want to use, as you see in Figure 1.5, where we're executing the expression //planet on ch01_01.xml. XPE will show you the results immediately, as you can see in the figure.

The XPath Tester

The XPath Tester is another Java tool for use with XPath, and you can get it for free at http://www.fivesight.com/downloads/xpathtester.asp. To start the XPath Tester, you use this command line (assuming java.exe is in your system's path and xpathtester_1_4_saxon.jar is in the current directory):

```
%java -jar xpathtester_1_4_saxon.jar
```

The XPath Tester displays a File Open dialog that lets you select the XML document to work with and then opens that document as you see in Figure 1.6.

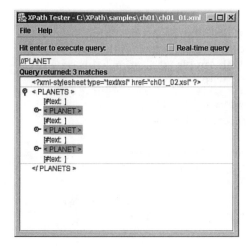

FIGURE 1.6 The XPath Tester.

Now you can enter the XPath expression you want to execute and press Enter to execute it, as you see in Figure 1.6. When you do, the XPath Tester will display the results, as you see in the figure.

The Xalan XPath Application

Another Java tool you can use to evaluate XPath expressions is a sample application that comes with the Xalan XSLT processor created by the Apache group. You can download Xalan at `http://xml.apache.org/xalan-j/index.html`.

The name of this example is ApplyXPath, and it's in the Java Archive file `xalansamples.jar` that comes with Xalan. We'll use this JAR file by first setting the Java `classpath` variable, which tells Java where to look for applications to run, to `xalansamples.jar`. Next, you can run the ApplyXPath application, passing it the name of the XML file to use and the XPath expression to evaluate, like this:

```
%set classpath=xalansamples.jar
%java ApplyXPath ch01_01.xml //planet
```

You can see the results in Figure 1.7, where you see that the application displays the elements matching the XPath expression we're testing.

FIGURE 1.7 Using Xalan's ApplyXPath.

We're not going to expect that you know Java or .NET in this book. But if you do happen to know Java, you can take a look at the source code for the ApplyXPath example to see how to use XPath in Java. For example, here's some Java code that applies the XPath expression //planet to ch01_01.xml, adapted from the ApplyXPath sample application—this code isn't difficult, and it shows the Java classes you use to work with XPath:

```
InputSource in = new InputSource(new FileInputStream("ch01_01.xml"));
DocumentBuilderFactory dfactory = DocumentBuilderFactory.newInstance();
Document doc = dfactory.newDocumentBuilder().parse(in);
Transformer serializer = TransformerFactory.newInstance().newTransformer();
NodeIterator nl = XPathAPI.selectNodeIterator(doc, "//planet");


Node n;
while ((n = nl.nextNode())!= null)
{
    if (isTextNode(n)) {
        StringBuffer sb = new StringBuffer(n.getNodeValue());
        for (Node nn = n.getNextSibling(); isTextNode(nn);
            nn = nn.getNextSibling())
        {
            sb.append(nn.getNodeValue());
        }
        System.out.print(sb);
    }
}
```

Besides the ones we've taken a look at, there are other XPath tools out there as well, such as the popular XML editor, XML Spy, which also includes an XPath tool. You can get XML Spy at http://www.xmlspy.com/download.html.

XPath with XSLT

For many people, the whole idea behind XPath is to be able to use XSLT, so we'll take a look at XSLT in overview now. XSLT and XPath are natural to use together, and we'll see quite a few XSLT examples in this book. For that reason, we'll take a look at enough XSLT here to get started. You won't have to know how XSLT works in detail—you'll just have to know how things work in overview, and what XSLT templates do. We'll see XSLT examples that use XPath in Chapters 3 and 4. And Chapter 5 is dedicated to XSLT and XPath.

For more information, you can find

- The W3C XSLT 1.0 recommendation at http://www.w3.org/TR/xslt

- The current XSLT 2.0 specification at http://www.w3.org/TR/xslt20/

XSLT centers around the stylesheets that XSLT processors (such as the one in Internet Explorer) can use to transform XML documents into HTML, other XML documents, plain text, and so on. You can assign XPath expressions to the `match` and `select` attributes in XSLT elements—but note that while the `select` attribute can handle any XPath expression, the `match` attribute can only handle XPath expressions that use the `child` or `attribute` axes.

As you might expect, XSLT stylesheets must be well-formed XML documents, so you start a stylesheet with the XML declaration. Next, you use a `<stylesheet>` element; by convention, XSLT stylesheets use the namespace `xsl`, which is "http://www.w3.org/1999/XSL/Transform". You must also include the `version` attribute in the `<stylesheet>` element; here, we'll use version 1.0:

```
<?xml version="1.0"?>
<xsl:stylesheet version="1.0" xmlns:xsl="http://www.w3.org/1999/XSL/Transform">
    .
    .
    .
```

Creating a Template

That's how you start an XSLT stylesheet. To work with specific nodes in an XML document, XSLT is a programming language that uses *templates*. When you match or select nodes, a template tells the XSLT processor how to transform the node for output. For example, say that you want to replace the root node with a whole new HTML document. You can start by creating a template with the `<xsl:template>` element, setting the `match` attribute to the XPath expression for the root node, `"/"`:

```
<?xml version="1.0"?>
<xsl:stylesheet version="1.0" xmlns:xsl="http://www.w3.org/1999/XSL/Transform">

    <xsl:template match="/">
        .
        .
        .
    </xsl:template>

</xsl:stylesheet>
```

When the root node is matched, the template is applied to that node. In this example, we'll replace the root node with an HTML document, so we'll just include that HTML document directly as the content of the `<xsl:template>` element, as you see in Listing 1.3.

LISTING 1.3 A Sample XSLT Document That Replaces the Root Node (`ch01_03.xsl`)

```xml
<?xml version="1.0"?>
<xsl:stylesheet version="1.0" xmlns:xsl="http://www.w3.org/1999/XSL/Transform">

    <xsl:template match="/">
        <HTML>
            <HEAD>
                <TITLE>
                    A Transformation Example
                </TITLE>
            </HEAD>
            <BODY>
                This entire document has been replaced!.
            </BODY>
        </HTML>
    </xsl:template>

</xsl:stylesheet>
```

And that's all it takes; by using the <xsl:template> element, we've set up a *rule* in the stylesheet. When the XSLT processor reads the document, the first node it sees is the root node. This rule matches that root node, so the XSLT processor replaces it with the HTML document, producing this result:

```
<HTML>
    <HEAD>
        <TITLE>
            A trivial transformation
        </TITLE>
    </HEAD>
    <BODY>
        This transformation has replaced
        the entire document.
    </BODY>
</HTML>
```

That's our first, rudimentary transformation. All we've done is to replace the entire document with another one. But of course, that's just the beginning of the power you have using XSLT and XPath.

The `xsl:apply-templates` Element

The template used in the preceding section only applied to one node—the root node, and performed a trivial action, replacing the entire XML document with an HTML document. However, you can also apply templates to the *children* of a node that you've matched, and you do that with the <xsl:apply-templates> element.

For example, say that you want to convert `ch01_01.xml` to HTML. The document element in that document is <planets>, so we can match that element with a template, setting the match attribute to the name of the element we want to match, and then replace the <planets> element with an <HTML> element, like this:

```
<?xml version="1.0"?>
<xsl:stylesheet version="1.0" xmlns:xsl="http://www.w3.org/1999/XSL/Transform">

    <xsl:template match="planets">
        <HTML>

            .

            .

            .

        </HTML>
    </xsl:template>

    .

    .

    .

</xsl:stylesheet>
```

But what about the children of the <planets> element? To make sure they are transformed correctly, you use the <xsl:apply-templates> element this way:

```
<?xml version="1.0"?>
<xsl:stylesheet version="1.0" xmlns:xsl="http://www.w3.org/1999/XSL/Transform">

    <xsl:template match="planets">
        <HTML>
            <xsl:apply-templates/>
        </HTML>
    </xsl:template>

    .

    .

    .

</xsl:stylesheet>
```

Now you can provide templates for the child nodes. In this case, we'll just replace each of the three <planet> elements with some text, which we place directly into the template for the <planet> element as you see in Listing 1.4.

LISTING 1.4 A Sample XSLT Document That Replaces <planet> Elements with Text (ch01_04.xsl)

```
<?xml version="1.0"?>
<xsl:stylesheet version="1.0" xmlns:xsl="http://www.w3.org/1999/XSL/Transform">

    <xsl:template match="planets">
        <HTML>
            <xsl:apply-templates/>
        </HTML>
    </xsl:template>

    <xsl:template match="planet">
        <P>
            Placeholder text for planet data...
        </P>
    </xsl:template>

</xsl:stylesheet>
```

And that's it—now the <planets> element is replaced by an <HTML> element, and the <planet> elements are also replaced:

```
<HTML>
    <P>
        Placeholder text for planet data...
    </P>

    <P>
        Placeholder text for planet data...
    </P>

    <P>
        Placeholder text for planet data...
    </P>
</HTML>
```

You can see that this transformation works, but it's still less than useful; all we've done is to replace the <planet> elements with some text. What if we wanted to access some of the data in the <planet> element? For example, say that we wanted to place the text from the <name> element in each <planet> element in the output document:

```
<planet>
    <name>Mercury</name>
    <mass units="(Earth = 1)">.0553</mass>
    <day units="days">58.65</day>
    <radius units="miles">1516</radius>
    <density units="(Earth = 1)">.983</density>
    <distance units="million miles">43.4</distance><!--At perihelion-->
</planet>
```

To gain access to this kind of data, you can use the select attribute of the <xsl:value-of> element.

Getting the Value of Nodes with `xsl:value-of`

In this example, we'll extract the name of each planet and insert that name into the output document. To get the name of each planet, we'll use the <xsl:value-of> element in a template targeted at the <planet> element, and select the <name> element with the select attribute as you can see in Listing 1.5.

LISTING 1.5   A Sample XSLT Document That Uses the Names of <planet> Elements (ch01_05.xsl)

```
<?xml version="1.0"?>
<xsl:stylesheet version="1.0" xmlns:xsl="http://www.w3.org/1999/XSL/Transform">

    <xsl:template match="planets">
        <HTML>
            <UL>
            <LI><xsl:apply-templates/></LI>
            </UL>
        </HTML>
    </xsl:template>

    <xsl:template match="planet">
        <xsl:value-of select="name"/>
    </xsl:template>

</xsl:stylesheet>
```

Applying the stylesheet ch01_05.xsl, the <xsl:value-of select="name"/> element directs the XSLT processor to insert the name of each planet into the output document, and so the results look like this:

```
<HTML>
    <UL>
        <LI>Mercury</LI>
        <LI>Venus</LI>
        <LI>Earth</LI>
    </UL>
</HTML>
```

How do you run XSLT examples like this? You might not think you have an XSLT processor handy, but you do if you have Internet Explorer. To connect an XSLT stylesheet to an XML document in Internet Explorer, you use the href attribute of a <?xml-stylesheet?> XML processing instruction as you see in ch01_06.xml (Listing 1.6). In that example, we're connecting our sample XML document to the XSLT stylesheet ch01_05.xsl.

LISTING 1.6 A Sample XML Document for Internet Explorer (ch01_06.xml)

```
<?xml version="1.0"?>
<?xml-stylesheet type="text/xsl" href="ch01_05.xsl"?>
<planets>

    <planet>
        <name>Mercury</name>
        <mass units="(Earth = 1)">.0553</mass>
        <day units="days">58.65</day>
        <radius units="miles">1516</radius>
        <density units="(Earth = 1)">.983</density>
        <distance units="million miles">43.4</distance><!--At perihelion-->
    </planet>

    <planet>
        <name>Venus</name>
        <mass units="(Earth = 1)">.815</mass>
        <day units="days">116.75</day>
        <radius units="miles">3716</radius>
        <density units="(Earth = 1)">.943</density>
        <distance units="million miles">66.8</distance><!--At perihelion-->
    </planet>

    <planet>
        <name>Earth</name>
```

LISTING 1.6 Continued

```
            <mass units="(Earth = 1)">1</mass>
            <day units="days">1</day>
            <radius units="miles">2107</radius>
            <density units="(Earth = 1)">1</density>
            <distance units="million miles">128.4</distance><!--At perihelion-->
        </planet>


</planets>
```

And that's all it takes—now you can run XSLT examples using XPath in Internet Explorer.

Working with Attributes

What if you wanted to use XSLT and XPath to display not only the value of each of the `<name>`, `<mass>`, and `<radius>` elements, but also the *units* for each value, such as "miles" for the `<radius>` element? We can recover the units from each element by getting the value of the units attribute of that element—you can see what we're aiming for in Figure 1.8, where the results are displayed in an HTML table.

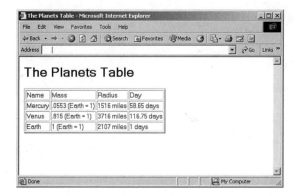

FIGURE 1.8 Displaying planetary data and units.

To create this result, we've got to use more than just the `<xsl:value-of select="name"/>` type of elements we've been using up to now, because we want to display the units for each measurement as well. We can start by creating the HTML for the table you see in Figure 1.8, matching the `<planets>` element and applying templates for the children of this element:

```
<xsl:template match="/planets">
    <HTML>
        <HEAD>
```

```
            <TITLE>
                The Planets Table
            </TITLE>
        </HEAD>
        <BODY>
            <H1>
                The Planets Table
            </H1>
            <TABLE BORDER="2">
                <TR>
                    <TD>Name</TD>
                    <TD>Mass</TD>
                    <TD>Radius</TD>
                    <TD>Day</TD>
                </TR>
                <xsl:apply-templates/>
            </TABLE>
        </BODY>
    </HTML>
</xsl:template>
```

Next, we match each `<planet>` element and invoke a new template on each element that has units we need to display:

```
<xsl:template match="planet">
    <TR>
        <TD><xsl:value-of select="name"/></TD>
        <TD><xsl:apply-templates select="mass"/></TD>
        <TD><xsl:apply-templates select="radius"/></TD>
        <TD><xsl:apply-templates select="day"/></TD>
    </TR>
</xsl:template>
```

In each of these additional templates, such as the one for the `<mass>` element, we want to get both the value of the element and its units. To refer to the current element, we can use ".", which refers to the context node:

```
<xsl:template match="mass">
    <xsl:value-of select="."/>
         .
         .
         .
</xsl:template>
```

This recovers the value of the current element. Next, we insert a space, using the `<xsl:text>` element like this:

```
<xsl:template match="mass">
    <xsl:value-of select="."/>
    <xsl:text> </xsl:text>
        .
        .
        .
</xsl:template>
```

Finally, we get the value of the `units` attribute for the `<mass>` element, which displays the units for the element's value (the `<xsl:text>` element lets us insert whitespace as needed here—more on that in Chapter 5) :

```
<xsl:template match="mass">
    <xsl:value-of select="."/>
    <xsl:text> </xsl:text>
    <xsl:value-of select="@units"/>
</xsl:template>
```

And that's all it takes—you can see the final XSLT stylesheet, `ch01_07.xsl`, in Listing 1.7.

LISTING 1.7   Accessing Attributes in a Stylesheet (`ch01_07.xsl`)

```
<?xml version="1.0"?>
<xsl:stylesheet version="1.1"
xmlns:xsl="http://www.w3.org/1999/XSL/Transform">

    <!-- This template matches all planets elements -->
    <xsl:template match="/planets">
        <HTML>
            <HEAD>
                <TITLE>
                    The Planets Table
                </TITLE>
            </HEAD>
            <BODY>
                <H1>
                    The Planets Table
                </H1>
                <TABLE BORDER="2">
                    <TR>
                        <TD>Name</TD>
```

LISTING 1.7   Continued

```
                          <TD>Mass</TD>
                          <TD>Radius</TD>
                          <TD>Day</TD>
                       </TR>
                       <xsl:apply-templates/>
                   </TABLE>
               </BODY>
          </HTML>
     </xsl:template>

     <xsl:template match="planet">
        <TR>
            <TD><xsl:value-of select="name"/></TD>
            <TD><xsl:apply-templates select="mass"/></TD>
            <TD><xsl:apply-templates select="radius"/></TD>
            <TD><xsl:apply-templates select="day"/></TD>
        </TR>
     </xsl:template>

     <xsl:template match="mass">
         <xsl:value-of select="."/>
         <xsl:text> </xsl:text>
         <xsl:value-of select="@units"/>
     </xsl:template>

     <xsl:template match="radius">
         <xsl:value-of select="."/>
         <xsl:text> </xsl:text>
         <xsl:value-of select="@units"/>
     </xsl:template>

     <xsl:template match="day">
         <xsl:value-of select="."/>
         <xsl:text> </xsl:text>
         <xsl:value-of select="@units"/>
     </xsl:template>

</xsl:stylesheet>
```

And you can see the results in Figure 1.8. That covers the XSLT in overview that we'll use for our XPath example—you won't need an in-depth knowledge of XSLT here, but an acquaintance will help because our XPath examples will sometimes use XSLT.

XPath with XQuery

Besides XSLT, XPath is very popular in W3C's XQuery specification. In fact, XQuery contains XPath as a proper sublanguage—all of XPath is contained in XQuery. They are more integrally linked than XPath and XSLT, because you could replace XPath in XSLT with another language and XSLT would still work, but XQuery itself may be thought of as an extension of XPath. XQuery lets you work with XML documents, treating them as databases. You can find information on XQuery at `http://www.w3.org/XML/Query`.

A lot of XQuery's data-accessing power is considered very important by W3C, which is why much of it is being incorporated into XPath 2.0. (We'll see how XPath and XQuery work together in Chapter 6.) Here's an example where we'll take a look at all books published by Sams since 1990, as stored in a database named `books.xml`. Here's what the XQuery query might look like:

```
<books>
{
    for $book in doc("http://www.starpowder.com/books.xml")
    where $book/publisher = "Sams" and $book/@year > 1990
    return
        <book year={$book/@year}>
        {$book/title}
        </book>
}
</books>
```

In this case, `$book` stands for the root node of `books.xml`, and you can create XPath expressions using `$book` such as `$book/publisher`, which stands for the value of child `<publisher>` elements, or `$book/@year`, which stands for the value of year attributes. Here's what the results of this query might look like:

```
<books>
    <book year="1990">
        <title>Title 1</title>
    </book>
    <book year="1991">
        <title>Title 2</title>
    </book>
        .
        .
        .
</books>
```

XPath with XPointer and XLink

Another use for XPath is with the XPointer and XLink specifications. XLinks specify how one document links to another document, and XPointers specify locations inside a document. We'll see both of these in Chapter 6, but it's worth getting an overview now.

The XLink specification is a W3C recommendation, released on June 27, 2001. You can find the most current version of this recommendation at www.w3.org/TR/xlink. You use XLinks to link one document to another. Here's an example to give you an idea what an XLink looks like; unlike HTML hyperlinks, any element can be a link in XML. You specify that an element is a link with the attribute xlink:type like this, where we're creating a simple XLink:

```
<MOVIE_REVIEW xmlns:xlink = "http://www.w3.org/1999/xlink"
    xlink:type = "simple"
    xlink:show = "new"
    xlink:href = "http://www.starpowdermovies.com/reviews.xml">
    Mr. Blandings Builds His Dream House
</MOVIE_REVIEW>
```

In this case, we're creating a simple XLink, which is much like an HTML hyperlink, by setting the xlink:type attribute to "simple". We're also setting the xlink:show attribute to "new", which means that XLink-aware software should open the linked-to document in a new window or other display context, and setting the xlink:href attribute to the URI of the new document (which can be quite general and need not be in the URL form we've used here).

XLinks let you link to a particular document, but you often need to be more precise than that. XPointers let you point to specific locations inside a document—without having to modify that document by embedding special tags or markers. To point to a specific location in a document, the XPointer specification builds on the XPath specification. XPointers are in the W3C Working Draft stage, and you can learn more about them at www.w3.org/TR/xptr-framework/.

How do you add an XPointer to a document's URI to specify a specific location in a document? You can append # (following the HTML usage for URLs that specify link targets) and then xpointer(), placing the XPath expression you want to use in the parentheses. Here's an example:

```
<MOVIE_REVIEW xmlns:xlink = "http://www.w3.org/1999/xlink"
    xlink:type = "simple"
    xlink:show = "new"
    xlink:href = "http://www.starpowdermovies.com/reviews.xml#xpointer(/child::*[126])">
    Mr. Blandings Builds His Dream House
</MOVIE_REVIEW>
```

As you can see, XPath is central to a number of XML specifications. We'll see how XPath is used in these specifications in more detail, and with examples, later in the book.

XPath Resources

Before finishing this chapter, it's worth noting that a great number of XPath resources are available online. Here's a starter set listing the applicable W3C specifications:

- `http://www.w3.org/TR/xpath`—The XPath 1.0 specification

- `http://www.w3.org/TR/xpath20/`—The XPath 2.0 specification

- `http://www.w3.org/TR/query-datamodel/`—The XPath 2.0 data model

- `http://www.w3.org/TR/xquery-operators/`—The XPath 2.0 functions and operators specification

- `http://www.w3.org/TR/xslt20/`—The XSLT 2.0 specification

- `http://www.w3.org/TR/xquery/`—The XQuery specification

- `http://www.w3.org/TR/REC-xml`—The XML 1.0 specification

- `http://www.w3.org/TR/xslt`—The XSLT 1.0 specification

Plenty of XPath tutorials are out there online, too—here are a few:

- `http://www.w3schools.com/xpath/default.asp`—The W3Schools tutorial, fairly comprehensive

- `http://www.zvon.org/xxl/XPathTutorial/General/examples.html`—A tutorial by Miloslav Nic and Jiri Jirat

- `http://www.developer.com/xml/article.php/1156211 Developer.com's XPath tutorial`—A good tutorial, but just an overview

A number of XPath quick reference pages are also available on the Internet—here's a starter list:

- `www.mulberrytech.com/quickref/XSLTquickref.pdf`—An XPath reference in PDF format

- `http://www.vbxml.com/xsl/xpathref.asp`—A good XPath reference

- `http://www.finetuning.com/xpathfaq.html`—An XPath Frequently Asked Questions (FAQ) list in HTML format

- `http://www.mulberrytech.com/quickref/`—Another good XPath quick reference

And, as we've already seen, there are a number of XPath tools out there, free and ready to download. Here's a list of their URLs:

- `http://www.fivesight.com/downloads/xpathtester.asp`—The XPath tester

- `http://www.vbxml.com/xpathvisualizer/`—The XPath Visualiser

- `http://www.logilab.org/xpathvis/`—Logilab's XPath Visualizer (spelled with a "z"—not the same as the XPath Visualiser)

- `http://sourceforge.net/project/showfiles.php?group_id=54719&release_id=98894`—The XPath Explorer

- `http://www.xmlspy.com/download.html`—An XPath tool for XML Spy

In Brief

Here are the crucial concepts for this chapter:

- XPath expressions can be evaluated to create a result.

- Location steps indicate a single step in a location path.

- Location paths are used to locate data and return node-sets.

- Axes let you specify how you want a location step to locate data.

- Predicates are optional parts of location steps that let you be more specific about the data you want.

- Nodes are the fundamental building blocks of XML documents.

- Root nodes are the topmost nodes in documents.

- A context node is the current node that is being processed.

The XPath Data Model

Understanding the XPath 1.0 Data Types

To let you work with the contents of an XML document, XPath lets you model the data in that document in a specific way called the *data model*. The data model specifies how XPath sees a document, and that's essential to know if you want XPath to find the data you're looking for.

For example, if you have an XML document and want to pick out all the <friend> elements, you need to know how XPath sees that document to be able to instruct it to do what you want. In this chapter, we're going to take a look at how XPath 1.0 sees the contents of an XML document— that is, we'll be discussing the XPath 1.0 data model.

To handle the data in an XML document, XPath 1.0 lets you work with four different data *types*. For example, by defining a *string* data type, XPath lets you handle text strings in XML elements and work with them directly. For instance, if you use the XPath expression //planet[name="Venus"], XPath will return all <planet> children in a document that have <name> children with text equal to "Venus". This works because XPath lets you work with text strings like "Venus". You can also work with *numbers*, like this: //planet[position()=3], which lets you specify that you want the third <planet> element in the document.

There are other data types available besides strings and numbers that you can work with in XPath, and we'll take a look at all the allowable data types here. Then we'll be ready to use those data types with the XPath data model to create XPath expressions of the type XPath processors will be able to understand and use to extract data from XML documents.

Here are the data types in XPath 1.0 (XPath 2.0 adds many more data types, as we'll see in the second half of the book):

- A number—stored as a floating-point number

- A string—a sequence of characters

- A Boolean—a true or false value

- A node-set—an unordered collection of unique nodes

XPath expressions are the fundamental building blocks of XPath, and an XPath expression is anything XPath can evaluate to yield a result (which is not an error). For example, here's an XPath expression: `//planet[position() > 3]`. This expression returns a node-set containing all the `<planet>` elements in a document after the first three.

All XPath 1.0 expressions must evaluate to a value that is one of the four data types—number, string, Boolean, or node-set. For example, not only is `//planet[position() > 3]` an XPath expression (this expression results in a node-set), but so is `position()` (which results in a number)—and so is 3, all by itself, as well as `position() > 3` (this expression yields a Boolean true/false value depending on whether the tested node's position is greater than three).

Let's take a look at all the allowed data types in more detail now.

Numbers

First of all, you can use numbers as XPath expressions. For example, in the XPath expression `//planet[position()=7]` (which you might use to match the seventh `<planet>` element in an XML document), the number 7 is a valid XPath expression, evaluating to itself.

NUMBERS IN XPATH 1.0

In XPath 1.0, a number represents a floating-point number. A number can have any double-precision 64-bit format that conforms to IEEE 754. These include a special "Not-a-Number" (NaN) value, positive and negative infinity, and positive and negative zero.

The `position()` function also evaluates to a number—the position of the current node among its sibling nodes. And there are other functions that evaluate to numbers—for example, the XPath 1.0 `floor` function returns the largest integer less than the argument you pass to it. That means that `floor(4.6)` would return a value of 4, for instance, so `floor(4.6)` is an XPath expression that evaluates to a number.

All of which is to say that numbers are a valid data type in XPath 1.0—you can use them directly, and expressions can be evaluated to yield a number.

Strings

XPath expressions can also be text strings (defined in XPath as "a sequence of zero or more characters," where the characters are Unicode characters by default). For example, in the XPath expression //planet[name="Mars"], which returns all <planet> children in a document that have <name> children with text equal to "Mars", "Mars" is an XPath expression of data type string.

Here's another example—if you have an XML element like this: <planet color = "RED">Mars</planet>, the XPath expression attribute::color would return the string "RED".

So as you can see, XPath expressions can also be of the string type.

Booleans

Besides numbers and strings, XPath expressions can also be Boolean true/false values. For example, take a look at the XPath expression position()=3. The position() function returns the position of a node among its siblings, and if position() returns 3, the XPath expression position()=3 is true. Otherwise, the expression position()=3 is false.

Here's another example—in the XPath expression //planet[attribute::color = "RED"], which returns all <planet> elements that have a color attribute with value of "RED", attribute::color = "RED" is an XPath expression that returns a Boolean value. In fact, in the expression //planet[attribute::color], the expression attribute::color is itself a Boolean expression. It's true if the current <planet> element has a color attribute, but false otherwise.

Booleans, then, make up the third data type that XPath expressions can evaluate to, in addition to numbers and strings.

Node-Sets

The fourth data type, node-sets, is where all the excitement lies in XPath 1.0. A node-set holds zero or more nodes (note that a node-set might contain only a single node), and working with node-sets is what really lets you work with the data in an XML document.

For example, the XPath expression //planet[position() > 3] returns all the <planet> elements after the first three. That means you get a node-set of <planet> elements when you evaluate this expression. Node-sets are the most interesting data type because a node-set holds actual nodes from the XML document. For example, you can filter a set of nodes that you want to work with into your node-set, ignoring all the rest of the data in the XML document. And treating a whole collection of nodes as one single data item—a node-set—is very handy.

Here's another example—the expression `child::planet[attribute::color = "RED"]` will return a node-set containing all `<planet>` children of the context node that have a `color` attribute with value of "RED".

DATA TYPES IN XPATH 2.0

The data types in XPath 1.0 are pretty primitive—just numbers, strings, Booleans, and node-sets. Augmenting these types was one of the big pushes behind XPath 2.0, which supports data types taken from XML schemas, as we're going to see in the second half of the book. Schemas support a great many data types, such as `boolean`, `byte`, `date`, `dateTime`, `int`, `long`, `nonPositiveInteger`, `normalizedString`, `positiveInteger`, `short`, `unsignedByte`, `unsignedInt`, `unsignedLong`, `unsignedShort`, and many more.

Node-sets are data types that are unique to XPath—you may be familiar with strings, numbers, and Booleans already, but node-sets are where the real meat of XPath is. A node-set is really a collection, not just a single data item like a string or a number; a node-set can hold either a single node or multiple nodes, but either way it's still called a node-set.

If an XPath expression returns a node-set containing multiple nodes, the XPath processor software will return all those nodes to you, as we've seen in the XPath Visualiser.

So what about the actual nodes in a node-set? What kinds of nodes can you have? That's where the data model comes in, and we're going to turn to that topic next.

Understanding Nodes

XPath models an XML document as a *tree of nodes*. This way of looking at an XML document is called XPath's data model. Different types of nodes are available in XPath, such as element nodes, attribute nodes, and text nodes, and we're going to take a look at the various possibilities now.

XPath Node Types

There are seven types of nodes in XPath 1.0:

- Root nodes
- Element nodes
- Attribute nodes
- Processing instruction nodes
- Comment nodes

- Text nodes

- Namespace nodes

We'll take a look at each of these node types here, using our XML document that holds planetary data, renumbered ch02_01.xml for this chapter, as you can see in Listing 2.1.

LISTING 2.1   Our Sample XML Document (ch02_01.xml)

```
<?xml version="1.0"?>
<planets>

    <planet>
        <name>Mercury</name>
        <mass units="(Earth = 1)">.0553</mass>
        <day units="days">58.65</day>
        <radius units="miles">1516</radius>
        <density units="(Earth = 1)">.983</density>
        <distance units="million miles">43.4</distance>
        <!--At perihelion-->
    </planet>

    <planet>
        <name>Venus</name>
        <mass units="(Earth = 1)">.815</mass>
        <day units="days">116.75</day>
        <radius units="miles">3716</radius>
        <density units="(Earth = 1)">.943</density>
        <distance units="million miles">66.8</distance>
        <!--At perihelion-->
    </planet>

    <planet>
        <name>Earth</name>
        <mass units="(Earth = 1)">1</mass>
        <day units="days">1</day>
        <radius units="miles">2107</radius>
        <density units="(Earth = 1)">1</density>
        <distance units="million miles">128.4</distance>
        <!--At perihelion-->
    </planet>

</planets>
```

We'll begin with the root node.

The Root Node

The *root node* is the root of the XPath tree for an XML document. This node is not the same as the <planets> element in ch02_01.xml—<planets> is the *document element* for the XML document, and people often confuse the two.

The root node is really a logical node that serves simply as the root of the whole XPath node tree. The root node gives you access to the whole tree, and in XPath, you use / to stand for the root node. When you use an XPath expression like /planets, you're starting at the root node and searching for <planets> elements that are direct children of the root node. In fact, you can see this XPath expression at work in our XML document in Figure 2.1 in the XPath Visualiser, as we first saw in Chapter 1.

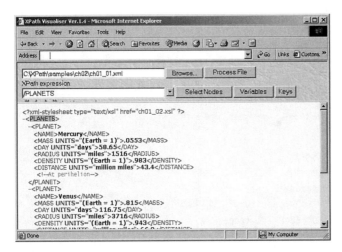

FIGURE 2.1   The <planets> child of the root node.

Because the root node is the root of the XPath tree, the root node is the same as the entire document, as far as many applications go. Note also that the root node includes not only the document element (and therefore all its children as well), but also any processing instructions, namespace declarations, and so on that are at the same level as the document element.

Element Nodes

We're already familiar with element nodes because they correspond to the elements in an XML document—there is one element node in the XPath node tree for every element in the original XML document. You can see plenty of elements in our sample XML document, ch02_01.xml, such as <planets>, <planet>, and so on:

```
<?xml version="1.0"?>
<planets>

    <planet>
        <name>Mercury</name>
        <mass units="(Earth = 1)">.0553</mass>
        <day units="days">58.65</day>
        <radius units="miles">1516</radius>
        <density units="(Earth = 1)">.983</density>
        <distance units="million miles">43.4</distance>
        <!--At perihelion-->
    </planet>

        .
        .
        .
```

Element nodes can also have children, of course. The children of each element node can include element nodes, comment nodes, processing instruction nodes, and text nodes.

Element nodes can also have a unique identifier (ID). For example, if the XML document has an attribute declared to be of type ID, that attribute can serve as the element's ID value. On the other hand, if you do not declare any attributes to be of type ID, no elements can have IDs.

In XPath, you can use an element's name (such as planet for the <planets> element) to match an element, or * to match any element. For example, you can see the XPath expression //* at work in Figure 2.2, matching all element nodes in ch02_01.xml.

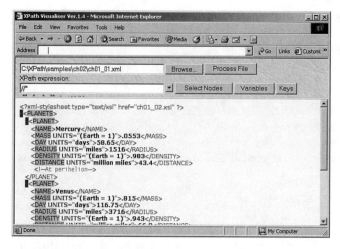

FIGURE 2.2   Matching element nodes.

Note that if you use an expression such as /planet, you'll get not only a <planet> element (if there is one), but also all its contents. Take a look at this example:

```
<planet>
    <name>Mercury</name>
    <mass units="(Earth = 1)">.0553</mass>
</planet>
```

In this case, /planet will return the <planet> element, which includes all that element's contents. In other words, what you get includes a newline character, some whitespace, the <name> element, another newline character, and some additional whitespace, the <mass> element, and a newline character. So the entire element and all its contents are returned. (As we'll see in Chapter 4, you can suppress leading and trailing whitespace with the normalize-space function.)

Attribute Nodes

We're already familiar with attribute nodes because they correspond to element attributes in XML. For example, this element in ch02_01.xml has an attribute named units with the value "days":

```
<?xml version="1.0"?>
<planets>

    <planet>
        <name>Mercury</name>
        <mass units="(Earth = 1)">.0553</mass>
        <day units="days">58.65</day>
        <radius units="miles">1516</radius>
        <density units="(Earth = 1)">.983</density>
        <distance units="million miles">43.4</distance>
        <!--At perihelion-->
    </planet>

        .
        .
        .
```

Elements can have more than one attribute, of course, and therefore more than one attribute node:

```
<day units="days" COPYRIGHT="(c) 2003 Steve">1</day>
```

In XPath terms, the element is the parent of each of its attribute nodes—however, an attribute node is *not* considered a child of its parent element. Note that this is different from the W3C XML Document Object Model (DOM), which does not treat the element with an attribute as the parent of the attribute.

In XML, you can also have *default attributes*, where attributes are given default values. For example, some attributes, like `xml:lang` and `xml:space`, affect all elements that are descendants of the element with the attribute—but that does not affect where attribute nodes appear in the tree. These attributes, like any other, are *only* considered attributes of their parent elements in XPath.

In XPath, you can refer to attributes using the `attribute` axis or its shorthand version, `@`. For example, to recover the value of the `units` attribute for an element, you can use the term `@units`, as we've seen in Chapter 1. To match all attributes in a document, you can use the XPath expression `//@*`, and you can see that expression at work on `ch02_01.xml` in the XPath Visualiser in Figure 2.3.

NO ATTRIBUTE NODES FOR NAMESPACE ATTRIBUTES

Bear in mind, however, that there are no attribute nodes in XPath corresponding to attributes that declare namespaces.

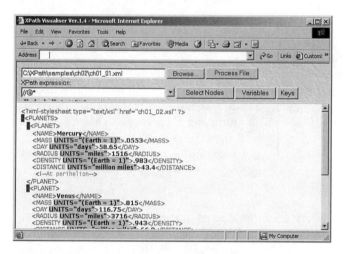

FIGURE 2.3 Matching attribute nodes.

Processing Instruction Nodes

There is a processing instruction node for every XML processing instruction. For example, there's a processing instruction in `ch02_01.xml`, `<?xml-stylesheet?>`, which looks like this:

```
<?xml version="1.0"?>
<?xml-stylesheet type="text/xsl" href="ch01_02.xsl"?>
<planets>

    <planet>
        <name>Mercury</name>
        .
        .
        .
```

THE XML DECLARATION IS NOT A PROCESSING INSTRUCTION

It's important to realize that the XML declaration is not a processing instruction. That means that there is no processing instruction node corresponding to the XML declaration.

ACCESSING A PROCESSING INSTRUCTION'S PSEUDO-ATTRIBUTES

Although you can't directly address the value of a processing instruction's pseudo-attributes using XPath, you can use the string-handling functions we'll see in Chapter 4 to get their values.

Processing instructions are not under the control of any namespace, so they do not have namespace nodes. Also, in XML, their attributes are really *pseudo-attributes*, which means that XPath will not recognize them as attributes. From an XPath 1.0 point of view, the value of a processing instruction is everything following the processing instruction's *target* (xml-stylesheet here) up to the final ?. For example, the value of <?xml-stylesheet type="text/xsl" href="ch01_02.xsl"?> is type="text/xsl" href="ch01_02.xsl".

You can use the processing-instruction node test to match processing instructions in XPath, which means that you can match all processing instructions in a document with the expression //processing-instruction()—as you can see in Figure 2.4.

Comment Nodes

As you'd expect, comment nodes in XPath correspond to comments in XML documents, which are delimited with <!-- and -->. As far as XPath is concerned, the value of a comment node is the text between <!-- and -->. In an XPath document tree, there is a comment node for every comment (except for any comment that occurs in a DTD or schema).

Our XML document contains a few comments, and you can see one of them here:

```
<?xml version="1.0"?>
<planets>

    <planet>
        <name>Mercury</name>
```

```
        <mass units="(Earth = 1)">.0553</mass>
        <day units="days">58.65</day>
        <radius units="miles">1516</radius>
        <density units="(Earth = 1)">.983</density>
        <distance units="million miles">43.4</distance>
        <!--At perihelion-->
    </planet>
          .
          .
          .
```

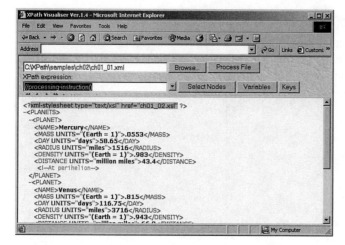

FIGURE 2.4   Matching processing instruction nodes.

In XPath, you can match comments with the comment node test, which means that the expression //comment() matches all comment nodes in a document. You can see this expression at work in the XPath Visualiser in Figure 2.5, where it is matching comment nodes.

Text Nodes

XPath also gives you the means of handling text data in elements as *text nodes*. For example, the value of the text node in the <name> element here is "Mercury":

```
<?xml version="1.0"?>
<planets>

    <planet>
        <name>Mercury</name>
```

```
        <mass units="(Earth = 1)">.0553</mass>
        <day units="days">58.65</day>
        <radius units="miles">1516</radius>
        <density units="(Earth = 1)">.983</density>
        <distance units="million miles">43.4</distance>
        <!--At perihelion-->
    </planet>
            .
            .
            .
```

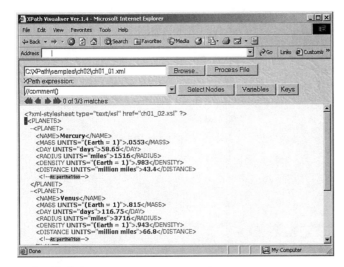

FIGURE 2.5   Matching comment nodes.

HANDLING TEXT IN XML CDATA SECTIONS

How does XPath handle text in XML CDATA sections? Each character within a CDATA section is treated as character data. In other words, a CDATA section is treated as if the <![CDATA[and]]> were removed and every occurrence of markup like < and & was replaced by the corresponding character entities like < and &.

Also, characters inside comments, processing instructions, and attribute values do not produce text nodes.

A text node of an element is just the PCDATA data of that element. Note that if an element contains other elements, processing instructions, or comments, that can break up text into multiple text nodes. For example, the element <planet>Mars<HR/>The Red Planet</planet> contains two text nodes, "Mars" and "The Red Planet".

In XPath, you can match text nodes with the text node function, which means that you can match all text nodes throughout a document with the expression //text(), as you see in the XPath Visualiser in Figure 2.6.

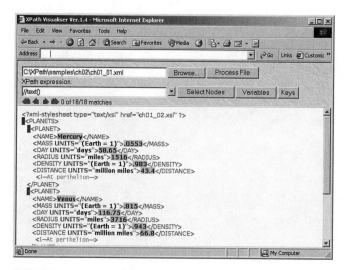

FIGURE 2.6   Matching text nodes.

Namespace Nodes

Namespace nodes are a little different from other nodes—they're not visible in the same way in a document. Each element has a set of namespace nodes, one for each distinct namespace prefix that is in scope for the element (including the standard XML prefix, which is implicitly declared by the XML Namespaces Recommendation) and one for the default namespace if one is in scope for the element. The element itself is the parent of each of these namespace nodes; however, a namespace node is not considered a child of its parent element. An element will have a namespace node

- For every attribute in the element that declares a namespace (that is, whose name starts with `xmlns:`).

- For every attribute in a containing element whose name starts `xmlns:` (unless the element itself or a nearer ancestor redeclares the prefix).

- For an `xmlns` attribute, if the element or some containing element has an `xmlns` attribute, and the value of the `xmlns` attribute for the nearest such element is not empty.

Namespace nodes are not directly visible in an XML document, so there's no XPath Visualiser example here. But take a look at this XSLT stylesheet, which includes two explicit namespace declarations:

```
<?xml version="1.0"?>
<xsl:stylesheet version="1.0"
    xmlns:xsl="http://www.w3.org/1999/XSL/Transform"
    xmlns="http://www.w3.org/1999/xhtml">

    <xsl:template match="//planets">
        <html>
            <xsl:apply-templates/>
        </html>
    </xsl:template>

    <xsl:variable name="myPosition" select="3"/>

    <xsl:template match="planet">
        <p>
            <xsl:value-of select="$myPosition"/>
        </p>
    </xsl:template>

</xsl:stylesheet>
```

In this case, the prefix xsl is associated with the URI
"http://www.w3.org/1999/XSL/Transform", and any elements whose names are prefixed with
xsl will have a namespace node with the value "http://www.w3.org/1999/XSL/Transform".
There's also a default namespace here, "http://www.w3.org/1999/xhtml", used for any non-
prefixed elements. And there's another default namespace here, the implicit XML namespace,
which is in effect for all XML elements. The URI for the implicit XML namespace is
"http://www.w3.org/XML/1998/namespace".

That completes our overview of the seven types of nodes in XPath 1.0: root nodes, element
nodes, attribute nodes, processing instruction nodes, comment nodes, text nodes, and namespace nodes. However, there's more about nodes to understand from XPath's point of view—
nodes can also have various kinds of names, as well as string values, for example.

Node Names

Most nodes have names—in fact, there are three different types of names that XPath uses:

- Qualified names, also called QNames—This term comes from www.w3.org/TR/REC-xml-
  names, and it's the name of the node including any applicable namespace prefix. For
  example, the element <STARS> has the QName "STARS", and the element <map:STARS>
  has the QName "map:STARS".

- Local name—The local name is the same as the QName minus any namespace prefix. For example, the element <STARS> has the local name "STARS", and the element <map:STARS> also has the local name "STARS".

- Expanded name—If a node has both a local name and is associated with a namespace, its expanded name is made of a pair of the namespace's URI and the local name.

The most common names are qualified names (QNames) and local names.

USING EXPANDED-NAME PAIRS

How does the expanded-name pair work, exactly? That's still an open question. There are XPath functions to return a node's local name and QName, but none to return its expanded name. The editor for the XPath 1.0 specification, James Clark, says at http://xml.coverpages.org/clarkNS-980804.html that the expanded name is made up of the namespace URI, a "+", and the local name, like this: http://www.starpowder.com+planets. In fact, XPath processors are more likely to use the format {http://www.starpowder.com}planets. So the real answer here is—it's still up to the software you're using.

Here's how to find the various names for the different types of nodes:

- Root nodes—The root node's local name is an empty string, "". It does not have an expanded name.

- Element nodes—An element node has a local name that is simply the name of the element without any namespace prefix, a QName that includes any namespace prefix, and an expanded name computed by expanding the QName of the element with the applicable namespace URI.

- Attribute nodes—Like elements, attributes have local names, QNames, and expanded names. But here's something to note—the namespace prefix of the color attribute in <my:planet color="RED"> is not my—there is no namespace prefix for this attribute. (In the QName and expanded name for attributes, you only use the actual namespace prefix for the attribute itself, not the element it's an attribute of.)

- Processing instruction nodes—The local name is the processing instruction's target. For example, in the processing instruction <?xml-stylesheet type="text/xsl" href="ch01_02.xsl"?>, the local name is xml-stylesheet. Because processing instructions don't have namespaces, the namespace part in processing instruction QNames and expanded names is null.

- Comment nodes—A comment node does not have a local name, a QName, or an expanded name.

- Text nodes—A text node does not have a local name, QName, or expanded name.

- Namespace nodes—The local name of a namespace node is the namespace prefix itself. A namespace node has an expanded name and QName as well—the local part is the namespace prefix, and the namespace URI is always null.

Besides node names, XPath also specifies that nodes have *string values*.

Node String Values

In addition to giving most nodes names, each node in XPath is considered to have a string (that is, text) value. For example, the string value of a comment node is the simple text content of the comment itself. Here's how to get the string value for each of the various types of nodes:

- Root nodes—The string value is the concatenated (joined) string value of all text nodes.

- Element nodes—The string value is the concatenated value of all contained text nodes, including the text nodes in descendant elements.

- Attribute nodes—The string value is the normalized attribute value. (The normalized value of a text string is the same text with leading and trailing whitespace removed, as well as converting multiple consecutive whitespace into a single whitespace character—unless the text string is considered XML character data, CDATA, in which case whitespace is not removed.)

- Processing instruction nodes—The string value is everything in the processing instruction between the target and the closing ?>. For example, in the processing instruction `<?xml-stylesheet type="text/xsl" href="ch01_02.xsl"?>`, the string value is `"type="text/xsl" href="ch01_02.xsl"`.

- Comment nodes—The string value is the comment's content.

- Text nodes—The string value is simply the character data in the text node.

- Namespace nodes—The string value is the namespace URI.

For example, take a look at this short XML document:

```
<?xml version="1.0"?>
<!--Here are the words-->
<words copyright = "(c) 2003 Starpowder Inc.">
    <term>Hello</term>
    <term>there.</term>
</words>
```

The string value of the root node of this XML document is the joined string value of the document's text nodes. That looks like this (including whitespace) :

```
Hello
there.
```

So far, then, we've seen how XPath views the nodes in an XML document. But how are those nodes arranged? There are a few different ways of looking at the order of nodes in an XML document, and the first one we should discuss is *document order*.

Document Order

In document order, the nodes in an XML document retain the order in which they appear in the XML document. Some elements contain other elements, and that hierarchical structure is maintained. In addition, the order of *sibling* nodes, at the same level in the document hierarchy, is preserved. For example, in document order, Mercury's <planet> element comes before Venus's <planet> element here:

```
<?xml version="1.0"?>
<planets>

    <planet>
        <name>Mercury</name>
        <mass units="(Earth = 1)">.0553</mass>
        <day units="days">58.65</day>
        <radius units="miles">1516</radius>
        <density units="(Earth = 1)">.983</density>
        <distance units="million miles">43.4</distance>
        <!--At perihelion-->
    </planet>

    <planet>
        <name>Venus</name>
        <mass units="(Earth = 1)">.815</mass>
        <day units="days">116.75</day>
        <radius units="miles">3716</radius>
        <density units="(Earth = 1)">.943</density>
        <distance units="million miles">66.8</distance>
        <!--At perihelion-->
    </planet>
        .
        .
        .
```

In other words, document order simply refers to the order in which nodes appear in an XML document. There's no question about the order when you're dealing with elements that enclose other elements, for example, but when you're dealing with elements on the same

MORE ON DOCUMENT ORDER

Here's one more thing to know about document order—attribute nodes are not in any special order, even in document order. That is, document order says nothing about the order of attributes in an element.

level—sibling elements—document order specifies that they should be ordered as they were in the original XML document.

XPath also organizes nodes into node-sets as well as node trees, the next step up from simple document order.

Working with Node-Sets

As you know, node-sets are XPath's way of dealing with multiple nodes. For example, you can see the node-set returned by the expression //planet on our sample XML document in the XPath Visualiser in Figure 2.7. But there's more to know about node-sets.

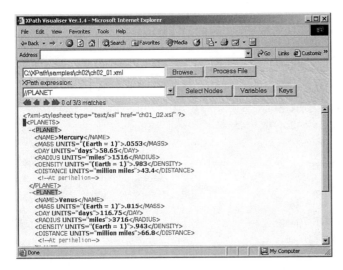

FIGURE 2.7   A node-set.

When you're working with a node-set, XPath gives you a variety of resources that are available at any time called the XPath *context*. You'll see more about what's in the XPath context in the upcoming chapters; here's what in it:

■ The *context node*, which is the XML node in the XML document that the XPath expression was invoked on. In other words, XPath expressions are executed starting from the context node. We'll see how to use relative expressions in XPath soon, and such expressions are always relative to the context node.

- The *context position*, which is a nonzero positive integer indicating the position of a node in a node-set. The first node has position 1, the next position 2, and so on.

- The *context size*, which is also a nonzero positive integer, the context size gives the maximum possible value of the context position. (It's the same as the number of nodes in a node-set.)

- A set of *variables*—you can use variables to hold data in XSLT, and if you do, those variables are stored in the expression's context, which can be accessed in XPath.

- A *function library* full of functions ready for you to call, such as the sum function, which returns the sum of the numbers you pass it.

- The set of *XML namespace declarations* available to the expression.

In addition to these context items, there is also the current node, which we've already discussed. The current node is not the same as the *context node*. The context node is set *before* you start evaluating an XPath expression—it's the node the expression is invoked on. However, as the XPath processor evaluates an XPath expression, it can work on various parts of that expression piece by piece, and the node that the XPath processor is working on at the moment is called the current node.

Here's an example showing how to work with context nodes and positions. Say that you apply the XPath expression /planets/planet to our planetary data:

```xml
<?xml version="1.0"?>
<planets>

    <planet>
        <name>Mercury</name>
        <mass units="(Earth = 1)">.0553</mass>
        <day units="days">58.65</day>
        <radius units="miles">1516</radius>
        <density units="(Earth = 1)">.983</density>
        <distance units="million miles">43.4</distance>
        <!--At perihelion-->
    </planet>

    <planet>
        <name>Venus</name>
        <mass units="(Earth = 1)">.815</mass>
        <day units="days">116.75</day>
        <radius units="miles">3716</radius>
```

```
        <density units="(Earth = 1)">.943</density>
        <distance units="million miles">66.8</distance>
        <!--At perihelion-->
    </planet>
        .
        .
        .
```

The first / in /planets/planet makes the root node the context node for the rest of the expression. The planets part makes the <planets> element the context node for the rest of the expression after that point. That means that the remainder of this expression, /planet, will be evaluated with respect to the <planets> element, so the <planets> element is the context node for the /planet part of this XPath expression.

The whole expression, /planets/planet, matches and returns the three <planet> elements in a node-set. The first <planet> element will have the context position 1, the next will have context position 2, and so on. The context size of the node-set containing the three <planet> elements is three.

Here's an example showing how to work with the variables present in a node-set context. XPath doesn't let you define variables. However, you can create variables in an XSLT stylesheet with the <xsl:variable> element like this, where I'm creating a variable named myPosition with the value 3:

```
<xsl:variable name="myPosition" select="3"/>
```

This new XSLT variable, myPosition, *can* be used in XPath expressions. For example, as we saw in Chapter 1, you can assign XPath expressions to the XSLT <xsl:value-of> element's select attribute. And in XPath, you can refer to the value in a variable by prefacing the variable's name with a $, as you see in ch02_02.xsl in Listing 2.2.

LISTING 2.2   Using an XSLT Variable (ch02_02.xsl)

```
<?xml version="1.0"?>
<xsl:stylesheet version="1.0" xmlns:xsl="http://www.w3.org/1999/XSL/Transform">

    <xsl:template match="//planets">
        <HTML>
            <xsl:apply-templates/>
        </HTML>
    </xsl:template>

    <xsl:variable name="myPosition" select="3"/>
```

LISTING 2.2 Continued

```
    <xsl:template match="planet">
        <P>
            <xsl:value-of select="$myPosition"/>
        </P>
    </xsl:template>

</xsl:stylesheet>
```

This will insert the value of myPosition into the document. This stylesheet just replaces each <planet> element with the value in myPosition, which is 3, in a <P> element, this way:

```
<HTML>
    <P>
    3
    </P>
    <P>
    3
    </P>
    <P>
    3
    </P>
</HTML>
```

And we've already seen some of the XPath functions, such as the position function, which we've used like this: //planet[position()=3], where we're using the position() function to return the current node's context position. All the XPath 1.0 functions are coming up in Chapter 4.

String Value of Node-Sets

We've already seen that nodes have string values, and it turns out that node-sets also have string values in XPath—but a node-set's string value might surprise you. If you followed the discussion earlier about the string value of a root node, which is the concatenation of text nodes in the document, you might expect the string-value of a node-set to be made up of the concatenated string-values of all the nodes in the set.

But that's not so—in XPath, the string-value of a node-set is simply the string-value of the *first* node in the node set only. For example, if you apply the XPath expression //planet to our planets example, ch02_01.xml, you'll get a node-set holding the three <planet> elements in that document, in document order. However, the string value of this node-set is the string value of the first element only, the Mercury element:

```
<planet>
    <name>Mercury</name>
    <mass units="(Earth = 1)">.0553</mass>
    <day units="days">58.65</day>
    <radius units="miles">1516</radius>
    <density units="(Earth = 1)">.983</density>
    <distance units="million miles">43.4</distance>
    <!--At perihelion-->
</planet>
```

Here's the string value of this element, and therefore of the entire //planets node-set:

```
Mercury
.0553
58.65
1516
.983
43.4
```

That completes our look at nodes and node-sets. The next step up in organization in XPath is to start thinking in terms of *node trees*.

XPath Node Trees

Working with XML documents as node trees is a conceptual way of looking at them. As you can tell from the name, the root node is at the base of the tree, and all other nodes are in a tree structure beginning at the root. Considering XML documents as node trees means that XPath can work with the relationships between nodes in different ways, and those ways are the XPath axes. When you use an axis, you tell XPath what relationships you want to explore in the node tree, starting with the context node—we'll see all the axes at work in Chapter 3.

Let's take a look at an example. You can see a short XML document holding the names of two books in ch02_03.xml in Listing 2.3.

LISTING 2.3   A Short XML Document (ch02_03.xml)

```
<?xml version="1.0"?>
<library>
    <book>
        <title>
            I Love XPath
        </title>
        <title>
```

LISTING 2.3   Continued

```
            XPath is the BEST
        </title>
    </book>
</library>
```

Here's how the XML document we just saw looks to an XPath processor as a tree of nodes:

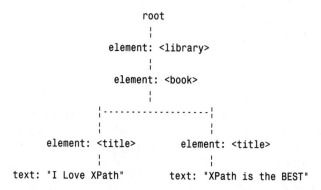

Actually, the preceding tree diagram does not represent the whole picture from an XPath processor's point of view. I've left out one type of node that causes a great deal of confusion—text nodes that contain only whitespace. Because this causes so much confusion in XPath, it's worth taking a look at. The sample XML document we've been working on so far is nicely indented to show the hierarchical structure of its elements, like this:

```
<?xml version="1.0"?>
<library>
    <book>
        <title>
            I Love XPath
        </title>
        <title>
            XPath is the BEST
        </title>
    </book>
</library>
```

However, from an XPath point of view, the whitespace we've used to indent elements in this example actually represents text nodes. That means that by default, those spaces will be copied to the output document. The way whitespace works is a major source of confusion in XPath, so we'll see how it works in this example.

Four characters are treated as whitespace: spaces, carriage returns, line feeds, and tabs. That means that from an XSLT processor's point of view, the input document looks like this:

```
<?xml version="1.0"?>
<library>⏎
....<book>⏎
........<title>⏎
............I Love XPath⏎
........</title>⏎
........<title>⏎
............XPath is the BEST⏎
........</title>⏎
....</book>⏎
</library>
```

All the whitespace between the elements is treated as whitespace text nodes in XPath. That means that there are five whitespace text nodes we have to add to our diagram: one before the `<book>` element, one after the `<book>` element, as well as one before, after, and in between the `<title>` elements:

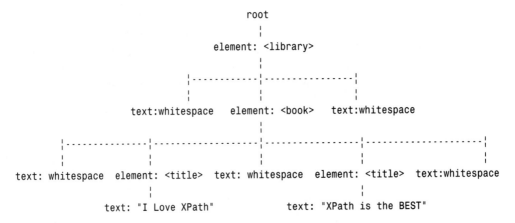

Whitespace nodes like these are text nodes that contain nothing but whitespace. XPath processors preserve this whitespace by default. Note that text nodes that contain characters other than whitespace are not considered whitespace nodes, and so will never be stripped from a document.

As we know, attributes are treated as nodes as well. Although attribute nodes are not considered child nodes of the elements in which they appear, the element is considered their parent node. Suppose you add an attribute to an element like this:

```
<?xml version="1.0"?>
<library>
    <book>
        <title>
            I Love XPath
        </title>
        <title pub_date="2003">
            XPath is the BEST
        </title>
    </book>
</library>
```

Here's how this attribute would appear in the document tree:

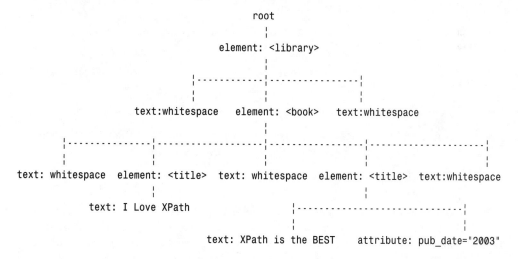

When you consider an XML document as a tree of nodes, there are various relationships between those nodes. For example, take our simple example:

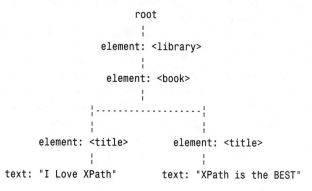

The root node is at the very top of the tree, followed by the root element's node, corresponding to the `<library>` element. This is followed by the `<book>` node, which has two `<title>` node children. These two `<title>` nodes are *grandchildren* of the `<library>` element. The parents, grandparents, and great-grandparents of a node, all the way back to and including the root node, are that element's *ancestors*. The nodes that are descended from a node—its children, grandchildren, great-grandchildren, and so on—are called its *descendants*. As we've seen, nodes on the same level are called *siblings*.

XPath 1.0 formalizes these relationships with its 13 axes, which we're going to start using in Chapter 3. These axes include the `child` axis, which lets you indicate that you're interested in children of the context node, the `descendant` axis, which points to descendants of the context node, and so on.

You use these axes to navigate from the context node along the branches of the node tree to the node(s) you want. Here are a few examples:

- `/descendant::planet[position() = 3]`—Returns the third `<planet>` element in the document.

- `preceding-sibling::name[position() = 2]`—Returns the second previous `<name>` sibling element of the context node.

- `ancestor::planet`—Returns all `<planet>` ancestors of the context node.

- `ancestor-or-self::planet`—Returns the `<planet>` ancestors of the context node. If the context node is a `<planet>` as well, also returns the context node.

- `child::*/child::planet`—Returns all `<planet>` grandchildren of the context node.

That completes our look at the XPath data model in this chapter. We started by taking a look at the various data types you can use in XPath—numbers, strings, Booleans, and node-sets. Then we took a closer look at the different types of XPath nodes that you can use in node-sets, and saw that when nodes are arranged into trees, you can use XPath axes to access them.

Now that we know how the XPath data model works—that is, how XPath views the data in an XML document—and have an introduction to using XPath axes to take advantage of the relationships that XPath knows about between nodes, we're ready to start working with real XPath expressions, and we'll do that in Chapter 3.

Before we finish with data models entirely, however, it's worth noting that there are other XML data models than the XPath data model—the Infoset and DOM models, for example—and we'll take a look at them and how they impact XPath 1.0 next. (If you prefer, you can skip this material and go directly to Chapter 3, or skim over it—I've added it for the sake of completeness for readers who use the Infoset and DOM data models.)

XPath and XML Infosets

An *XML infoset* is intended to hold all the information in an XML document in compact form. Reducing an XML document to its infoset is intended to make comparisons between all kinds of XML documents easier by presenting the data in those documents in a standard way. You can find the official XML Information Set specification at www.w3.org/TR/xml-infoset.

To understand what infosets are and what they're used for, imagine searching for data on the World Wide Web. You may want to search for a particular topic, such as XML, and you'd turn up millions of matches. How could you possibly write software to compare those documents? The data in those documents isn't stored in any way that's directly comparable.

That's where infosets come in because the idea is to regularize how data is stored in an XML document, which will, ultimately, let you work with thousands of such documents. The idea behind infosets is to set up an abstract way of looking at an XML document that allows it to be compared to others.

XML infosets have their own data model, which is not the same as the XPath data model. An XML infoset can contain 15 different types of information items:

- A document information item
- Element information items
- Attribute information items
- Processing instruction information items
- Reference to skipped entity information items
- Character information items
- Comment information items
- A document type declaration information item
- Entity information items
- Notation information items
- Entity start marker information items
- Entity end marker information items
- CDATA start marker information items
- CDATA end marker information items
- Namespace declaration information items

Each of these information items themselves have a set of properties, which contain more information—for example, the document information item has properties that let you access the children of the root node.

Over time, several XML standards have developed their own data model, and W3C is trying to get them all reconciled. You won't have to know about infosets in this book, but if you're already familiar with them, it's useful to know how you can derive the nodes in the XPath data model from the information items provided by an XML infoset. Here's how that works:

- The root node comes from the Infoset document information item. The children of the root node come from the `children` and `children-comments` properties.

- Element nodes come from Infoset element information items. The children of an element node come from the `children` and `children-comments` properties. The attributes of an element node come from the `attributes` property.

- Attribute nodes come from `attribute` information items. The string-value of the node comes from concatenating the character code property of each member of the `children` property.

- Text nodes come from one or more consecutive `character` information items. The string-value of the node comes from concatenating the character code property of each of the `character` information items.

- Processing instruction nodes come from `processing instruction` information items. The local part of the expanded name of the node comes from the `target` property. The string value of the node comes from the `content` property.

- Comment nodes come from `comment` information items. The string value of the node comes from the `content` property.

- Namespace nodes come from a `namespace` declaration information item. The local part of the expanded-name of the node comes from the `prefix` property. The string value of the node comes from the `namespace` URI property.

In fact, one of the tasks of XPath 2.0 was to reconcile the data models used in XPath and the XML Infoset specifications, and we'll discuss that later in Chapter 7.

DOM Level 3 XPath

There's another popular way of looking at the data in an XML document—the Document Object Model (DOM). If you've done any programming that extracted data from XML documents, you're probably familiar with the DOM, because the DOM specifies a set of programming objects and functions that lets you work with the data in an XML document (the DOM objects are implemented in programming languages like JavaScript and Java). You can find more information on the DOM at www.w3.org/DOM/DOMTR.

Like the XPath data model, the DOM lets you consider an XML document as a tree of nodes, although these nodes are not exactly the same as in XPath. Here are the node types in the DOM:

- Element
- Attribute
- Text
- CDATA section
- Entity reference
- Entity
- Processing instruction
- Comment
- Document
- Document type
- Document fragment
- Notation

Each of these node types corresponds to a programming object with its own methods that let you navigate from node to node or recover the text in a node.

In an attempt to reconcile the data model in the DOM with XPath 1.0, W3C created a version of XPath called "Document Object Model XPath," and you can find it at www.w3.org/TR/DOM-Level-3-XPath/. The idea was to support the creation of XPath functions that would work with standard DOM objects—in other words, to let you work with a DOM tree of nodes using XPath functions. To do that, the DOM version of XPath connects DOM and XPath nodes by first treating XPath nodes in terms of infosets.

The DOM XPath specification is now in Candidate Recommendation status, and you can read all about it at www.w3.org/TR/DOM-Level-3-XPath/. It's never really become very popular, however, because most people consider it just an interim way of relating the XPath and DOM models.

In fact, as you can see, the situation with XPath 1.0, XML infosets, and the DOM data models is a problem because each of these data models is different. W3C has worked on bringing things together in XPath 2.0, however, with the XPath 2.0 data model (more properly called the W3C XQuery 1.0 and XPath 2.0 Data Model). The XPath 2.0 data model forms the basis of data models for a number of XML-related specification—XPath and others, such as XSLT and XQuery. In this way, W3C is doing what it should have done from the beginning—creating one standard data model that will let you treat the data in an XML document as a tree of nodes. More on the XPath 2.0 data model in Chapter 7.

In Brief

- There are four data types in XPath 1.0:

  - Numbers

  - Strings

  - Booleans

  - Node-sets

- These node types are supported in XPath 1.0:

  - The root node

  - Element nodes

  - Attribute nodes

  - Processing instruction nodes

  - Comment nodes

  - Text nodes

  - Namespace nodes

- Here are some additional concepts from this chapter:

  - Document order is the order of nodes as they appear in the original document.

  - Documents are handled by XML processors as node trees.

  - Infosets hold the data that an XML document contains in standard form.

Location Steps and Paths

3

Understanding Location Steps and Paths

How do location paths work? We took a look at location paths in the overview in Chapter 1, where we saw that location paths look much like directory paths. For example, you might store section one of chapter one of part one of a novel in a directory with this path if you're using Windows:

```
\novel\part1\section1\chapter1
```

or this path if you're using Unix:

```
/novel/part1/section1/chapter1
```

The idea behind XPath location paths is very much the same except that, as we'll see in this chapter and the next, the XPath syntax can get much more complex and detailed than directory paths. Like directory paths, you build location paths out of individual steps, called *location steps*, separated by / or //. You use these steps to specify the data you want, just as you use successive directories in a file path to get to the location of a file.

For example, in the XPath location path `/library/book/title[2]/text()`, we begin with a /, which matches the root node of the document, followed by, in order:

- The location step library, which matches the child `<library>` element of the root node

- The location step book, which matches the child `<book>` element of the `<library>` element

- The location step `title[2]`, which matches the second `<title>` element of the `<book>` element

- `text()`, which matches the text in the `<title>` element

In fact, the XPath location path `/library/book/title[2]/text()` uses abbreviated XPath syntax, which we're going to see in this chapter. Here's the full version of this XPath location path, where the child element nature of each successive location step is spelled out:

```
/child::library/child::book/child::title[position()=2]/child::text
```

Okay—now let's get to the details.

The Parts of a Location Step

Each location step is made up of an *axis,* a *node test,* and zero or more *predicates,* like this (where the * symbol means "zero or more of"):

```
axis :: node-test [predicate]*
```

For example, in the location step `child::name[position() = 2]`, `child` is the name of the axis (which you follow with `::`), `name` is the node test and `[position() = 2]` is the predicate. In this case, the `child` axis selects child nodes of the node you start at, which is the context node. We're going to take a look at axes, node tests, and predicates in detail in this chapter. This location step can also be abbreviated, using the abbreviated syntax we'll see in this chapter, as `name[2]` (this works because the child axis is the default axis, and when you use position predicates like `[position() = 2]`, XPath lets you abbreviate them as simply `[2]`).

Location paths can be made up of one or more location steps, such as `child::name[position() = 2]/child::firstName`, which selects all the `<firstName>` elements that are children of the second `<name>` child element of the context node. This location path can also be abbreviated as `name[2]/firstName`.

When you start the location path (not a location step) with `/` or `//`, the location path is called an *absolute location path* because you're specifying the path from the root node of the XML document (just as starting a file path with `/` in Unix starts the path from the root directory and makes the path an absolute one). Otherwise, the location path is *relative,* starting with the context node.

For example, take a look at this node tree again:

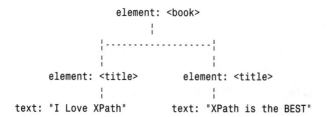

Beginning a location path with / (or //, as we'll see) makes that path start with the document's root node, making this an absolute location path and making the root node the context node for the first location step in the path. To move to the child `<library>` element, you add the location step `library` like this: `/library` (using unabbreviated syntax, that would be `/child::library`). That makes the context node for the next location step the `<library>` element. To move to the `<book>` element starting from the `<library>` context node, you add `book` (or `child::book`) to the location path like this: `/library/book` and so on, all the way down to the text in the second `<title>` element, which you reach with `/library/book/title[2]/text()`. These are all absolute location paths, starting from the root node.

On the other hand, if you've got a context node already set—some XPath software lets you specify context nodes—your location paths can be relative. For example, if you've set the context node to the `<library>` element, the relative location path `book/title[2]/text()` will locate the text in the second `<title>` element in the document.

Now it's time to get systematic about our study of location steps, which we're going to do by taking a look at what kind of axes, node tests, and predicates XPath are available.

XPath Axes

We're going to take a look at all 13 XPath 1.0 axes in this chapter. For example, in the location step `child::planet`, which refers to all `<planet>` elements that are children of the context node, `child` is the axis (and as you now know, you can also abbreviate this location step as `planet`, because `child` is the default axis). Here are all the XPath 1.0 axes:

- The `ancestor` axis holds the ancestors of the context node; the ancestors of the context node are the parent of context node and the parent's parent and so forth, back to and including the root node.

- The `ancestor-or-self` axis holds the context node and the ancestors of the context node.

- The `attribute` axis holds the attributes of the context node.

- The `child` axis holds the children of the context node.

- The `descendant` axis holds the descendants of the context node. A descendant is a child or a child of a child and so on.

- The descendant-or-self axis contains the context node and the descendants of the context node.

- The following axis holds all nodes in the same document as the context node that come after the context node.

- The following-sibling axis holds all the following siblings of the context node. A sibling is a node on the same level as the context node.

- The namespace axis holds the namespace nodes of the context node.

- The parent axis holds the parent of the context node.

- The preceding axis contains all nodes that come before the context node.

- The preceding-sibling axis contains all the preceding siblings of the context node. A sibling is a node on the same level as the context node.

- The self axis contains the context node.

Each XPath location step must specify an axis (or use the default child axis), as in this location path we've already seen: /child::library/child::book/child::title[2]/child::text.

You can also see the various XPath axes listed in Table 3.1, which lists the support for these axes by XML processors in Internet Explorer. The XML processor in Internet Explorer is called MSXML; MSXML 2.0 was the version in Internet Explorer 5.0, early versions of Internet Explorer 6.0 used MSXML3, and the current version is MSXML4. If you're using the .NET platform, your version of MSXML is MSXML.NET.

TABLE 3.1
The XPath Axes

AXIS	ABBREVIATION	MSXML2	MSXML3	MSXML4	MSXML.NET
ancestor			X	X	X
ancestor-or-self			X	X	X
attribute	@		X	X	X
child	(default)	X	X	X	X
descendant	//	X	X	X	X
descendant-or-self		X	X	X	X
following			X	X	X
following-sibling		X	X	X	
namespace			X	X	X
parent	..	X	X	X	X
preceding			X	X	X
preceding-sibling		X	X	X	
self		X	X	X	X

XPath Node Tests

When you use an axis in a location step, you're telling XPath where to look and identifying a set of nodes. A node test tells XPath which of the nodes in that set you're interested in.

There are a number of ways to create node tests. You can use names of nodes as node tests, or the wildcard * to select element or attribute nodes (note especially that * matches only elements and attributes, not just any kind of node). For example, the location step `child::*/child::name` selects all <name> elements that are grandchildren of the context node. To match attributes, you'd use the attribute axis like this: `attribute::*`. Besides node names and the wildcard character, you can also use these node tests in XPath 1.0:

- The * wildcard character matches any element or attribute name.

- A name matches a node with that name (for example, `planet` will match a <planet> element).

- The `comment()` node test selects comment nodes.

- The `node()` node test selects any type of node.

- The `processing-instruction()` node test selects a processing instruction node. You can specify the name of the processing instruction to select in the parentheses.

- The `text()` node test selects a text node.

You can see the XPath 1.0 node tests in Table 3.2, along with the XML processor version that supports them in the Internet Explorer.

TABLE 3.2

The XPath Node Tests

AXIS	MSXML2	MSXML3	MSXML4	MSXML.NET
*	x	x	x	x
name	x	x	x	x
comment()	x	x	x	x
node()	x	x	x	x
processing-instruction()	x	x	x	x
text()	x	x	x	x

The node test lets you specify what nodes you want to work with in an XPath location step. For example, take a look at our sample node tree:

```
root
 |
element: <library>
```

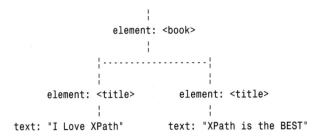

You can start at the root node with /, and then use the child axis and the node test library to move to the <library> element—giving you the location path /child::library. You can see this at work in the XPath Visualiser in Figure 3.1.

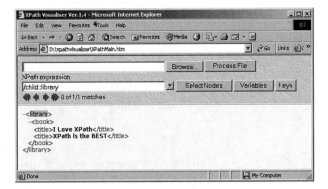

FIGURE 3.1   Using the XPath location step /child::library.

And you can move to the <book> element under the <library> element with another location step involving this child axis and a node test like this: /child:library/child:book. You can see what this looks like in the XPath Visualiser in Figure 3.2.

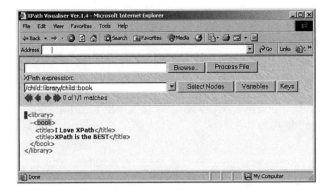

FIGURE 3.2   Using the XPath location step /child::library/child::book.

The next level down in the node tree holds two `<title>` elements, however. What if we only want to work with the second one? If we used the location path `/child::library/child::book/child::title`, we'd match both `<title>` elements, so we need more than a node test here—we need to use a predicate.

XPath Predicates

The next part of a location step, which follows the node text, is the predicate. A location step doesn't need a predicate, but if you use a predicate, you can specify even more about the node or nodes you want to match.

You often use one of the built-in XPath functions in predicates. For example, take a look at the location step `child::planet[position() = 2]`. In this case, the predicate, which is always enclosed between [and], is `position() = 2`. This means that the value the built-in XPath function `position()` returns must indicate that this is the second `<planet>` child in order for the location step to match (this location step can also be abbreviated as `planet[2]`). In this way, this predicate narrows down the search from the node-set of all `<planet>` children of the context node down to the second `<planet>` child.

Now we're in a position to select the second `<title>` element in our XML document that has this node tree:

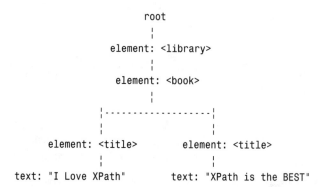

To move to the second `<title>` element, we can use the location path `/child::library/child::book/child::title[2]`, as you see in the XPath Visualiser in Figure 3.3 (this location path can also be abbreviated as `/library/book/title[2]`).

As you can see, expressions in predicates can let you narrow down the search from a whole node-set to just the nodes you're looking for.

Here's another node-test example—to select the `<title>` element that contains the text "I Love XPath", you can use this XPath location path with the `text()` node test: `/child::library/child::book/child::title[text()="I Love XPath"]`, as you see in Figure 3.4.

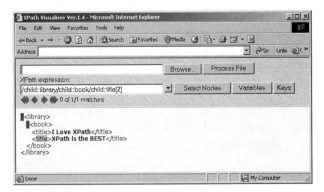

FIGURE 3.3   Using the location step `/child::library/child::book/child::title[2]`.

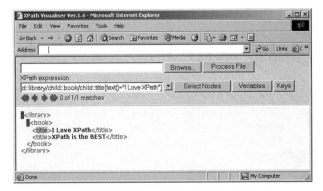

FIGURE 3.4   Selecting a `<title>` element.

Now we're able to construct XPath location paths like `/child::library/child::book/child::title[2]` using axes, node tests, and predicates. Each part of a location step, the axis, node test, and predicate, narrows down the set of nodes you're working with.

You can also build up XPath expressions much as you can location paths. For example, the `text()` node test will return the text in a node, so if you want to extract the text of the `<title>` element, you can use the XPath expression `/child::library/child::book/child::title[2]/text()`, which evaluates not to a node-set, but to a text string, "XPath is the BEST", as you can see in Figure 3.5.

You can use multiple predicates in the same location step—for example, say that we added a `language` attribute to each `<planet>` element in our planetary data XML document, as you see in `ch03_01.xml` (see Listing 3.1).

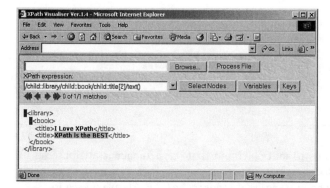

FIGURE 3.5 Using /child::library/child::book/child::title[2]/text().

LISTING 3.1 Adding a Language Attribute (ch03_01.xml)

```xml
<?xml version="1.0" encoding="utf-8"?>
<planets>

    <planet language="English">
        <name>Mercury</name>
        <mass units="(Earth = 1)">.0553</mass>
        <day units="days">58.65</day>
        <radius units="miles">1516</radius>
        <density units="(Earth = 1)">.983</density>
        <distance units="million miles">43.4</distance><!--At perihelion-->
    </planet>

    <planet language="English">
        <name>Venus</name>
        <mass units="(Earth = 1)">.815</mass>
        <day units="days">116.75</day>
        <radius units="miles">3716</radius>
        <density units="(Earth = 1)">.943</density>
        <distance units="million miles">66.8</distance><!--At perihelion-->
    </planet>

    <planet language="English">
        <name>Earth</name>
        <mass units="(Earth = 1)">1</mass>
        <day units="days">1</day>
```

LISTING 3.1 Continued

```
        <radius units="miles">2107</radius>
        <density units="(Earth = 1)">1</density>
        <distance units="million miles">128.4</distance><!--At perihelion-->
    </planet>

</planets>
```

What if we wanted to reach the second `<planet>` element that has a `language` attribute set to "English"? We could do that with a location path like this: `/planets/planet[attribute::language = "English"][position() = 2]`, as you see in Figure 3.6. In this way, you can handle multiple conditions with multiple predicates.

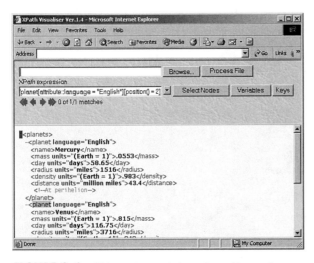

FIGURE 3.6 Using `/planets/planet[attribute::language = "English"][position() = 2]`.

Some Examples of XPath Location Paths

There's nothing like seeing all this at work to understand what's going on, so here are a number of location path examples:

- `child::planet`—Returns the `<planet>` element children of the context node.

- `child::*`—Returns all element children (* only matches elements, or attributes if you use it with the `attribute` axis) of the context node.

- `child::text()`—Returns all text node children of the context node.

- `child::node()`—Returns all the children of the context node, no matter what their node type is.

- `attribute::units`—Returns the units attribute of the context node.

- `descendant::planet`—Returns the `<planet>` element descendants of the context node.

- `ancestor::planet`—Returns all `<planet>` ancestors of the context node.

- `ancestor-or-self::planet`—Returns the `<planet>` ancestors of the context node. If the context node is a `<planet>` as well, also returns the context node.

- `descendant-or-self::planet`—Returns the `<planet>` element descendants of the context node. If the context node is a `<planet>` as well, also returns the context node.

- `self::planet`—Returns the context node if it is a `<planet>` element.

- `child::name/descendant::planet`—Returns the `<planet>` element descendants of the child `<name>` elements of the context node.

- `child::*/child::planet`—Returns all `<planet>` grandchildren of the context node.

- `/`—Returns the root node (that is, the parent of the document element).

- `/descendant::planet`—Returns all the `<planet>` elements in the document.

- `/descendant::planet/child::name`—Returns all the `<name>` elements that have a `<planet>` parent.

- `child::planet[position() = 3]`—Returns the third `<planet>` child of the context node.

- `child::planet[position() = last()]`—Returns the last `<planet>` child of the context node.

- `/descendant::planet[position() = 3]`—Returns the third `<planet>` element in the document.

- `child::planets/child::planet[position() = 4 ]/child::name[position() = 3]`—Returns the third `<name>` element of the fourth `<planet>` element of the `<planets>` element.

- `child::planet[position() > 3]`—Returns last() location path> last()> all the `<planet>` children of the context node after the first three.

- `preceding-sibling::name[position() = 2]`—Returns the second previous `<name>` sibling element of the context node.

- `child::planet[attribute::color = "RED"]`—Returns all `<planet>` children of the context node that have a color attribute with value of "RED".

- `child::planet[attribute::color = "RED"][position() = 3]`—Returns the third `<planet>` child of the context node that has a `color` attribute with value of "RED".

- `child::planet[position() = 3][attribute::color="RED"]`—Returns the third `<planet>` child of the context node, only if that child has a `color` attribute with value of "RED".

- `child::planet[child::name]`—Returns the `<planet>` children of the context node that have `<name>` children.

As you can see, some of this syntax is pretty involved, and a little lengthy to type. However, there is an abbreviated form of XPath syntax, and we'll look at that next.

Using XPath Abbreviated Syntax

There are a number of abbreviations you can take advantage of in XPath syntax. Here are the rules:

- `self::node()` can be abbreviated as .

- `parent::node()` can be abbreviated as ..

- `child::`*nodename* can be abbreviated as *nodename*

- `attribute::`*nodename* can be abbreviated as @*nodename*

- `/descendant-or-self::node()/` can be abbreviated as `//`

You can also abbreviate predicate expressions like `[position() = 3]` as `[3]`. Using the abbreviated syntax makes XPath expressions a lot easier to write. For example, `attribute::units` can be abbreviated as `@units`, you can refer to the context node itself as simply ., and you can refer to the current node and any descendants as `//`.

The `//` syntax in particular is useful and important. Take a look at `ch03_01.xml`, for example, the XML document where we're storing planetary data. In that XML document, we have three `<planet>` elements as children of the main `<planets>` element:

```
<planets>

    <planet language="English">
        <name>Mercury</name>
        <mass units="(Earth = 1)">.0553</mass>
        <day units="days">58.65</day>
        .
        .
        .
```

```
<planet language="English">
    <name>Venus</name>
    <mass units="(Earth = 1)">.815</mass>
    <day units="days">116.75</day>
    .
    .
    .

<planet language="English">
    <name>Earth</name>
    <mass units="(Earth = 1)">1</mass>
    <day units="days">1</day>
    .
    .
    .
```

To select all three <planet> elements, you can use the absolute XPath expression /planets/planet, which starts at the XML document's root node, finds the <planets> element, and then matches the three <planet> child elements. That's fine if you know exactly where in the XML document the elements you want are and so can specify a direct path to them.

But you can also use //planet to select all three <planet> elements, because //planet will find the <planet> elements by checking the root node and all descendants for <planet> elements. That's the power of //—when you want to search for nodes that may be anywhere in a document, use //.

How about some examples of location paths using abbreviated syntax? Here are a number of examples:

- planet—Returns the <planet> element children of the context node.

- *—Returns all element children of the context node.

- text()—Returns all text node children of the context node.

- @units—Returns the units attribute of the context node.

- @*—Returns all the attributes of the context node.

- planet[3]—Returns the third <planet> child of the context node.

- planet[first()]—Returns the first <planet> child of the context node.

- */planet—Returns all <planet> grandchildren of the context node.

- /planets/planet[3]/name[2]—Returns the second <name> element of the third <planet> element of the <planets> element.

- `//planet`—Returns all the `<planet>` descendants of the root node.

- `planets//planet`—Returns the `<planet>` element descendants of the `<planets>` element children of the context node.

- `//planet/name`—Returns all the `<name>` elements that have a `<planet>` parent.

- `.`—Returns the context node itself.

- `.//planet`—Returns the `<planet>` element descendants of the context node.

- `..`—Returns the parent of the context node.

- `../@units`—Returns the units attribute of the parent of the context node.

- `planet[name]`—Returns the `<planet>` children of the context node that have `<name>` children.

- `planet[name="Venus"]`—Returns the `<planet>` children of the context node that have `<name>` children with text equal to "Venus".

Using the XPath Axes

There are 13 axes to master, and we'll take a look at them here, complete with examples. To understand how something like XPath works, there's no better way than seeing it at work as much as possible.

We'll take a look at various examples using XPath Visualiser, and we'll also take a look at some examples using the XPath axes with XSLT. You don't really have to understand the XSLT at this point—you can just pick out the XPath expression inside the example. But XSLT is important when working with XPath, as we're going to see in Chapter 5, and here it will help us out when XPath Visualiser can't (as with the namespace axis, which XPath Visualiser doesn't display visually). We're already familiar with the `child` and `attribute` axes, so we won't introduce them here, but we will introduce all the other axes now, beginning with the ancestor axis.

Using the `ancestor` Axis

The `ancestor` axis contains all the ancestors of the context node, including its parents, grandparents, great-grandparents, and so on. This axis always contains the root node (unless the context node is the root node).

Here's an example using XPath Visualiser. In this case, we'll use the location path `//planet/day` to select the `<day>` elements in our planetary data example, `ch03_01.xml`. Then we'll work backward with the `ancestor` axis to find the `<planet>` ancestor of each `<day>` element like this: `//planet/day/ancestor::planet`. You can see the results in Figure 3.7 (note that we're only searching for `<planet>` ancestors with this location path, so only `<planet>` ancestors are selected).

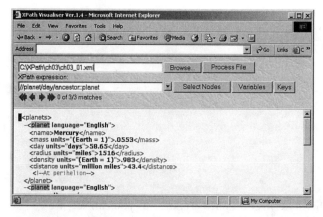

FIGURE 3.7   Using the ancestor axis.

Here's an example doing the same thing using XSLT. As discussed in Chapter 1, in XSLT you create a template with an <xsl:template> element to match nodes. In this case, we want to match <day> elements:

```
<xsl:template match="day">
        .
        .
        .
</xsl:template>
```

Now we'll use an <xsl:for-each> element to loop over all ancestors of the <day> element, using the XPath ancestor axis:

```
<xsl:template match="day">
    <xsl:for-each select="ancestor::*">
        .
        .
        .
    </xsl:for-each>
</xsl:template>
```

To display the name of the ancestor element, we can use the XSLT <xsl:value-of> element. We can extract the name of the current planet with the XPath expression ./name, where . selects the context node. Here's what that looks like in XSLT:

```
<?xml version="1.0" encoding="utf-8"?>
<xsl:stylesheet version="1.1"
xmlns:xsl="http://www.w3.org/1999/XSL/Transform">
<xsl:output method="xml"/>
```

```
<xsl:template match="day">
    <xsl:for-each select="ancestor::*">
        <xsl:value-of select="./name"/>
    </xsl:for-each>
</xsl:template>

<xsl:template match="planet">
    <xsl:apply-templates select="day"/>
</xsl:template>

</xsl:stylesheet>
```

And here's the result when you use this stylesheet on ch03_01.xml—as you can see, we've been able to pick out the names of the ancestors of the <day> elements in our document:

```
<?xml version="1.0" encoding="utf-8"?>
    Mercury
    Venus
    Earth
```

Using the ancestor-or-self Axis

The ancestor-or-self axis contains all the ancestors of the context node, and the context node itself. That means, among other things, that this axis always contains the root node.

Here's an example using XPath Visualiser. In this case, we'll use this axis to select all ancestors of <day> elements, as well as the <day> element itself this way: /planet/day/ancestor-or-self::*. You can see the results in Figure 3.8.

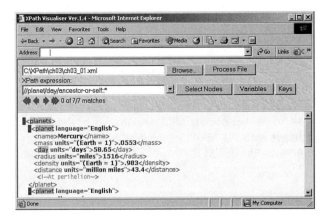

FIGURE 3.8 Using the ancestor-or-self axis.

Here's an example using XSLT and the `ancestor-or-self` axis. In this case, we're going to add author attributes set to "Thaddeus" throughout our document like this:

```
<?xml version="1.0" encoding="utf-8"?>
<?xml-stylesheet type="text/xml" href="planets.xsl"?>
<planets author="Thaddeus" >

    <planet author="Thaddeus" language="English">
        <name>Mercury</name>
        <mass units="(Earth = 1)">.0553</mass>
        <day author="Thaddeus" units="days">58.65</day>
        <radius units="miles">1516</radius>
        <density units="(Earth = 1)">.983</density>
        <distance units="million miles">43.4</distance><!--At perihelion-->
    </planet>


    <planet author="Thaddeus" language="English">
        <name>Venus</name>
        <mass units="(Earth = 1)">.815</mass>
        <day units="days">116.75</day>
        <radius units="miles">3716</radius>
        <density units="(Earth = 1)">.943</density>
        <distance units="million miles">66.8</distance><!--At perihelion-->
    </planet>

    <planet language="English">
        <name>Earth</name>
        <mass units="(Earth = 1)">1</mass>
        <day units="days">1</day>
        <radius units="miles">2107</radius>
        <density units="(Earth = 1)">1</density>
        <distance units="million miles">128.4</distance><!--At perihelion-->
    </planet>

</planets>
```

Now say that you want to list by name all ancestors of <day> elements that have an author attribute—as well as the current <day> element if it has an author attribute. To do that, you can use the XPath location path `ancestor-or-self::*[@author]`, which matches all nodes and ancestors that have an author attribute. Here's what it looks like in XSLT:

```
<?xml version="1.0" encoding="utf-8"?>
<xsl:stylesheet version="1.1"
xmlns:xsl="http://www.w3.org/1999/XSL/Transform">
<xsl:output method="xml"/>
```

```
<xsl:template match="day">
    <xsl:for-each select="ancestor-or-self::*[@author]">
        <xsl:value-of select="local-name(.)"/>
        <xsl:text> </xsl:text>
    </xsl:for-each>
</xsl:template>

<xsl:template match="planet">
    <xsl:apply-templates select="day"/>
</xsl:template>

</xsl:stylesheet>
```

Here's the result, showing the matching ancestors of all three <day> elements that have author attributes, including the <day> element itself, which has an author attribute:

```
<?xml version="1.0" encoding="UTF-8"?>

planets planet day
planets planet
planets
```

Using the descendant Axis

The descendant axis contains all the descendants of the context node. Note that this does not include any attributes or namespace nodes.

Here's an example using XPath Visualiser. In this case, we'll select all descendants of <planet> elements with the location path //planet/descendant::*, as you see in Figure 3.9.

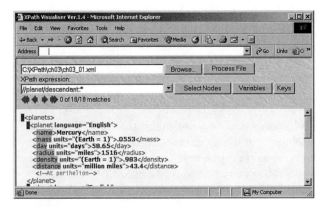

FIGURE 3.9   Using the descendant axis.

Here's an example using XSLT. In this case, we'll check a document to see if it includes a <planet> element for Mercury, and if so, we'll include this element in the result: <info>Sorry, Mercury cannot be found at this time.</info>. To match Mercury's <planet> element, all you have to do is to check whether any text node descendant of a <planet> element holds the string "Mercury" this way:

```xml
<?xml version="1.0" encoding="utf-8"?>
<xsl:stylesheet version="1.0"
xmlns:xsl="http://www.w3.org/1999/XSL/Transform">
<xsl:output method="xml"/>

<xsl:template match="planet[descendant::text()='Mercury']">
    <info>Sorry, Mercury cannot be found at this time.</info>
</xsl:template>

  <xsl:template match="*">
      <xsl:apply-templates select="*"/>
  </xsl:template>

</xsl:stylesheet>
```

That's all it takes. Here's the result, showing the <info> element:

```xml
<?xml version="1.0" encoding="utf-8"?>
<info>Sorry, Mercury cannot be found.</info>
```

Using the descendant-or-self Axis

The descendant-or-self axis contains all the descendants of the context node, and the context node itself. Note, however, that it does not contain any attributes or namespace nodes.

You can see an example in Figure 3.10, where we're selecting all <planet> elements and their descendants with the XPath location path //planet/descendant-or-self::*.

Here's an example doing the same thing using XSLT. In this case, we'll use an XSLT template to match all <planet> elements and then loop over all nodes in the node-set returned by using the descendant-or-self axis, displaying each node's name:

```xml
<?xml version="1.0" encoding="utf-8"?>
<xsl:stylesheet version="1.0"
xmlns:xsl="http://www.w3.org/1999/XSL/Transform">
<xsl:output method="xml"/>
```

```
<xsl:template match="planet">
    <xsl:for-each select="descendant-or-self::*">
        <xsl:value-of select="local-name()"/>
        <xsl:text> </xsl:text>
    </xsl:for-each>
</xsl:template>

</xsl:stylesheet>
```

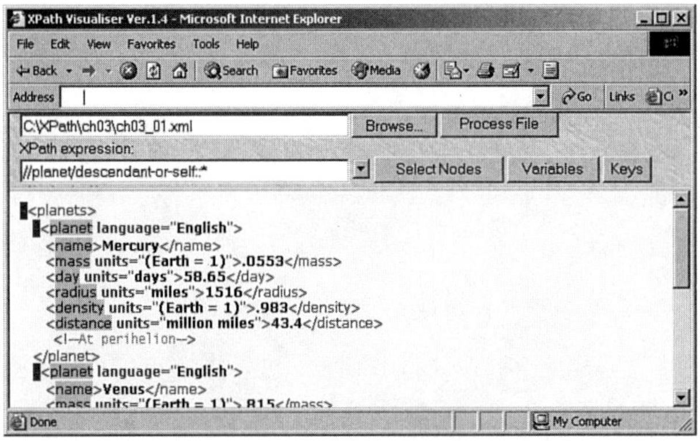

FIGURE 3.10   Using the descendant-or-self axis.

That's all it takes. Here's the result, where we've been able to list the name of all the descendants of `<planet>` elements, as well as the `<planet>` elements themselves, using the descendant-or-self axis:

```
<?xml version="1.0" encoding="UTF-8"?>
    planet name mass day radius density distance
    planet name mass day radius density distance
    planet name mass day radius density distance
```

Using the following Axis

The `following` axis contains all nodes that come after the context node in document order, excluding any of the context node's descendants—and also excluding attribute nodes and namespace nodes.

You can see an example in the XPath Visualiser in Figure 3.11, where we're using this axis to select the following elements after the `<mass>` element in the first `<planet>` element, using the XPath location path `/planets/planet[1]/mass/following::*`.

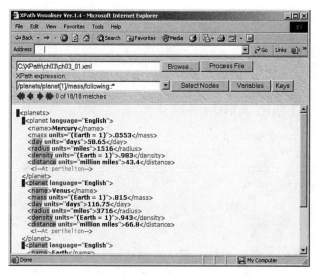

FIGURE 3.11 Using the `following` axis to extract data.

Here's an example using XSLT to do the same thing. In this case, we're matching the first
`<planet>` element in an XSLT template and displaying the names of the following elements:

```xml
<?xml version="1.0" encoding="utf-8"?>
<xsl:stylesheet version="1.1"
xmlns:xsl="http://www.w3.org/1999/XSL/Transform">
<xsl:output method="xml"/>

<xsl:template match="planet[1]">
    <xsl:for-each select="mass/following::*">
        <xsl:value-of select="local-name()"/>
        <xsl:text> </xsl:text>
    </xsl:for-each>
</xsl:template>

  <xsl:template match="*">
     <xsl:apply-templates select="*"/>
  </xsl:template>

</xsl:stylesheet>
```

Here's what the result looks like. Note that we've been able to get all the elements following
the `<mass>` element in the first `<planet>` element, and then all the following elements in the
rest of the document:

```
<?xml version="1.0" encoding="UTF-8"?>
day radius density distance
planet name mass day radius density distance
planet name mass day radius density distance
```

Using the `following-sibling` Axis

The `following-sibling` axis contains all the following siblings of the context node. You can see an example in the XPath Visualiser in Figure 3.12, where we're using the XPath location path `/planets/planet[1]/mass/following-sibling::*` to select all following sibling nodes of the <mass> element in the first <planet> element.

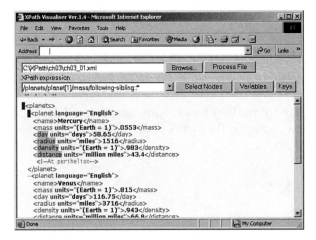

FIGURE 3.12   Using the `following-sibling` axis.

Here's how this example works in XSLT; in this case, we're also matching the first <planet> element's <mass> element and then getting its following sibling elements:

```
<?xml version="1.0" encoding="utf-8"?>
<xsl:stylesheet version="1.1"
xmlns:xsl="http://www.w3.org/1999/XSL/Transform">
<xsl:output method="xml"/>

<xsl:template match="planet[1]">
    <xsl:for-each select="mass/following-sibling::*">
        <xsl:value-of select="local-name()"/>
        <xsl:text> </xsl:text>
    </xsl:for-each>
</xsl:template>
```

```
<xsl:template match="*">
    <xsl:apply-templates select="*"/>
</xsl:template>

</xsl:stylesheet>
```

Here's the result—as you can see, we've caught all the siblings following the <mass> element in the first <planet> element:

```
<?xml version="1.0" encoding="UTF-8"?>
day radius density distance
```

Using the namespace Axis

The namespace axis contains the namespace nodes of the context node—note that the axis will be empty unless the context node is an element. An element will have a namespace node for

- Every attribute of the element whose name starts with "xmlns:".

- Every attribute of an ancestor element whose name starts "xmlns:" (unless, of course, the element itself or a nearer ancestor redeclares the namespace).

- An xmlns attribute, if the element, or some ancestor, has an xmlns attribute.

XPath Visualiser doesn't handle this axis visually, so we'll rely on XSLT here. Here, we'll add an XML namespace declaration to the <planets> element, using the namespace "http://www.XPathCorp.com" like this:

```
<?xml version="1.0" encoding="utf-8"?>
<?xml-stylesheet type="text/xml" href="planets.xsl"?>
<planets xmlns="http://www.XPathCorp.com">

    <planet>
        <name>Mercury</name>
        <mass units="(Earth = 1)">.0553</mass>
        <day units="days">58.65</day>
        <radius units="miles">1516</radius>
        <density units="(Earth = 1)">.983</density>
        <distance units="million miles">43.4</distance><!--At perihelion-->
    </planet>
        .
        .
        .
```

In XSLT, we can check the namespaces used in the `<planets>` element like this:

```
<?xml version="1.0" encoding="utf-8"?>
<xsl:stylesheet version="1.1"
xmlns:xsl="http://www.w3.org/1999/XSL/Transform">
<xsl:output method="xml"/>

<xsl:template match="planets">
    <xsl:value-of select="namespace::*"/>
</xsl:template>

</xsl:stylesheet>
```

And here's the result, showing that we can indeed pick out the namespace:

```
<?xml version="1.0" encoding="UTF-8"?>
http://www.XPathCorp.com
```

Using the `parent` Axis

The `parent` axis contains the parent (and only the parent) of the context node, if there is one.

You can see an example in XPath Visualiser in Figure 3.13. Here, we're picking out the parent elements of all `<day>` elements with the XPath location path `//day/parent::*`.

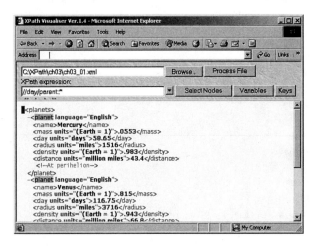

FIGURE 3.13 Using the parent axis to extract data.

And here's the same example in XPath. In this case, we'll match all <day> elements and get the names of their parent elements. Here's what it looks like:

```
<?xml version="1.0" encoding="utf-8"?>
<xsl:stylesheet version="1.1"
xmlns:xsl="http://www.w3.org/1999/XSL/Transform">
<xsl:output method="xml"/>

<xsl:template match="//day">
    <xsl:for-each select="parent::*">
        <xsl:value-of select="local-name()"/>
        <xsl:text> </xsl:text>
    </xsl:for-each>
</xsl:template>

<xsl:template match="*">
    <xsl:apply-templates select="*"/>
</xsl:template>

</xsl:stylesheet>
```

And here's the result:

```
<?xml version="1.0" encoding="UTF-8"?>
planet planet planet
```

> **USING THE ABBREVIATION ..**
>
> Remember that you can also use the abbreviation . . to stand for the parent of the context node.

Using the preceding Axis

The preceding axis contains all nodes that are before the context node in document order, excluding any ancestors of the context node, and also excluding attribute nodes and namespace nodes.

Here's an example using XPath Visualiser. In this case, we'll select all elements preceding the <density> element in the first planet element with the XPath location path //planet[1]/density/preceding::*, as you can see in Figure 3.14.

Let's give this axis a try in XSLT. In this case, say that we want to set the content of the <distance> element to the text "This planet is farther than Mercury from the sun." if the current planet is indeed farther from the sun than Mercury. One way to do that is to see if Mercury comes before the current planet in document order, using the preceding axis:

```
<?xml version="1.0" encoding="utf-8"?>
<xsl:stylesheet version="1.1"
xmlns:xsl="http://www.w3.org/1999/XSL/Transform">
<xsl:output method="xml"/>
```

```
<xsl:template match="distance[preceding::*/name='Mercury']">
    <distance>This planet is farther than Mercury from the sun.</distance>
</xsl:template>

<xsl:template match="@*¦node()">
  <xsl:copy>
    <xsl:apply-templates select="@*¦node()"/>
  </xsl:copy>
</xsl:template>

</xsl:stylesheet>
```

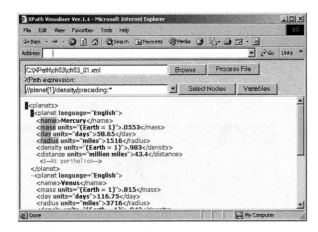

FIGURE 3.14 Using the preceding axis to select elements.

If the current planet does come after Mercury, this example inserts the message in its <distance> element, as you see in this result:

```
<?xml version="1.0" encoding="utf-8"?>
<?xml-stylesheet type="text/xml" href="planets.xsl"?>
<planets>

    <planet>
        <name>Mercury</name>
        <mass units="(Earth = 1)">.0553</mass>
        <day units="days">58.65</day>
        <radius units="miles">1516</radius>
        <density units="(Earth = 1)">.983</density>
        <distance units="million miles">43.4</distance>
        <!--At perihelion-->
    </planet>
```

```
<planet>
    <name>Venus</name>
    <mass units="(Earth = 1)">.815</mass>
    <day units="days">116.75</day>
    <radius units="miles">3716</radius>
    <density units="(Earth = 1)">.943</density>
    <distance>This planet is farther than Mercury from the sun.</distance>
    <!--At perihelion-->
</planet>

<planet>
    <name>Earth</name>
    <mass units="(Earth = 1)">1</mass>
    <day units="days">1</day>
    <radius units="miles">2107</radius>
    <density units="(Earth = 1)">1</density>
    <distance>This planet is farther than Mercury from the sun.</distance>
    <!--At perihelion-->
</planet>

</planets>
```

Using the `preceding-sibling` Axis

The `preceding-sibling` axis contains all the preceding siblings of the context node. Note that if the context node is an attribute node or namespace node, the `preceding-sibling` axis won't hold anything.

You can see an example in the XPath Visualiser in Figure 3.15, where we're using the XPath location path `//planet[2]/preceding-sibling::*` to select all preceding siblings of the second `<planet>` element. Note that just the first `<planet>` element is selected. On the other hand, if we had used `//planet[2]/preceding::*`, not only would the first `<planet>` element be selected, but all that element's child elements would be selected as well.

Here's a more advanced example using XSLT. In this case, we'll replace the `<distance>` element in Mercury's `<planet>` element with `<distance>This planet is the closest to the sun.</distance>`. If we're matching `<distance>` elements, how can we make sure that we've got Mercury's `<distance>` element? We can check the current `<distance>` element's preceding siblings and look for the text "Mercury". Here's what it looks like in XSLT:

```
<?xml version="1.0"?>
<xsl:stylesheet version="1.0"
xmlns:xsl="http://www.w3.org/1999/XSL/Transform">
<xsl:output method="xml"/>
```

```
<xsl:template match="distance[preceding-sibling::*='Mercury']">
  <distance>This planet is the closest to the sun.</distance>
</xsl:template>

<xsl:template match="@*|node()">
  <xsl:copy>
    <xsl:apply-templates select="@*|node()"/>
  </xsl:copy>
</xsl:template>

</xsl:stylesheet>
```

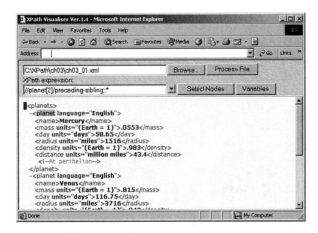

FIGURE 3.15   Using the `preceding-sibling` axis to extract data.

And here's the result:

```
<?xml version="1.0" encoding="utf-8"?>
<?xml-stylesheet type="text/xml" href="planets.xsl"?>
<planets>

    <planet language="English">
        <name>Mercury</name>
        <mass units="(Earth = 1)">.0553</mass>
        <day units="days">58.65</day>
        <radius units="miles">1516</radius>
        <density units="(Earth = 1)">.983</density>
        <distance>This planet is the closest to the sun.</distance>
        <!--At perihelion-->
    </planet>
```

```
<planet language="English">
    <name>Venus</name>
    <mass units="(Earth = 1)">.815</mass>
    <day units="days">116.75</day>
    <radius units="miles">3716</radius>
    <density units="(Earth = 1)">.943</density>
    <distance units="million miles">66.8</distance><!--At perihelion-->
</planet>

<planet language="English">
    <name>Earth</name>
    <mass units="(Earth = 1)">1</mass>
    <day units="days">1</day>
    <radius units="miles">2107</radius>
    <density units="(Earth = 1)">1</density>
    <distance units="million miles">128.4</distance><!--At perihelion-->
</planet>

</planets>
```

Using the `self` Axis

The `self` axis contains just the context node, and you can abbreviate "`self::node()`" as "`.`". This is a useful axis to know about, because as you know, if you omit the axis, the default is `child::`, but sometimes you want to refer to the current node instead. For example, `[self::planet]` is true only if the context node is a `<planet>` element.

You can see an example using this axis in XPath Visualiser in Figure 3.16, where we're using the XPath location path `//*[self::radius]` to select `<radius>` elements in ch03_01.xml (this location path is equivalent to `//radius`).

Here's an example using XSLT. In this case, we'll use one template to match *both* `<name>` and `<day>` elements in the same template. We can do that by matching name ¦ day in a template like this (more on how this works in the next section):

```
<xsl:template match="name ¦ day">
    .

    .

    .
</xsl:template>
```

At this point, we've matched both `<name>` and `<day>` elements—but suppose that in the body of the template we actually want to treat these elements differently. To do that, we have to check if we're dealing with a `<name>` element or a `<day>` element, which we can do with the

XSLT element <xsl:if>, where you assign the condition to test to this element's test attribute. Here's what it looks like in XSLT:

```
<xsl:template match="name ¦ day">

    <xsl:if test="self::name">
        <xsl:value-of select="."/>
    </xsl:if>

    <xsl:if test="self::day">
        <xsl:value-of select="."/>
        <xsl:text> </xsl:text>
        <xsl:value-of select="@units"/>
    </xsl:if>

</xsl:template>
        .
        .
        .
```

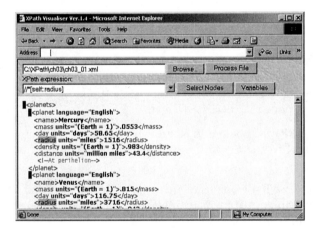

FIGURE 3.16   Using the self axis to select <radius> elements.

So now we've taken a look at all 13 axes, from the ancestor axis to the self axis. Note that you can combine location paths with the ¦ operator—we'll take a closer look at that now.

Creating Compound Location Paths

In XPath, you can combine location paths with the ¦, or "pipe" character. We've already seen that at work like this:

```
<xsl:template match="name ¦ day">
     .
     .
     .
</xsl:template>
```

You can use any kind of location paths with the pipe character, like this:

```
<xsl:template match="name/firstName ¦ day/author/lastName">
     .
     .
     .
</xsl:template>
```

When you use a compound location path, each path is evaluated separately—that is, the context node for the first path doesn't affect the context node for the other path. And you're not restricted to two paths; you can connect as many as you like with pipes:

```
<xsl:template match=
     "name/firstName ¦ day/author/lastName ¦ distance ¦ mass/kilograms">
     .
     .
     .
</xsl:template>
```

When it comes to *predicates*, however, the situation is different. In XPath, you combine conditions in a predicate with the and and or operators. For example, if you wanted to match all <distance> elements that have units attributes set to "million miles" *and* language attributes set to "English", you could use the and operator like this:

```
<xsl:template
match="distance[@units='million miles'
and @language='English']">
     <distance>This is the planet Mercury,
closest to the Sun.</distance>
</xsl:template>
```

USING QUOTATION MARKS

Notice the quotation marks here—to avoid confusing the XSLT processor, we're using single quotes to surround the attribute values here, because the whole XPath expression is surrounded in double quotes. You could also use the or operator if you wanted to match <distance> elements that have units attributes set to "million miles" *or* language attributes set to "English", like this:

```
<xsl:template match="distance[@units='mil
lion miles' and @language='English']">
     <distance>This is the planet Mercury,
closest to the Sun.</distance>
</xsl:template>
```

Here's another example: `child::*[self::name or self::mass]`, which returns both the `<name>` and `<mass>` children of the context node.

You can connect as many conditions in a predicate as you want using and and or. And if it gets confusing, you can use parentheses like this:

```
<xsl:template match="author[(@firstName='Cary') and (@lastName='Grant)]">
    <distance>This is the planet Mercury, closest to the Sun.</distance>
</xsl:template>
```

Note also that compound location paths can also have predicates, of course, including compound predicates.

Nesting Predicates

It's also legal to *nest* predicates. Here's how you might select all `<project>` elements that have `<name>` descendants that in turn have a preceding sibling `<active>` element:

```
//project[descendant::name[preceding-sibling::active]]
```

You can also nest predicates when using compound location paths and even compound predicates.

Using Predicates Without Operators

The predicates we've used so far usually use operators, as in the location step `author[position()=4]`, where we're using the = operator (we'll see all the available operators in the next chapter). However, you don't need to use operators at all in predicates if you just want to test for the existence of a node.

For example, if you want to find all `<notation>` elements that contain at least one `<author>` element, you can use this location path: `//notation[descendant::author]`.

That's it for this chapter on location steps and location paths. We saw how XPath works with the data model introduced in Chapter 2 by using location paths, which are made up of location steps. Each location step, in turn, is made up of an axis, a node test, and a predicate. In Chapter 4, we're going to get more details on creating location paths as we see the operators and functions you can use in XPath predicates.

In Brief

- Each location step is made up of an axis, a node test, and zero or more predicates.

- An axis indicates how to search for nodes. Here are the XPath 1.0 axes:

    - The `child` axis

    - The `attribute` axis

    - The `ancestor` axis

    - The `ancestor-or-self` axis

    - The `descendant` axis

    - The `descendant-or-self` axis

    - The `following` axis

    - The `following-sibling` axis

    - The `namespace` axis

    - The `parent` axis

    - The `preceding` axis

    - The `preceding-sibling` axis

    - The `self` axis

- You can use these node tests in XPath 1.0:

    - The `*` wildcard character matches any element or attribute name.

    - A name matches a node with that name (for example, `planet` will match a `<planet>` element).

    - The `comment()` node test selects comment nodes.

    - The `node()` node test selects any type of node.

    - The `processing-instruction()` node test selects a processing instruction node.

    - The `text()` node test selects a text node.

- Predicates are enclosed in [and] and may contain any valid XPath 1.0 expression.

XPath 1.0 Functions and Operators

4

The XPath Boolean Operators and Functions

You can use XPath logical operators to produce Boolean true/false results. These are the logical operators:

- != means "is not equal to."

- < means "is less-than" (use < in XML documents).

- <= means "is less-than or equal to" (use <= in XML documents).

- = means "is equal to" (C, C++, Java, and JavaScript programmers take note—this operator is one = sign, not two).

- > means "is greater-than."

- >= means "is greater-than or equal to."

And as we saw in Chapter 3, you can also use the and and or operators to connect Boolean clauses in predicates.

Here's an example using the logical operator >. This XPath location path selects all <planet> elements after the third one:

```
//planet[position() > 3]
```

XPath also supports a set of Boolean functions:

- boolean() converts its argument to a Boolean value.

- false() returns a value of false.

- lang() tests whether the language tag set with the xml:lang attribute is the same as the language passed to this function.

- not() reverses the true/false value of its argument.

- true() returns a value of true.

We'll take a look at these in more detail, starting with the boolean function.

The boolean Function

You use the boolean function to convert the argument you pass to it into a Boolean value. Here's what happens when you pass arguments of various XPath types to this function:

- boolean—The same value is returned.

- number—If the number is zero, the result is false. Otherwise the result is true.

- string—If the string is empty, the result is false; otherwise, the result is true.

- node-set—Empty node-set returns false, otherwise returns true.

The false Function

You can use the false function to return a value of false. That's really all there is to this function.

When do you use this function? XPath does not define any Boolean constants, so if you need to assign a value of false to an XSLT variable, you can use the false function.

The `lang` Function

The `lang` function tests whether the language of the context node (as defined by the `xml:lang` attribute) is the same as the language you pass to it. You pass this function a string that corresponds to a language tag in the XML specification, such as "en" for English, "de" for German, or "fr" for French.

Here's an example where we're checking to make sure that the source document was written in English. We'll start by copying over our planetary data XML document, `ch03_01.xml`, to `ch04_01.xml` in the downloadable code for this book so we can use it in this chapter. Then we set the `xml:lang` attribute in `ch04_01.xml` to English like this:

```xml
<?xml version="1.0" encoding="UTF-8"?>
<planets  xml:lang="en">

    <planet>
        <name>Mercury</name>
        <mass units="(Earth = 1)">.0553</mass>
        <day units="days">54.65</day>
        <radius units="miles">1516</radius>
        <density units="(Earth = 1)">.983</density>
        <distance units="million miles">43.4</distance><!--At perihelion-->
    </planet>
        .
        .
        .
```

You can see how we test the `lang` function with the XPath Visualiser and the location path `//*[lang("en")]`, which selects elements that have `xml:lang` set to "en". You can see the results in Figure 4.1—because we've set `xml:lang` to "en" in the document element, `<planets>`, all enclosed elements also have `xml:lang` set to "en".

Here's an example using the `lang` function in XSLT. Say that in this case you want to make sure that a source document's language is English before applying templates. You can use the `lang` function and the `<xsl:if>` element like this in XLST:

```xml
<?xml version="1.0" encoding="UTF-8"?>
<xsl:stylesheet version="1.1"
xmlns:xsl="http://www.w3.org/1999/XSL/Transform">

    <xsl:template match="/planets">
        <xsl:if test="lang('en')">
        <HTML>
        .
        .
        .
```

```
        </HTML>
        </xsl:if>
    </xsl:template>
            .
            .
            .

</xsl:stylesheet>
```

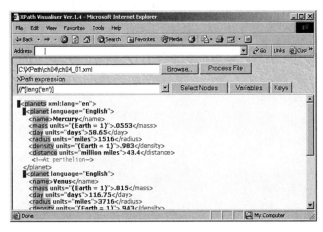

FIGURE 4.1   Using `lang('en')`.

The not Function

You use the `not` function to reverse the Boolean value of the argument you pass to it. If you pass it an argument whose logical value is true, this function will return `false`, and if you pass it a `false` argument, it returns `true`.

You can see an example in the XPath Visualiser in Figure 4.2, where we're selecting elements that do *not* have a `units` attribute, using the location path `//*[not(@units)]`.

Here's an XSLT example. In this case, we'll create two templates, one for `<planet>` elements that have *both* `color` and `rings` attributes, and another template for all other `<planet>` elements. That looks like this:

```
<?xml version="1.0" encoding="UTF-8"?>
<xsl:stylesheet version="1.1"
xmlns:xsl="http://www.w3.org/1999/XSL/Transform">

    <xsl:template match="planet[@color and @rings]">
            .
            .
            .
```

```
        </xsl:template>

    <xsl:template match="planet[not(@color) or not(@rings)]">
            .
            .
            .
        </xsl:template>

    </xsl:stylesheet>
```

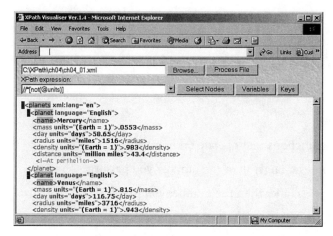

FIGURE 4.2   Using the not function while selecting elements.

The true() Function

The true function returns a value of true. And that's all it does.

XPath does not define any Boolean constants, so if you need to assign a value of true to an XSLT variable, you can use the true function.

The XPath Numeric Operators and Functions

XPath 1.0 has the following operators you can use on numbers:

- \+ performs addition.
- \- performs subtraction.
- * performs multiplication.

- `div` performs division (the / character, which stands for division in other languages, is already heavily used in XML and XPath).

- `mod` returns the modulus of two numbers (the remainder after dividing the first by the second).

For example, the location path `//planet[1 + 4]` will find the fifth `<planet>` element, `//planet[2 * 3]` will find the sixth, and so on. Here's an XSLT example—this example selects all planets whose radius (measured in miles) divided by its day (measured in earth days) is greater than 120:

```
<xsl:template match="planets">
    <HTML>
        <BODY>
            <xsl:apply-templates select="planet[radius div day > 120]"/>
        </BODY>
    </HTML>
</xsl:template>
```

In addition, XPath 1.0 supports these functions that operate on numbers:

- `ceiling()` returns the smallest integer larger than the number you pass it.

- `floor()` returns the largest integer smaller than the number you pass it.

- `round()` rounds the number you pass it to the nearest integer.

- `sum()` returns the sum of the numbers you pass it.

We'll take a look at each of these functions to become familiar with them.

The `ceiling` Function

You use the `ceiling` function to get the smallest integer that is larger than the number you pass it. For example, this expression returns 4:

```
ceiling(3.1415926535)
```

The `floor` Function

The `floor` function returns the largest integer that is smaller than the number you pass it. For example, this expression returns 3:

```
floor(3.1415926535)
```

You can see an XSLT example in ch04_02.xsl in Listing 4.1, where we're converting the data in the planetary data document, ch04_01.xml, using floor to convert the value of the <distance> element to an integer.

LISTING 4.1   Using the Floor Function (ch04_02.xsl)

```
<?xml version="1.0" encoding="UTF-8"?>
<xsl:stylesheet version="1.0"
xmlns:xsl="http://www.w3.org/1999/XSL/Transform">

    <xsl:template match="/planets">
        <HTML>
            <HEAD>
                <TITLE>
                    Planetary Data
                </TITLE>
            </HEAD>
            <BODY>
                <H1>
                    Planetary Data
                </H1>
                <TABLE BORDER="2">
                    <TR>
                        <TD>Name</TD>
                        <TD>Radius</TD>
                        <TD>Distance</TD>
                    </TR>
                    <xsl:apply-templates/>
                </TABLE>
            </BODY>
        </HTML>
    </xsl:template>

    <xsl:template match="planet">
        <TR>
            <TD><xsl:value-of select="name"/></TD>
            <TD><xsl:apply-templates select="mass"/></TD>
            <TD><xsl:apply-templates select="radius"/></TD>
            <TD><xsl:apply-templates select="distance"/></TD>
        </TR>
    </xsl:template>
```

LISTING 4.1   Continued

```
<xsl:template match="radius">
    <xsl:value-of select="."/>
    <xsl:text> </xsl:text>
    <xsl:value-of select="@units"/>
</xsl:template>

<xsl:template match="distance">
    <xsl:value-of select="floor(.)"/>
    <xsl:text> </xsl:text>
    <xsl:value-of select="@units"/>
</xsl:template>

</xsl:stylesheet>
```

And here's the result when ch04_02.xsl is applied to ch04_01.xml:

```
<HTML>
    <HEAD>
        <TITLE>
            Planetary Data

        </TITLE>
    </HEAD>
    <BODY>
        <H1>
            Planetary Data

        </H1>
        <TABLE BORDER="2">
            <TR>
                <TD>Name</TD>
                <TD>Radius</TD>
                <TD>Distance</TD>
            </TR>

            <TR>
                <TD>Mercury</TD>
                <TD>.0553</TD>
                <TD>1516 miles</TD>
                <TD>43 million miles</TD>
```

```
        </TR>

        <TR>
            <TD>Venus</TD>
            <TD>.815</TD>
            <TD>3716 miles</TD>
            <TD>66 million miles</TD>
        </TR>

        <TR>
            <TD>Earth</TD>
            <TD>1</TD>
            <TD>2107 miles</TD>
            <TD>128 million miles</TD>
        </TR>

    </TABLE>
  </BODY>
</HTML>
```

The number Function

The number function just converts its argument to a number. Here's an example, where we're passing the *string* "3.1415" to this function:

```
number("3.1415")
```

This expression returns the *number* 3.1415.

The round Function

The round function rounds its value and returns it. For example, round(3.1415926535) returns 3, round(5.5) returns 6, round(-2.5) returns -2, and so on.

The sum Function

The sum function adds together the numeric values of a set of nodes and returns the result. For example, we can find the average planetary mass using the expression sum(//mass) div count(//mass), where the count function is a node-set function we'll see later in this chapter that returns the number of nodes in a node-set. You can see the results displayed by the XPath Visualiser in Figure 4.3.

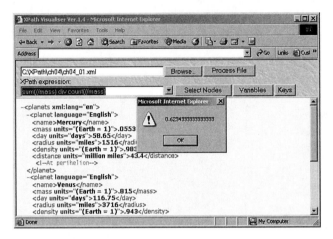

FIGURE 4.3   Using the sum function.

Here's how you can create the same result in XSLT:

```
<?xml version="1.0" encoding="UTF-8"?>
<xsl:stylesheet version="1.1"
xmlns:xsl="http://www.w3.org/1999/XSL/Transform">
<xsl:output method="xml"/>

<xsl:template match="planets">
    <HTML>
        <BODY>
            The average planetary mass is:
            <xsl:value-of select="sum(//mass) div count(//mass)"/>
        </BODY>
    </HTML>
</xsl:template>

</xsl:stylesheet>
```

And here's the result document:

```
<?xml version="1.0" encoding="UTF-8"?>
<HTML>
    <BODY>
        The average planetary mass is: 0.6234333333333334
    </BODY>
</HTML>
```

That finishes our look at the XPath 1.0 numeric operators and functions. Next, we'll take a look at the XPath 1.0 string operators and functions.

The XPath String Operators and Functions

XPath 1.0 doesn't have any operators that are specially designed to work with strings, but it does have many string functions:

- concat(string *string1*, string *string2*, ...)—This function returns all strings you pass to it concatenated (that is, joined) together.

- contains(string *string1*, string *string2*)—This function returns true if the first string contains the second one.

- normalize-space(string *string1*)—This function returns *string1* after leading and trailing whitespace is stripped and multiple consecutive whitespace is replaced with a single space.

- starts-with(string *string1*, string *string2*)—This function returns true if the first string starts with the second string.

- string(string *string1*) — Returns the argument you pass to it in string form.

- string-length(string *string1*) — This function returns the number of characters in *string1*.

- substring(string *string1*, number *offset*, number *length*) — This function returns *length* characters from the string, starting at *offset*.

- substring-after(string *string1*, string *string2*) — This function returns the part of *string1* after the first occurrence of *string2*.

- substring-before(string *string1*, string *string2*) — This function returns the part of *string1* up to the first occurrence of *string2*.

- translate(string *string1*, string *string2*, string *string3*)—This function returns *string1* with all occurrences of the characters that occur in *string2* replaced by corresponding characters (that is, characters that occur at the same location) in *string3*.

We'll take a look at these various string functions at work here.

The concat Function

The concat function concatenates (joins) as many strings together as you pass to it, returning the concatenated string. You can see XPath Visualiser evaluating concat("Now ", "is ", "the ", "time.") in Figure 4.4.

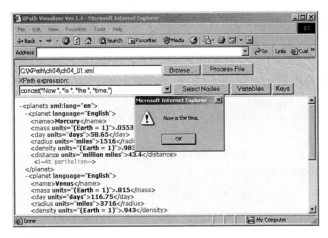

FIGURE 4.4   Using the concat function.

Here are some XSLT templates that concatenate the value of various elements in ch04_01.xml with their units:

```
<xsl:template match="radius">
    <xsl:value-of select="concat(., ' ', @units)"/>
</xsl:template>

<xsl:template match="mass">
    <xsl:value-of select="concat(., ' ', @units)"/>
</xsl:template>

<xsl:template match="day">
    <xsl:value-of select="concat(., ' ', @units)"/>
</xsl:template>

</xsl:stylesheet>
```

By concatenating the values of elements with their units, these templates display values such as 43.4 million miles, and so on.

The contains **Function**

The contains function checks to see if one string is contained inside another, and returns a value of true if so, false otherwise. Here's how you use this function: contains(*container-string*, *contained-string*).

Here's an example of a template using XSLT and the contains function; in this case, we'll search all attributes in the document for the word "days", and if found, will substitute the text "Why not use years instead?" in the result document:

```
<xsl:template match="//*[contains(@units, 'days')]">
    <xsl:text>Why not use years instead?</xsl:text>
</xsl:template>
```

Here's the result document:

```
<HTML>
    <HEAD>
        <TITLE>
            Planetary Data
        </TITLE>
    </HEAD>

    <BODY>
        <H1>
            Planetary Data
        </H1>

        <TABLE BORDER="2">
            <TR>
                <TD>Name</TD>
                <TD>Mass</TD>
                <TD>Radius</TD>
                <TD>Day</TD>
                <TD>Distance</TD>
            </TR>

            <TR>
                <TD>Mercury</TD>
                <TD>.0553 (Earth = 1)</TD>
                <TD>1516 miles</TD>
                <TD>Why not use years instead?</TD>
                <TD>43.4 million miles</TD>
            </TR>

            <TR>
                <TD>Venus</TD>
                <TD>.815 (Earth = 1)</TD>
```

```
                <TD>3716 miles</TD>
                <TD>Why not use years instead?</TD>
                <TD>66.8 million miles</TD>
            </TR>

            <TR>
                <TD>Earth</TD>
                <TD>1 (Earth = 1)</TD>
                <TD>2107 miles</TD>
                <TD>Why not use years instead?</TD>
                <TD>124.4 million miles</TD>
            </TR>

        </TABLE>
    </BODY>
</HTML>
```

The `normalize-space` Function

You use the `normalize-space` function to remove leading and trailing whitespace and condense all internal adjacent whitespace into a single space, returning the resulting string. You can see the XPath Visualiser evaluating the expression `normalize-space(" Now   is   the      time.   ")` in Figure 4.5.

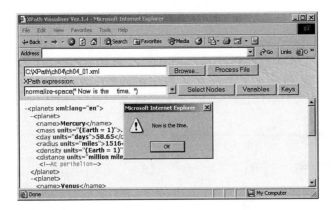

FIGURE 4.5   Using the `normalize-space` function.

Here's an example that uses XSLT; in this case, we might start by adding extra whitespace to the units attribute in all of the `ch04_01.xml` document's `<distance>` elements:

```
<?xml version="1.0" encoding="UTF-8"?>
<?xml-stylesheet type="text/xml" href="planets.xsl"?>
<planets>

    <planet>
        <name>Mercury</name>
        <mass units="(Earth = 1)">.0553</mass>
        <day units="days">54.65</day>
        <radius units="miles">1516</radius>
        <density units="(Earth = 1)">.983</density>
        <distance units="million        miles">43.4</distance><!--At perihelion-->
    </planet>
        .
        .
        .
```

You can remove this extra whitespace in XSLT using the `normalize-space` function like this:

```
<?xml version="1.0" encoding="UTF-8"?>
<xsl:stylesheet version="1.1"
xmlns:xsl="http://www.w3.org/1999/XSL/Transform">

    <xsl:template match="/planets">
        <HTML>
        .

        .

        .
        </HTML>
    </xsl:template>

    <xsl:template match="distance">
        <xsl:value-of select="."/>
        <xsl:text> </xsl:text>
        <xsl:value-of select="normalize-space(@units)"/>
    </xsl:template>
        .
        .
        .
```

You can see in the results that the extra whitespace has indeed been removed:

```
<HTML>
    <HEAD>
```

```
    <TITLE>
        Planetary Data
    </TITLE>
</HEAD>

<BODY>
    <H1>
        Planetary Data
    </H1>
    <TABLE BORDER="2">
        <TR>
            <TD>Name</TD>
            <TD>Mass</TD>
            <TD>Radius</TD>
            <TD>Distance</TD>
        </TR>

        <TR>
            <TD>Mercury</TD>
            <TD>.0553 (Earth = 1)</TD>
            <TD>1516 miles</TD>
            <TD>43.4 million miles</TD>
        </TR>
            .
            .
            .
```

This function is useful in string handling because when you extract text from elements, you're often left with extra spaces (as when the text is indented).

The starts-with Function

You use the starts-with function to determine whether one string starts with another. Here's how you use it—starts-with(*string-to-examine*, *possible-start-string*). This function returns a Boolean value of true if *string-to-examine* does indeed start with *possible-start-string*, and false otherwise.

Here's an example using XPath Visualiser. In this case, we'll look for text nodes whose text starts with the letter "E" like this: //text()[starts-with(., "E")] (recall that . refers to the context node). You can see the results in Figure 4.6, where we've located the Earth.

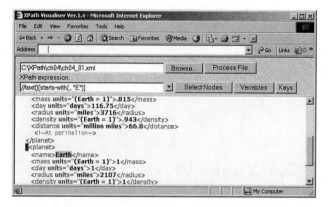

FIGURE 4.6   Using the `starts-with` function.

On the other hand, if we had wanted to locate elements whose text content starts with "E", we could have used this location path: `//*[starts-with(., "E")]`. This works because an element's string value is all its contained strings, which in this case is simply "Earth". We can make use of that fact in an XSLT template where we're matching elements whose text content starts with "E"—which means the Earth's `<planet>` element. In this example, we'll replace that element's text with "The Home Planet" like this:

```
<?xml version="1.0" encoding="UTF-8"?>
<xsl:stylesheet version="1.1"
xmlns:xsl="http://www.w3.org/1999/XSL/Transform">


    <xsl:template match="*[starts-with(., 'E')]">
        <xsl:text>The Home Planet</xsl:text>
    </xsl:template>

        .

        .

        .

</xsl:stylesheet>
```

And here's the result—note that the text for Earth has indeed become "The Home Planet":

```
<HTML>
    <HEAD>
        <TITLE>
            Planetary Data
        </TITLE>
    </HEAD>
```

```
<BODY>
    <H1>
        Planetary Data
    </H1>

    <TABLE BORDER="2">
        <TR>
            <TD>Name</TD>
            <TD>Mass</TD>
            <TD>Radius</TD>
            <TD>Day</TD>
        </TR>
        .
        .
        .
        <TR>
            <TD>The Home Planet</TD>
            <TD>1 (Earth = 1)</TD>
            <TD>2107 miles</TD>
            <TD>1 days</TD>
        </TR>
    </TABLE>
</BODY>
</HTML>
```

The string Function

The string function just converts the item you pass it to a string, and returns that string. In fact, you don't usually need to use this function, because conversions like this are made automatically. Even when an object is returned by an XPath function, it's converted automatically into a string if you want to display its value.

SHOP TALK

THE STRING FUNCTION

The truth is that the string function has almost no uses in XPath 1.0. The only use for it I've ever found is when you want to check a string value but node tests would give you a node-set instead.

Here's how that might work, using XSLT. Say that you wanted to keep track of the order of the singers at various performances, and so had <name> elements for the opera stars Mike, Todd, and Songlin, giving their singing order at various performances like this:

SHOP TALK

```xml
<?xml version="1.0" encoding="UTF-8"?>
<performances>

    <performance>
        <name>Mike</name>
        <name>Todd</name>
        <name>Songlin</name>
        <month>12</month>
        <day>24</day>
    </performance>

    <performance>
        <name>Todd</name>
        <name>Songlin</name>
        <name>Mike</name>
        <month>12</month>
        <day>24</day>
    </performance>

    <performance>
        <name>Songlin</name>
        <name>Mike</name>
        <name>Todd</name>
        <month>12</month>
        <day>24</day>
    </performance>

</performances>
```

Now what if you wanted to find the performance where Songlin was to sing first? A test like the following won't work, because name returns a node-set of *all* the context node's <name> children, and because every <performance> element has a child <name> element with the name Songlin in it, this test will always be true:

```xml
<xsl:template match="performance">
<xsl:if test="name='Songlin'">
    <TR>
        <TD><xsl:value-of select="name"/></TD>
        <TD><xsl:apply-templates select="month"/></TD>
        <TD><xsl:apply-templates select="day"/></TD>
    </TR>
</xsl:if>
</xsl:template>
```

SHOP TALK

Instead of working with a node-set, if you want to test only the first <name> element in each <performance> element, you can use the string function, which returns a string, not a node-set:

```
<?xml version="1.0" encoding="UTF-8"?>
<xsl:stylesheet version="1.1"
xmlns:xsl="http://www.w3.org/1999/XSL/Transform">

    <xsl:template match="/performances">
        <HTML>
        .
        .
        .
        </HTML>
    </xsl:template>

    <xsl:template match="performance">
    <xsl:if test="string(name)='Songlin'">
        <TR>
            <TD><xsl:value-of select="name"/></TD>
            <TD><xsl:apply-templates select="month"/></TD>
            <TD><xsl:apply-templates select="day"/></TD>
        </TR>
    </xsl:if>
    </xsl:template>

    <xsl:template match="month">
        <xsl:value-of select="."/>
    </xsl:template>
        .
        .
        .
    <xsl:template match="day">
        <xsl:value-of select="."/>
    </xsl:template>

</xsl:stylesheet>
```

Having said all this, however, note that you can solve the same problem by explicitly matching to name[1] in a template without having to use the string function at all.

The `string-length` Function

The `string-length` function returns the length of a string you pass to it. You can see an example in XPath Visualiser in Figure 4.7, where we're checking the length of the string "Now is the time."

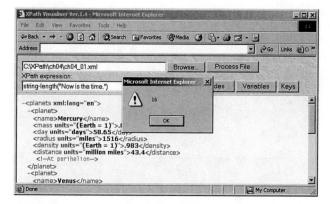

FIGURE 4.7 Using the `string-length` function.

You can see an example using this function in XSLT, where we're using `string-length` to determine the length of each planet's name, in `ch04_03.xsl` (see Listing 4.2).

LISTING 4.2 Using the `string-length` Function (`ch04_03.xsl`)

```xml
<?xml version="1.0" encoding="UTF-8"?>
<xsl:stylesheet version="1.1"
xmlns:xsl="http://www.w3.org/1999/XSL/Transform">

    <xsl:template match="/planets">
        <HTML>
            <HEAD>
                <TITLE>
                    Using string-length
                </TITLE>
            </HEAD>
            <BODY>
                <H1>
                    Using string-length
                </H1>
                    <xsl:apply-templates/>
```

LISTING 4.2   Continued

```
            </BODY>
        </HTML>
    </xsl:template>

    <xsl:template match="planet">
        <xsl:value-of select="name"/> is <xsl:value-of
            select="string-length(name)"/> letters in length.
        <BR/>
    </xsl:template>

    <xsl:template match="*">
    </xsl:template>

</xsl:stylesheet>
```

And here's the result of `ch04_03.xsl` when applied to `ch04_01.xml`:

```
<HTML>
    <HEAD>
        <TITLE>
            Using string-length
        </TITLE>
    </HEAD>

    <BODY>
        <H1>
            Using string-length
        </H1>

        Mercury is 7 letters in length.
        <BR>

        Venus is 5 letters in length.
        <BR>

        Earth is 5 letters in length.
        <BR>

    </BODY>
</HTML>
```

The `substring` Function

The `substring` function returns a substring from a string. This function returns the substring of the source string starting at the starting position and continuing for the number of characters you've specified—or to the end of the string if you haven't specified a number of characters to return. Here's how you use this function: `substring(source-string, start-position, number-of-characters)`. You pass this function a `source-string`, a `starting-position`, and, optionally, a `number-of-characters`. If you ask for more characters than it's possible to return from the string, an error occurs.

You can see an example in the XPath Visualiser in Figure 4.8, where we're evaluating the expression `substring("Now is the time.", 0, 3)`.

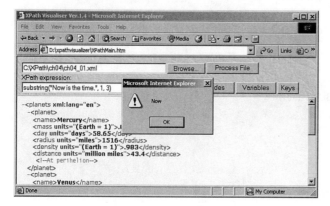

FIGURE 4.8   Using the `substring` function.

The `substring` function is one of three substring functions: `substring-before`, which returns the string preceding a matched substring; `substring` itself, which returns substrings that you specify; and `substring-after`, which returns the substring following a match. We'll see an XSLT example that uses all three functions after taking a look at the other two—`substring-after` and `substring-before`.

The `substring-after` Function

The `substring-after` function returns the substring following a matched string. You pass this function a source string, and a string to match inside the source string. It will return the substring of the source string following the match if there was a match, or an empty string (that is, "") otherwise. Here's how you use this function:

```
substring-after(string, string-to-match)
```

The `substring-before` Function

You can pass `substring-before` a source string, and a string to match inside the source string. It will return the substring in the source string preceding the match if there is a match; otherwise, it returns an empty string (that is, ""). Here's how you use `substring-before`:

`substring-before(string, string-to-match)`

You can see an XSLT example showing how to use the `substring-before`, `substring`, and `substring-after` functions in `ch04_04.xsl` (Listing 4.3). Here, we'll use `substring-before` to get the substring of "Earth" before the "r", the `substring` function to get the "r" itself, and `substring-after` to get the text after the "r".

LISTING 4.3   Using the `substring-before`, `substring`, and `substring-after` Functions (`ch04_04.xsl`)

```
<?xml version="1.0" encoding="UTF-8"?>
<xsl:stylesheet version="1.1"
xmlns:xsl="http://www.w3.org/1999/XSL/Transform">

    <xsl:template match="/planets">
        <HTML>
            <HEAD>
                <TITLE>
                    Planetary Information
                </TITLE>
            </HEAD>
            <BODY>
                <H1>
                    Planetary Information
                </H1>
                    <xsl:apply-templates/>
            </BODY>
        </HTML>
    </xsl:template>

    <xsl:template match="planet">
        <xsl:if test="name='Earth'">
        You are on
        <xsl:value-of
        select="concat(substring-before(name, 'r'), substring(name, 3, 1),
            substring-after(name, 'r'))"/>.
```

LISTING 4.3   Continued

```
            <BR/>
        </xsl:if>
    </xsl:template>

    <xsl:template match="*">
    </xsl:template>

</xsl:stylesheet>
```

Here's the result, where we've reassembled the Earth from its parts:

```
<HTML>
    <HEAD>
        <TITLE>
            Planetary Information
        </TITLE>
    </HEAD>

    <BODY>
        <H1>
            Planetary Information
        </H1>

          You are on Earth.
        <BR>

    </BODY>
</HTML>
```

The `translate` Function

You use the `translate` function to *translate* characters. You pass three strings—the first is the string to work on, the next is a list of characters to match, and the last is a list of characters to replace the matched characters with. Each character in the first string that matches a character in the match string is replaced with the character in the same position in the replace string. Here's how you use this function:

```
string translate(string, from-characters, to-characters)
```

For example, to convert "XSLT" (or any string) to lowercase, you could evaluate the expression `translate("XSLT", "ABCDEFGHIJKLMNOPQRSTUVWXYZ", "abcdefghijklmnopqrstuvwxyz")`, as you see in XPath Visualiser in Figure 4.9.

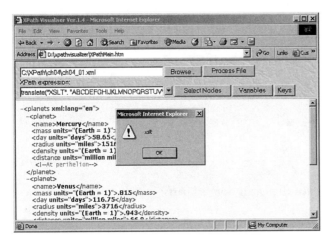

FIGURE 4.9   Using the translate function.

The XPath Node-Set Operators and Functions

XPath does have a few operators that are designed to work on node-sets. In Chapter 3, we saw that the ¦ operator computes the union of its operands, which must be node-sets. Here's an example of an XSLT template that uses this operator, which we saw in Chapter 3:

```
<xsl:template match="name ¦ day">
    .
    .
    .
</xsl:template>
```

Also, as you know, the / and // operators create location paths, and you must use these operators with expressions that evaluate to node-sets. You've already had plenty of practice with these operators.

Here are the XPath functions that work on node-sets:

- count(*node-set*)—This function returns the number of nodes in node-set.

- id(string *ID*)—This function returns a node-set of the element whose ID matches the string passed to the function, or an empty node-set if no element matches.

- last()—This function returns the number of nodes in a node-set that contains the context nodes and all its siblings.

- local-name(*node-set*)—This function returns the local name of the first node in the node-set.

- name(*node-set*)—This function returns the qualified name of the first node in the node-set.

- namespace-uri(*node-set*)—This function returns the URI of the namespace of the first node in the node-set.

- position()—This function returns the position of the context node in the context node-set, starting with 1.

We'll see these functions in more detail next.

The count Function

You use the count function to count the number of nodes in a node-set. All you have to do is to pass the node-set to this function, and it returns the number of nodes as a number.

You can see an example in the XPath Visualiser in Figure 4.10, where we're counting the number of <planet> elements.

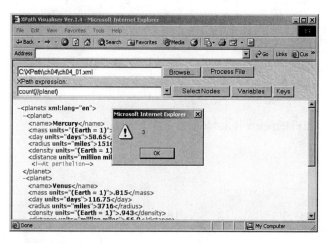

FIGURE 4.10 Using the count function.

Here's an example that we saw earlier in this chapter where we used the expression sum(//mass) div count(//mass), which uses the count function to determine the average planetary mass:

```
<?xml version="1.0" encoding="UTF-8"?>
<xsl:stylesheet version="1.1"
xmlns:xsl="http://www.w3.org/1999/XSL/Transform">
<xsl:output method="xml"/>
```

```
<xsl:template match="planets">
    <HTML>
        <BODY>
            The average planetary mass is:
                <xsl:value-of select="sum(//mass) div count(//mass)"/>
        </BODY>
    </HTML>
</xsl:template>

</xsl:stylesheet>
```

And here's the resulting document:

```
<?xml version="1.0" encoding="UTF-8"?>
<HTML>
    <BODY>
        The average planetary mass is: 0.6234333333333334
    </BODY>
</HTML>
```

The `id` Function

The `id` function returns a node-set where all the nodes have the same ID value as that passed to this function.

Here's an XSLT template that matches all elements that have the ID "expired":

```
<xsl:template match = "//*[id('expired')]">
    <xsl:value-of select="."/>
</xsl:template>
```

To make this work, XPath and XSLT processors usually require that you declare ID values as such in a DTD or XML schema. For example, if you wanted to create a DTD for `ch04_01.xml` that supported an `id` attribute of XML type ID, and set that attribute to "expired" in the `<planet>` element for Mercury, here's what that might look like:

```
<?xml version="1.0" encoding="UTF-8"?>
<!DOCTYPE planets [
<!ELEMENT planet (name, mass, radius,day)>
<!ELEMENT name (#PCDATA)>
<!ELEMENT mass (#PCDATA)>
<!ELEMENT radius (#PCDATA)>
<!ELEMENT day (#PCDATA)>
<!ATTLIST planet
```

```
      id ID #REQUIRED>
]>
<planets>
    <planet id='expired'>
        <name>Mercury</name>
        <mass units="(Earth = 1)">.0553</mass>
        <day units="days">54.65</day>
        <radius units="miles">1516</radius>
        <density units="(Earth = 1)">.983</density>
        <distance units="million miles">43.4</distance><!--At perihelion-->
    </planet>
             .
             .
             .
```

> ## BE CAREFUL WHEN MATCHING BY ID
>
> Some XPath processors and some XSLT processors won't match by ID because they won't read DTDs or XML schema.

The last Function

The last function returns the number of nodes in the node-set that contains the context node and its siblings, so its value is equal to the position of the last node. You can see an example in the XPath Visualiser in Figure 4.11 where in this case we're selecting the last element in each sibling group with the location path //*[last()].

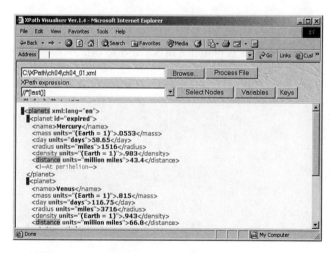

FIGURE 4.11   Using the last function.

Here's an XSLT example. In this case, we'll use the position and last functions to indicate the order of the planets, as you can see in ch04_05.xsl in Listing 4.4.

LISTING 4.4 Using the last Function (ch04_05.xsl)

```xml
<?xml version="1.0" encoding="UTF-8"?>
<xsl:stylesheet version="1.1" xmlns:xsl="http://www.w3.org/1999/XSL/Transform">
<xml:output method="xml"/>

<xsl:template match="planets">
<document>
    <planets>
        <xsl:apply-templates select="planet"/>
    </planets>
</document>
</xsl:template>

<xsl:template match="planet">
    <xsl:value-of select="name"/> is planet
    <xsl:text> </xsl:text>
    <xsl:value-of select="position()"/> of
    <xsl:text> </xsl:text>
    <xsl:value-of select="last()"/>
    <BR/>
</xsl:template>

</xsl:stylesheet>
```

Here's the result—"Mercury is planet 1 of 3", "Venus is planet 2 of 3", and so on:

```xml
<?xml version="1.0" encoding="UTF-8"?>
<document>
    <planets>
    Mercury is planet 1 of 3
    <BR/>
    Venus is planet 2 of 3
    <BR/>
    Earth is planet 3 of 3
    <BR/>
    </planets>
</document>
```

The local-name Function

You can use the local-name function to return the local (that is, unqualified) name of a node. You pass this function a node-set and it returns the local name of the first name in the node-set. If the node-set is empty, it returns the local name of the context node.

You can see an example in the XPath Visualiser in Figure 4.12, where we're finding all `<radius>` elements using the location path `//*[local-name()="radius"]`.

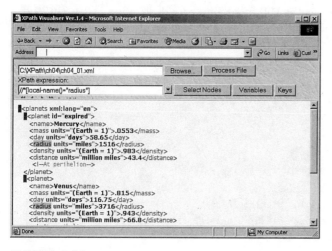

FIGURE 4.12 Using the `local-name` function.

The name Function

The name function is like the `local-name` function, except that it returns the fully qualified name of the node, including any namespace. For example, if you set the document element's namespace to the fictitious URI "http://www.XPathCorp.com" like this:

```
<?xml version="1.0" encoding="UTF-8"?>
<planets xmlns:ns="http://www.XPathCorp.com" xml:lang="en">

    <ns:planet>
        <ns:name>Mercury</ns:name>
        <ns:mass units="(Earth = 1)">.0553</ns:mass>
        <ns:day units="days">58.65</ns:day>
        .
        .
        .
```

Then all the child elements would have the namespace "http://www.XPathCorp.com". For example, the expression `name(//planet[1])` returns the full name of the first `<planet>` element. Different XPath processors have different ways of doing this—some will return "http://www.XPathCorp.com:planet", and some will return programming objects that you need to decipher with programming code.

The `namespace-uri` Function

You can use the `namespace-uri` function in XPath 1.0 to get a string containing the URI of the namespace in a node's name. This is the URI in a namespace declaration as set with the `xmlns` or `xmlns:prefix` attributes. You can only use this function on elements or attributes in node-sets.

For example, you might add a namespace, "pickle", to `ch04_01.xml`:

```
<?xml version="1.0" encoding="UTF-8"?>
<pickle:planets xmlns:pickle="http://XPathCorp.com">

    <pickle:planet>
        <pickle:name>Mercury</pickle:name>
        <pickle:mass units="(Earth = 1)">.0553</pickle:mass>
        <pickle:day units="days">54.65</pickle:day>
        <pickle:radius units="miles">1516</pickle:radius>
        <pickle:density units="(Earth = 1)">.983</pickle:density>
        <pickle:distance units="million miles">43.4</pickle:distance>
            <!--At perihelion-->
    </pickle:planet>

    <pickle:planet>
        <pickle:name>Venus</pickle:name>
        <pickle:mass units="(Earth = 1)">.815</pickle:mass>
        <pickle:day units="days">116.75</pickle:day>
        <pickle:radius units="miles">3716</pickle:radius>
        <pickle:density units="(Earth = 1)">.943</pickle:density>
        <pickle:distance units="million miles">66.8</pickle:distance>
            <!--At perihelion-->
    </pickle:planet>
        .
        .
        .
```

Then you could find the URI of this namespace in a stylesheet using `namespace-uri`:

```
<?xml version="1.0" encoding="UTF-8"?>
<xsl:stylesheet version="1.1"
xmlns:xsl="http://www.w3.org/1999/XSL/Transform"
xmlns:pickle="http://www.XPathCorp.com">
```

```
<xsl:template match="/planets">
    <xsl:value-of select="namespace-uri()"/>
</xsl:template>
```

    .

    .

    .

Here's what you'd see as the result:

```
<?xml version="1.0" encoding="UTF-8"?>
http://XPathCorp.com
```

The `position` Function

We've already seen the `position` function, which returns the position of the context node in the node-set that makes up the current context. This function is a favorite, and we've put it to work throughout the book already. Here's an example we've seen earlier in this chapter that uses the `position` function to display the location of each planet:

```
<?xml version="1.0" encoding="UTF-8"?>
<xsl:stylesheet version="1.1" xmlns:xsl="http://www.w3.org/1999/XSL/Transform">
<xml:output method="xml"/>

<xsl:template match="planets">
<document>
    <planets>
        <xsl:apply-templates select="planet"/>
    </planets>
</document>
</xsl:template>

<xsl:template match="planet">
    <xsl:value-of select="name"/> is planet
    <xsl:text> </xsl:text>
    <xsl:value-of select="position()"/> of
    <xsl:text> </xsl:text>
    <xsl:value-of select="last()"/>
    <BR/>
</xsl:template>

</xsl:stylesheet>
```

And here's the result:

```
<?xml version="1.0" encoding="UTF-8"?>
<document>
    <planets>
    Mercury is planet 1 of 3
    <BR/>
    Venus is planet 2 of 3
    <BR/>
    Earth is planet 3 of 3
    <BR/>
    </planets>
</document>
```

That completes the XPath 1.0 node-set functions, as well as our discussion on the operators and functions available in XPath 1.0. You can see the support for XPath 1.0 functions in Internet Explorer in Table 4.1, listed by XML processor, MSXML, version.

TABLE 4.1

The XPath 1.0 Functions in Internet Explorer

FUNCTION	MSXML2	MSXML3	MSXML4	MSXML.NET
boolean		X	X	X
ceiling		X	X	X
concat		X	X	X
contains		X	X	X
count		X	X	X
false		X	X	X
floor		X	X	X
id	X	X	X	X
lang		X	X	X
last	X	X	X	X
local-name		X	X	X
name		X	X	X
namespace-uri		X	X	X
normalize-space		X	X	X
not		X	X	X
number		X	X	X
position		X	X	X
round		X	X	X
starts-with		X	X	X
string		X	X	X

TABLE 4.1

Continued

FUNCTION	MSXML2	MSXML3	MSXML4	MSXML.NET
string-length		X	X	X
substring		X	X	X
substring-after		X	X	X
substring-before		X	X	X
sum		X	X	X
translate		X	X	X
true		X	X	X

That wraps up this chapter, where we've seen the available XPath 1.0 operators and functions. You'll see these operators and functions in XPath predicates all the time. In the next chapter, we'll take a look at working with XSLT with XPath.

In Brief

- The Boolean operators are logical operators like !=, <, >, >=, and so on. The boolean function converts its argument to a Boolean value, the false function returns a value of false, the lang function tests whether a node's language (set with the xml:lang attribute) is the same as the language passed to the function, the not function reverses the true/false value of its argument, and the true function returns a value of true.

- The XPath 1.0 numeric operators include +, -, *, div, and mod. There are also a number of numeric functions—ceiling() returns the smallest integer larger than the number you pass it, floor returns the largest integer smaller than the number you pass it, round rounds the number you pass it to the nearest integer, and sum returns the sum of the numbers you pass it.

- There aren't any string-specific XPath 1.0 operators, but there are plenty of functions:

  - The concat function returns all strings you pass to it joined together.

  - The contains function returns true if the first string contains the second one.

  - The normalize-space function returns the string you pass to it after leading and trailing whitespace is stripped and multiple consecutive whitespace is replaced with a single space.

  - The starts-with function returns true if the first string you pass it starts with the second string.

  - The string-length function returns the number of characters in a string.

- The `substring` function returns a substring from a string.

- The `substring-after` function returns a substring after another string.

- The `substring-before` function returns a substring before another string.

- The `translate` function returns a string with all occurrences of the characters in a second string replaced by matching characters in a third string.

XPath with XSLT

5

Working with XSLT

We've already been using Extensible Stylesheet Language Transformations (XSLT) throughout the book to show how XPath works, and in this chapter, we're going to take a closer look at XSLT. After all, XSLT is the major reason most people who use XPath 1.0 use XPath in the first place.

XSLT itself is really part of a larger specification, Extensible Stylesheet Language (XSL). XSLT is the most popular part of XSL, because it lets you work with the data in an XML document and transform it into other formats, including HTML or just plain text. You can also use XSLT to transform XML documents into other XML documents where you've arranged the data in a different way.

XSLT is an W3C specification and has been a recommendation since November 16, 1999. You can find the W3C recommendation for XSLT 1.0, the current version, at www.w3.org/TR/xslt. XSLT 2.0 is in the works, but it's only a working draft at this point (there actually was an XSLT 1.1, but it was not continued after the working draft stage). You can see the current version of the XSLT 2.0 Working Draft at http://www.w3.org/TR/xslt20/.

To use XSLT, you need two documents—an XML document that you want to transform, and an XSLT stylesheet that will direct how the transformation works (note that XSLT stylesheets are also XML documents). And you'll also need an XSLT processor.

We took a look at this process in Chapter 1, but we'll see it in more depth now. We'll start this chapter with our planetary data document, renamed ch05_01.xml so we can use it in this chapter, and an XSLT stylesheet that we first saw in Chapter 1, which you see in ch05_02.xsl in Listing 5.1.

LISTING 5.1   Transforming XML Data into HTML (ch05_02.xsl)

```
<?xml version="1.0" encoding="UTF-8"?>
<xsl:stylesheet version="1.1"
xmlns:xsl="http://www.w3.org/1999/XSL/Transform">

    <!-- This template matches all planets elements -->
    <xsl:template match="/planets">
        <HTML>
            <HEAD>
                <TITLE>
                    The Planets Table
                </TITLE>
            </HEAD>
            <BODY>
                <H1>
                    The Planets Table
                </H1>
                <TABLE BORDER="2">
                    <TR>
                        <TD>Name</TD>
                        <TD>Mass</TD>
                        <TD>Radius</TD>
                        <TD>Day</TD>
                    </TR>
                    <xsl:apply-templates/>
                </TABLE>
            </BODY>
        </HTML>
    </xsl:template>

    <xsl:template match="planet">
        <TR>
            <TD><xsl:value-of select="name"/></TD>
            <TD><xsl:apply-templates select="mass"/></TD>
            <TD><xsl:apply-templates select="radius"/></TD>
            <TD><xsl:apply-templates select="day"/></TD>
        </TR>
    </xsl:template>

    <xsl:template match="mass">
        <xsl:value-of select="."/>
        <xsl:text> </xsl:text>
        <xsl:value-of select="@units"/>
```

LISTING 5.1 Continued

```
    </xsl:template>

    <xsl:template match="radius">
        <xsl:value-of select="."/>
        <xsl:text> </xsl:text>
        <xsl:value-of select="@units"/>
    </xsl:template>

    <xsl:template match="day">
        <xsl:value-of select="."/>
        <xsl:text> </xsl:text>
        <xsl:value-of select="@units"/>
    </xsl:template>

</xsl:stylesheet>
```

This stylesheet extracts the XML data in `ch05_01.xml` and formats it into an HTML table. So how do you make this transformation happen?

Techniques for Performing XSLT Transformations

XSLT transformations can happen in three different places:

- In the server. A server program, such as a .NET or JavaServer Page (JSP) program that operates on a Web server, can use XSLT to transform an XML document and send it to the client program, such as a browser.

- In the client. A client program, such as an HTML browser, can perform XSLT transformations. For example, Internet Explorer has full XSLT 1.0 support.

- With a separate program. You can use standalone programs to perform your own XSLT transformations.

As a client program example, recall that Internet Explorer lets you perform XSLT 1.0 transformations. To make that transformation happen, you have to connect your stylesheet to the XML document to transform. You can do that using an `<?xml-stylesheet?>` processing instruction like this: `<?xml-stylesheet type="text/xsl" href="ch05_02.xsl"?>` (note that some other XSLT processors will require this attribute to be `type="text/xml"`, not `type="text/xsl"`). You can see Internet Explorer–enabled version of our sample XML document in `ch05_03.xml` (see Listing 5.2), where we're putting the `<?xml-stylesheet?>` processing instruction to work.

LISTING 5.2   An XML Document Holding Planetary Data (ch05_03.xml)

```xml
<?xml version="1.0" encoding="UTF-8"?>
<?xml-stylesheet type="text/xsl" href="ch05_02.xsl"?>
<planets>

    <planet>
        <name>Mercury</name>
        <mass units="(Earth = 1)">.0553</mass>
        <day units="days">58.65</day>
        <radius units="miles">1516</radius>
        <density units="(Earth = 1)">.983</density>
        <distance units="million miles">43.4</distance><!--At perihelion-->
    </planet>

    <planet>
        <name>Venus</name>
        <mass units="(Earth = 1)">.815</mass>
        <day units="days">116.75</day>
        <radius units="miles">3716</radius>
        <density units="(Earth = 1)">.943</density>
        <distance units="million miles">66.8</distance><!--At perihelion-->
    </planet>

    <planet>
        <name>Earth</name>
        <mass units="(Earth = 1)">1</mass>
        <day units="days">1</day>
        <radius units="miles">2107</radius>
        <density units="(Earth = 1)">1</density>
        <distance units="million miles">128.4</distance><!--At perihelion-->
    </planet>

</planets>
```

You can see the results in Figure 5.1. Using Internet Explorer like this is the most accessible way to perform XSLT transformations for most people.

You can also use standalone packages to perform XSLT transformations. For example, the Xalan XSLT processor mentioned in Chapter 1 lets you perform XSLT transformations. You can download Xalan at http://xml.apache.org/xalan-j/index.html. Note that you'll need to have Java installed; the current version as of this writing is 1.4, which you can download for free from http://java.sun.com/j2se/1.4/download.html.

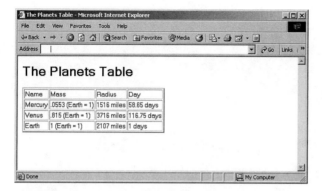

FIGURE 5.1 Using XSLT in the client.

Here's how you'd use Xalan to transform `ch05_01.xml`, using `ch05_02.xsl`, into a new result document, which we'll call `results.html`:

```
%xalan ch05_01.xml ch05_02.xsl results.html
```

And here's what `results.html` looks like when you do this (where we've indented the HTML to make it more readable):

```
<HTML>
    <HEAD>
        <META http-equiv="Content-Type" content="text/html; charset=UTF-8">
        <TITLE>
            The Planets Table
        </TITLE>
    </HEAD>

    <BODY>
        <H1>
            The Planets Table
        </H1>

        <TABLE BORDER="2">
            <TR>
                <TD>Name</TD>
                <TD>Mass</TD>
                <TD>Radius</TD>
                <TD>Day</TD>
            </TR>

            <TR>
```

```
            <TD>Mercury</TD>
            <TD>.0553 (Earth = 1)</TD>
            <TD>1516 miles</TD>
            <TD>58.65 days</TD>
        </TR>

        <TR>
            <TD>Venus</TD>
            <TD>.815 (Earth = 1)</TD>
            <TD>3716 miles</TD>
            <TD>116.75 days</TD>
        </TR>

        <TR>
            <TD>Earth</TD>
            <TD>1 (Earth = 1)</TD>
            <TD>2107 miles</TD>
            <TD>1 days</TD>
        </TR>

    </TABLE>
  </BODY>
</HTML>
```

Another popular XSLT processor that runs with Java is named Saxon, and you can download Saxon for free from `http://saxon.sourceforge.net/`. As we'll see in this chapter, Saxon can do some things that Xalan can't, such as indent output documents automatically. We're also going to see Saxon at work in the second half of this book, because it's the first XSLT processor to include any support for XPath 2.0 (Saxon is written by Michael Kay, who is on the XPath 2.0 W3C design committee.)

That's how you make XSLT transformations happen. Now let's get more details on how to create stylesheets.

Creating Stylesheets

Because XSLT documents are also XML documents, the XSLT 1.0 specification defines a number of elements to let you create stylesheets. XSLT uses XPath to let you specify exactly what data you want to work with in the XML document, and we'll be assigning XPath expressions to the match and select attributes of XSLT elements in this chapter.

As introduced in Chapter 1, XSLT stylesheets begin with an XML declaration and the `<xsl:stylesheet>` element (note that this is *not* the `<?xsl:stylesheet?>` processing instruction you can use in XML documents to connect stylesheets to XML documents). In this element, we associate the `xsl` namespace with the URI "http://www.w3.org/1999/XSL/Transform", which is the official namespace for XSLT:

```
<?xml version="1.0" encoding="UTF-8"?>
<xsl:stylesheet version="1.0" xmlns:xsl="http://www.w3.org/1999/XSL/Transform">
        .
        .
        .
```

To specify what elements you want to locate and work with, you use the `<xsl:template>` element to create XSLT templates.

Creating Templates

A template uses an XPath expression to match a node or nodes in your XML document and lets you specify what you want to do with the matched data. For example, to match the document element, `<planets>`, in our XML document, we use this `<xsl:template>` element:

```
<?xml version="1.0" encoding="UTF-8"?>
<xsl:stylesheet version="1.0" xmlns:xsl="http://www.w3.org/1999/XSL/Transform">

    <!-- This template matches all planets elements -->
    <xsl:template match="planets">
        .
        .
        .
    </xsl:template>
        .
        .
        .
</xsl:stylesheet>
```

The XSLT processor will look through the XML document and match the `<planets>` element to this template. The XSLT processor automatically opens the document, starts at the root node, and searches for templates that match the children of the root node. In this case, that means `<xsl:template match="planets">` will match, because `<planets>` is a child of the root node (but `<xsl:template match="planet">` would not match because `<planet>` is a *grandchild* of the root node).

The template replaces the node(s) you've matched with the content you specify. In this case, we want to create a new HTML table displaying our planetary data and use the `<xsl:apply-templates/>` to handle the child elements of the `<planets>` element:

```
<?xml version="1.0" encoding="UTF-8"?>
<xsl:stylesheet version="1.1"
xmlns:xsl="http://www.w3.org/1999/XSL/Transform">

    <!-- This template matches all planets elements -->
    <xsl:template match="/planets">
        <HTML>
            <HEAD>
                <TITLE>
                    The Planets Table
                </TITLE>
            </HEAD>
            <BODY>
                <H1>
                    The Planets Table
                </H1>
                <TABLE BORDER="2">
                    <TR>
                        <TD>Name</TD>
                        <TD>Mass</TD>
                        <TD>Radius</TD>
                        <TD>Day</TD>
                    </TR>
                    <xsl:apply-templates/>
                </TABLE>
            </BODY>
        </HTML>
    </xsl:template>
        .
        .
        .
```

Note in particular that you use the <xsl:apply-templates> element, as we've done here, to indicate that you've got other templates to use on the child nodes of the current node.

Applying Templates for Child Nodes

In our case, we're using <xsl:apply-templates> to work with the child nodes of the <planets> element, and we'll use a new template to indicate that we want to match <planet> elements like this:

```
<?xml version="1.0" encoding="UTF-8"?>
<xsl:stylesheet version="1.1"
xmlns:xsl="http://www.w3.org/1999/XSL/Transform">

    <!-- This template matches all planets elements -->
    <xsl:template match="/planets">
        <HTML>
            .
            .
            .
            <xsl:apply-templates/>
            .
            .
            .
        </HTML>
    </xsl:template>

    <xsl:template match="planet">
        <TR>
            <TD><xsl:value-of select="name"/></TD>
            <TD><xsl:apply-templates select="mass"/></TD>
            <TD><xsl:apply-templates select="radius"/></TD>
            <TD><xsl:apply-templates select="day"/></TD>
        </TR>
    </xsl:template>
```

In this new <planet> template, we're using <xsl:apply-templates> again to work with the child <mass>, <radius>, and <day> elements of the current <planet> element.

Note also that we're using one of the core XSLT elements here, <xsl:value-of>, to extract the value of the <name> element. (Also note that, because <planet> nodes are not direct child nodes of the root node, this new template would never match anything unless we specifically use a <xsl:apply-templates/> element in the <planets> template to invoke it on the child nodes of the <planets> node explicitly.)

Using <xsl:value-of>

The <xsl:value-of> element inserts the text value of the node you specify with the select attribute into the result document. In this case, we're assigning "name" to the select attribute, which inserts the text value of the current <planet> element's <name> element into the result document, which for us means our HTML table.

Although the `<xsl:template>` element uses the match attribute, `<xsl:value-of>` and `<xsl:apply-templates>` use the select attribute. We'll see that there's a significant difference here in a few pages—the XPath expressions you can use with match are far more restricted than the ones you can use with select.

And that completes the technology we need for the remainder of this stylesheet, because all that's left to do is to create templates for each of the values we want to display and displaying those values and the value of the units attribute like this (more on the `<xsl:text>` element later in this chapter) :

```
<xsl:template match="mass">
    <xsl:value-of select="."/>
```

```
    <xsl:text> </xsl:text>
    <xsl:value-of select="@units"/>
</xsl:template>

<xsl:template match="radius">
    <xsl:value-of select="."/>
    <xsl:text> </xsl:text>
    <xsl:value-of select="@units"/>
</xsl:template>

<xsl:template match="day">
    <xsl:value-of select="."/>
    <xsl:text> </xsl:text>
    <xsl:value-of select="@units"/>
</xsl:template>
```

We've already seen most of how this stylesheet works, but here's something to note—the select attribute only selects the first node that matches. What if you have multiple nodes that could match? We'll take a look at that next.

Using `<xsl:for-each>`

For example, say you have multiple `<name>` elements for each planet, as you see in ch05_04.xml in Listing 5.3.

LISTING 5.3   An XML Document with Multiple `<name>` Elements (ch05_04.xml)

```
<?xml version="1.0" encoding="UTF-8"?>
<?xml-stylesheet type="text/xsl" href="ch05_02.xsl"?>
<planets>

    <planet>
        <name>Mercury</name>
        <name>The Hottest Planet</name>
```

LISTING 5.3   Continued

```
            <mass units="(Earth = 1)">.0553</mass>
            <day units="days">58.65</day>
            <radius units="miles">1516</radius>
            <density units="(Earth = 1)">.983</density>
            <distance units="million miles">43.4</distance><!--At perihelion-->
        </planet>

        <planet>
            <name>Venus</name>
            <name>Planet of Love</name>
            <mass units="(Earth = 1)">.815</mass>
            <day units="days">116.75</day>
            <radius units="miles">3716</radius>
            <density units="(Earth = 1)">.943</density>
            <distance units="million miles">66.8</distance><!--At perihelion-->
        </planet>

        <planet>
            <name>Earth</name>
            <name>The Green Planet</name>
            <mass units="(Earth = 1)">1</mass>

            <day units="days">1</day>
            <radius units="miles">2107</radius>
            <density units="(Earth = 1)">1</density>
            <distance units="million miles">128.4</distance><!--At perihelion-->
        </planet>


</planets>
```

To catch all possible matches, you can use the XSLT `<xsl:for-each>` element as you see in `ch05_05.xsl` in Listing 5.4.

LISTING 5.4   An Example of an XSL Stylesheet with Multiple Matches (`ch05_05.xsl`)

```
<?xml version="1.0" encoding="UTF-8"?>
<xsl:stylesheet version="1.0" xmlns:xsl="http://www.w3.org/1999/XSL/Transform">

    <xsl:template match="planets">
        <HTML>
            <xsl:apply-templates/>
```

LISTING 5.4   Continued

```
            </HTML>
        </xsl:template>

    <xsl:template match="planet">
        <xsl:for-each select="name">
            <P>
                <xsl:value-of select="."/>
            </P>
        </xsl:for-each>
            <BR/>
    </xsl:template>

    </xsl:stylesheet>
```

This stylesheet will catch all <name> elements, place their values in a <P> element, and add them to the output document like this:

```
<HTML>

    <P>Mercury</P>
    <P>The Hottest Planet</P>
    <BR>

    <P>Venus</P>
    <P>Planet of Love</P>
    <BR>

    <P>Earth</P>
    <P>The Green Planet</P>
    <BR>

</HTML>
```

As you can see, <xsl:for-each> is designed to let you handle node-sets that contain multiple nodes. At this point, then, we've been able to handle some of the XSLT basics. Two of the most important aspects are the match attribute in the <xsl:template> element and the select attribute in the <xsl:value-of> element. Much of being able to work with XSLT involves knowing what values you can assign to these attributes. You can assign XPath expressions to both of these attributes, but there are restrictions on what XPath expressions you can use with the match attribute. We'll take a look at the match attribute first, followed by the select attribute.

Understanding the `match` and `select` Attributes

There are two different XSLT attributes that you assign XPath expressions to—the `match` and the `select` attributes. You can use the `match` attribute with the `<xsl:template>` element, and the `select` attribute can be used in the `<xsl:apply-templates>`, `<xsl:value-of>`, `<xsl:for-each>`, `<xsl:copy-of>`, and `<xsl:sort>` XSLT elements.

The `match` attribute is restricted to using the current node or direct child nodes. In other words, you can only use the `self` and the `child` axes—just those two—with the `match` attribute. So in XSLT, `match=axis::node-test[predicate]` is legal only if *axis* is the `self` or the `child` axis. This restriction was made to make implementing XSLT processors easier.

SHOP TALK

SHOP TALK: AN XSLT LOOPHOLE

On the other hand, there's a surprising loophole here—the *predicate* part of `match=axis::node-test[predicate]` can hold any XPath expression at all: there's no limitation on which axes you can use. One gets the impression that in the original XSLT 1.0, the committee overlooked this possibility when they put the restriction on the `match` attribute.

As a result, you're not actually restricted to the `self` and the `child` axes in `match` expressions, because you can use completely general XPath expressions in the predicate of the XPath expression you assign to the `match` attribute.

So all you have to do is to use the `self` axis and put the general XPath expression you want to use in the predicate of the location path you assign to the `match` attribute. (Note, however, that not all XSLT processors may be able to handle completely general XPath expressions, even though they are legal here.)

This is one of the curiosities of XSLT 1.0, and we'll see whether the situation changes in XSLT 2.0 when it's released as a final recommendation.

There are no restrictions on the XPath expressions you can assign to the `select` attribute. This attribute can be used in the `<xsl:apply-templates>`, `<xsl:value-of>`, `<xsl:for-each>`, `<xsl:copy-of>`, and `<xsl:sort>` XSLT elements, and we'll see most of these elements in this chapter.

Copying Nodes

It's often useful to be able to simply copy nodes from the input document to the output document without making any changes, and we'll take a look at how that works here, with examples. There are two elements that you can use to copy nodes in XSLT—<xsl:copy> and <xsl:copy-of>.

Using the <xsl:copy> Element

The <xsl:copy> element lets you copy a node from the source tree to the output tree. Note that this is a *shallow* copy, however, which means that it does not copy any of the node's descendants. No attributes of elements are copied either.

This element can contain a template body, which is used only when the node to copy is a root node or an element.

You can see an example in ch05_06.xsl in Listing 5.5—all this example does is to copy all elements from the source document to the result document, using <xsl:copy>.

LISTING 5.5   An XSLT Stylesheet That Copies Elements (ch05_06.xsl)

```
<?xml version="1.0" encoding="UTF-8"?>
<xsl:stylesheet version="1.1"
xmlns:xsl="http://www.w3.org/1999/XSL/Transform">
    <xsl:output method="xml"/>

    <xsl:template match="*">
        <xsl:copy>
            <xsl:apply-templates/>
        </xsl:copy>
    </xsl:template>
</xsl:stylesheet>
```

However, note that <xsl:copy> does not copy attributes, so here's the result when we use this stylesheet on ch05_01.xml:

```
<?xml version="1.0" encoding="UTF-8"?>
<planets>

    <planet>
        <name>Mercury</name>
        <mass>.0553</mass>
        <day>58.65</day>
        <radius>1516</radius>
        <density>.983</density>
```

```
            <distance>43.4</distance>
        </planet>

        <planet>
            <name>Venus</name>
            <mass>.815</mass>
            <day>116.75</day>
            <radius>3716</radius>
            <density>.943</density>
            <distance>66.8</distance>
        </planet>

        <planet>
            <name>Earth</name>
            <mass>1</mass>
            <day>1</day>
            <radius>2107</radius>
            <density>1</density>
            <distance>128.4</distance>
        </planet>

</planets>
```

You can also copy attributes if you find a way to apply `<xsl:copy>` to each of an element's attributes. That can be done, for example, with `<xsl:for-each>`, as you see in ch05_07.xsl in Listing 5.6.

LISTING 5.6   An XSLT Stylesheet That Copies Elements and Attributes (ch05_07.xsl)

```
<?xml version="1.0" encoding="UTF-8"?>
<xsl:stylesheet version="1.1"
xmlns:xsl="http://www.w3.org/1999/XSL/Transform">
    <xsl:output method="xml"/>

    <xsl:template match="*">
        <xsl:copy>
            <xsl:for-each select="@*">
                <xsl:copy/>
            </xsl:for-each>
            <xsl:apply-templates/>
        </xsl:copy>
    </xsl:template>
</xsl:stylesheet>
```

Here's the result—note that this time, the attributes are intact:

```
<?xml version="1.0" encoding="UTF-8"?>
<planets>

    <planet>
        <name>Mercury</name>
        <mass units="(Earth = 1)">.0553</mass>
        <day units="days">58.65</day>
        <radius units="miles">1516</radius>
        <density units="(Earth = 1)">.983</density>
        <distance units="million miles">43.4</distance>
    </planet>

    <planet>
        <name>Venus</name>
        <mass units="(Earth = 1)">.815</mass>
        <day units="days">116.75</day>
        <radius units="miles">3716</radius>
        <density units="(Earth = 1)">.943</density>
        <distance units="million miles">66.8</distance>
    </planet>

    <planet>
        <name>Earth</name>
        <mass units="(Earth = 1)">1</mass>
        <day units="days">1</day>
        <radius units="miles">2107</radius>
        <density units="(Earth = 1)">1</density>
        <distance units="million miles">128.4</distance>
    </planet>

</planets>
```

However, there's an easier way of making sure that you copy all the children, attributes, and other descendants of nodes—you can use `<xsl:copy-of>` instead of `<xsl:copy>`.

The `<xsl:copy-of>` Element

The `<xsl:copy-of>` element lets you make a *deep* copy of nodes, which means that the node and all its attributes and descendants are copied. This element has one attribute, `select`, which is mandatory and specifies the node or node-set you want copied. This element is empty, and takes no content.

Here's an example showing how this works; in this case, we'll just replace the <xsl:for-each> element in the preceding example with an <xsl:copy-of> element that specifically selects all attributes of the context element to copy. You can see what this looks like in ch05_08.xsl in Listing 5.7.

LISTING 5.7   An XSLT Stylesheet That Copies Elements and Attributes (ch05_08.xsl)

```
<?xml version="1.0" encoding="UTF-8"?>
<xsl:stylesheet version="1.1"
xmlns:xsl="http://www.w3.org/1999/XSL/Transform">
    <xsl:output method="xml"/>

    <xsl:template match="*">
        <xsl:copy>
            <xsl:copy-of select="@*"/>
            <xsl:apply-templates/>
        </xsl:copy>
    </xsl:template>

</xsl:stylesheet>
```

This works as the example in the previous section did, copying all elements and attributes. In fact, we don't need to modify the previous example at all—we can simply use <xsl:copy-of> to copy the entire document by matching the root node and copying all descendants of that node like this:

```
<?xml version="1.0" encoding="UTF-8"?>
<xsl:stylesheet version="1.1"
xmlns:xsl="http://www.w3.org/1999/XSL/Transform">
    <xsl:output method="xml"/>

    <xsl:template match="/">
        <xsl:copy-of select="*"/>
    </xsl:template>
</xsl:stylesheet>
```

You can also use <xsl:copy-of> to copy particular nodes and their descendants instead of matching the wildcard "*". For example, this rule copies all <density> elements and their descendants:

```
<xsl:template match="density">
    <xsl:copy-of select="."/>
</xsl:template>
```

You could even be tricky and replace the `<density>` element with a `<mass>` element like this when you perform the copy:

```
<xsl:template match="density">
    <xsl:copy-of select="mass"/>
</xsl:template>
```

Handling Whitespace

Handling spaces is always something of an involved topic in XSLT. Inserting a single space, " ", isn't difficult if you use the `<xsl:text>` element, which you use to insert text directly into the output document. This element only has one attribute: `disable-output-escaping`. Set this attribute to "yes" to make sure characters like < and > are output literally rather than as < and >. The default is "no".

This element can only contain a text node. Here's an example where we're using `<xsl:text>` to insert a space between an element value and the element's units:

```
<xsl:template match="mass">
    <xsl:value-of select="."/>
    <xsl:text> </xsl:text>
    <xsl:value-of select="@units"/>
</xsl:template>
```

Using `<xsl:text>` explicitly like this lets you insert whitespace into the output document—otherwise, the XSLT processor would delete extra whitespace like this by default. You can use this element to insert any text in the output document, not just whitespace, but because non-whitespace text is usually copied by default, this element is often used to handle whitespace.

Formally speaking, whitespace nodes are text nodes that only contain whitespace (that is, spaces, carriage returns, line feeds, and tabs). These nodes are copied by default when they come from the source document. However, you can also have whitespace nodes in your stylesheets as well, as here:

```
<xsl:template match="planets">
    <xsl:copy>
        <xsl:apply-templates select="planet"/>
    </xsl:copy>
</xsl:template>
```

Here, we're using spaces to indent the stylesheet elements, as well as carriage returns, to spread things out. Pure whitespace nodes like these are *not* copied from the stylesheet to the output document.

Note, however, that the whitespace in this `<TITLE>` element in the source document will be copied to the output, because it's not a pure whitespace node (it also contains the text "My Summer Vacation"):

```
<xsl:template match="/data">
    <HTML>
        <HEAD>
            <TITLE>
                    My Summer Vacation
            </TITLE>
            .
            .
            .
```

If you want to eliminate whitespace, you could use empty `<xsl:text>` elements so the remaining whitespace becomes pure whitespace nodes, like this:

```
<xsl:template match="/data">
    <HTML>
        <HEAD>
            <TITLE>
                <xsl:text/>My Summer Vacation<xsl:text/>
            </TITLE>
            .
            .
            .
```

Pure whitespace nodes are not copied from the stylesheet to the output document unless it's inside an `<xsl:text>` element, or an enclosing element has the `xml:space` attribute set to "preserve".

On the other hand, by default, XSLT 1.0 preserves whitespace text nodes in the source document and copies them to the result document. That what's happening in the example of copying stylesheets that we've already seen:

```
<?xml version="1.0" encoding="UTF-8"?>
<xsl:stylesheet version="1.1"
xmlns:xsl="http://www.w3.org/1999/XSL/Transform">
    <xsl:output method="xml"/>
    <xsl:template match="*">
        <xsl:copy>
            <xsl:apply-templates/>
        </xsl:copy>
    </xsl:template>
</xsl:stylesheet>
```

When you apply this stylesheet to ch05_01.xml, all the whitespace we've used in ch05_01.xml is copied over to the result document as well:

```
<?xml version="1.0" encoding="UTF-8"?>
<planets>

    <planet>
        <name>Mercury</name>
        <mass units="(Earth = 1)">.0553</mass>
        <day units="days">58.65</day>
        <radius units="miles">1516</radius>
        <density units="(Earth = 1)">.983</density>
        <distance units="million miles">43.4</distance><!--At perihelion-->
    </planet>

        .
        .
        .
```

However, there are times you want to remove the whitespace used to format input documents, and you can do that with the <xsl:strip-space> element. There is only one attribute for this element: elements, which is mandatory and which specifies elements to strip the whitespace from. You set this attribute to a whitespace-separated list of names or names with wildcards. This element contains no content.

You can see an example that strips all whitespace nodes from ch05_01.xml using <xsl:strip-space elements="*"/> in ch05_09.xsl in Listing 5.8.

LISTING 5.8   An XSLT Stylesheet That Copies Elements and Attributes (ch05_09.xsl)

```
<?xml version="1.0" encoding="UTF-8"?>
<xsl:stylesheet version="1.1"
xmlns:xsl="http://www.w3.org/1999/XSL/Transform">
    <xsl:strip-space elements="*"/>
    <xsl:output method="xml"/>
    <xsl:template match="*">
        <xsl:copy>
            <xsl:apply-templates/>
        </xsl:copy>
    </xsl:template>
</xsl:stylesheet>
```

Here's the result document you get when you apply this stylesheet to ch05_01.xml—note that all whitespace has been stripped out, including all carriage returns (a few had to be added to fit this result on the page—the actual result is just one long string):

```
<?xml version="1.0" encoding="UTF-8"?>
<planets><planet><name>Mercury</name><mass>.0553</mass><day>58.65</day><radius>
1516</radius><density>.983</density><distance>43.4</distance></planet><planet>
<name>Venus</name><mass>.815</mass><day>116.75</day><radius>3716</radius>
<density>.943</density><distance>66.8</distance></planet><planet><name>Earth
</name><mass>1</mass><day>1</day><radius>2107</radius><density>1</density>
<distance>128.4</distance></planet></planets>
```

On the other hand, you might not want to remove all the whitespace nodes throughout a document, and you can use the `<xsl:preserve-space>` element to indicate which elements you want to preserve whitespace nodes in. This element has the same attribute as `<xsl:strip-space>`, elements.

What this means is that if you've used `<xsl:strip-space>`, you can still indicate what element or elements you want whitespace nodes preserved in by setting the elements attribute in `<xsl:preserve-space>` to a list of elements like this:

> ### PRESERVING WHITESPACE BY DEFAULT
>
> Using `<xsl:preserve-space>` is actually the default for all elements in XSLT—in other words, whitespace is preserved from the input document.

```
<?xml version="1.0" encoding="UTF-8"?>
<xsl:stylesheet version="1.1"
xmlns:xsl="http://www.w3.org/1999/XSL/Transform">
    <xsl:strip-space elements="*"/>
    <xsl:preserve-space elements="name distance"/>
    <xsl:output method="xml"/>
    <xsl:template match="*">
        <xsl:copy>
            <xsl:apply-templates/>
        </xsl:copy>
    </xsl:template>
</xsl:stylesheet>
```

There's also an easy way to work with whitespace if you just want to indent the result document. The `<xsl:output>` element supports an attribute called indent, which you can set to "yes" or "no", and indicates to the XSLT processor whether you want the result document indented.

Often, indenting the result document doesn't matter very much, because that document is targeted to an application that doesn't care about indenting, such as a browser. But there are times when you'd like to view the result document as straight text, and in such cases, indenting that document can help.

How an XSLT processor uses the indent attribute varies by processor, because it's not specified by W3C. Say, for example, that you have a version of ch05_01.xml without any indentation at all, which appears in ch05_10.xml in Listing 5.9.

LISTING 5.9   An XML Document with No Indentation (ch05_10.xml)

```
<?xml version="1.0" encoding="UTF-8"?>
<?xml-stylesheet type="text/xml" href="planets.xsl"?>
<planets>

<planet>
<name>Mercury</name>
<mass units="(Earth = 1)">.0553</mass>
<day units="days">58.65</day>
<radius units="miles">1516</radius>
<density units="(Earth = 1)">.983</density>
<distance units="million miles">43.4</distance><!--At perihelion-->
</planet>

<planet>
<name>Venus</name>
<mass units="(Earth = 1)">.815</mass>
<day units="days">116.75</day>
<radius units="miles">3716</radius>
<density units="(Earth = 1)">.943</density>
<distance units="million miles">66.8</distance><!--At perihelion-->
</planet>

<planet>
<name>Earth</name>
<mass units="(Earth = 1)">1</mass>
<day units="days">1</day>
<radius units="miles">2107</radius>
<density units="(Earth = 1)">1</density>
<distance units="million miles">128.4</distance><!--At perihelion-->
</planet>

</planets>
```

To indent this document, you can use an XSLT processor that supports the <xsl:output
indent="yes"/> element. A stylesheet that uses this element appears in ch05_11.xsl in
Listing 5.10.

LISTING 5.10   Using <xsl:output indent="yes"/> (ch05_11.xsl)

```
<?xml version="1.0" encoding="UTF-8"?>
<xsl:stylesheet version="1.1"
xmlns:xsl="http://www.w3.org/1999/XSL/Transform">
    <xsl:output indent="yes"/>

    <xsl:template match="/planets">
<HTML>
<HEAD>
<TITLE>
         The Planets Table
     </TITLE>
</HEAD>
<BODY>
<H1>
         The Planets Table
     </H1>
<TABLE BORDER="2">
<TD>Name</TD>
<TD>Mass</TD>
<TD>Radius</TD>
<TD>Day</TD>
<xsl:apply-templates/>
</TABLE>
</BODY>
</HTML>
</xsl:template>

<xsl:template match="planet">
<TR>
<TD><xsl:value-of select="name"/></TD>
<TD><xsl:value-of select="mass"/></TD>
<TD><xsl:value-of select="radius"/></TD>
<TD><xsl:value-of select="day"/></TD>
</TR>
</xsl:template>

</xsl:stylesheet>
```

Xalan doesn't indent documents this way, but the Saxon XSLT processor will. Here's the result using Saxon, indented as we wanted:

```
<HTML>
  <HEAD>
    <meta http-equiv="Content-Type" content="text/html; charset=utf-8">

    <TITLE>
        The Planets Table

    </TITLE>
  </HEAD>
  <BODY>
    <H1>
        The Planets Table

    </H1>
    <TABLE BORDER="2">
        <TD>Name</TD>
        <TD>Mass</TD>
        <TD>Radius</TD>
        <TD>Day</TD>


        <TR>
            <TD>Mercury</TD>
            <TD>.0553</TD>
            <TD>1516</TD>
            <TD>58.65</TD>
        </TR>


        <TR>
            <TD>Venus</TD>
            <TD>.815</TD>
            <TD>3716</TD>
            <TD>116.75</TD>
        </TR>


        <TR>
            <TD>Earth</TD>
            <TD>1</TD>
            <TD>2107</TD>
```

```
            <TD>1</TD>
        </TR>


        </TABLE>
    </BODY>
</HTML>
```

As you can see, handling whitespace takes a little bit of thought in XSLT, but it's easier if you know what's going on.

People often use XSLT to work with the data in XML documents without resorting to programming, but in fact, you can do a bit of programming using XSLT when you use the <xsl:if> and <xsl:choose> elements. We'll take a look at these XSLT elements next.

Making Choices with <xsl:if> and <xsl:choose>

The <xsl:if> element lets you make choices. To use this element, you assign its test attribute a value that evaluates to a Boolean value of true or false. If it evaluates to true, the enclosed XSLT elements are also evaluated, but they are not evaluated if test evaluates to false.

Let's take a look at an example. In this case, we'll list the three planets in ch05_01.xml, and use <xsl:if> to add two horizontal rule elements (<HR) both above and below this list to offset the list visually. You can see how this works, using the position function to determine the top and bottom of the list, in ch05_12.xsl in Listing 5.11.

LISTING 5.11   Using <xsl:if> (ch05_12.xsl)

```
<?xml version="1.0" encoding="UTF-8"?>
<xsl:stylesheet version="1.0" xmlns:xsl="http://www.w3.org/1999/XSL/Transform">

    <xsl:template match="planets">
        <HTML>
            <HEAD>
                <TITLE>
                    The First Three Planets
                </TITLE>
            </HEAD>
            <BODY>
                <H1>
                    The First Three Planets
```

LISTING 5.11   Continued

```
            </H1>
            <xsl:apply-templates select="planet"/>
        </BODY>
    </HTML>
</xsl:template>

<xsl:template match="planet">
    <xsl:if test="position() = 1"><HR/><HR/></xsl:if>
    <P>
        Number <xsl:value-of select="position()"/>. <xsl:value-of select="name"/>
    </P>
    <xsl:if test="position() = last()"><HR/><HR/></xsl:if>
</xsl:template>

</xsl:stylesheet>
```

Here's what you get when you use this new stylesheet—note the two <HR> elements before and after the list of planets:

```
<HTML>
    <HEAD>
        <TITLE>
            The First Three Planets
        </TITLE>
    </HEAD>

    <BODY>
        <H1>
            The First Three Planets
        </H1>
        <HR>
        <HR>
        <P>Number 1. Mercury</P>
        <P>Number 2. Venus</P>
        <P>Number 3. Earth</P>
        <HR>
        <HR>
    </BODY>
</HTML>
```

You can see what this looks like in Figure 5.2.

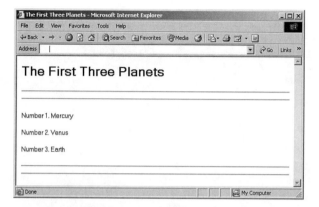

FIGURE 5.2   Making choices with <xsl:if>.

Besides <xsl:if>, you can also use <xsl:choose> to make decisions. This element lets you compare a test value against several possibilities.

For example, say that we want to color-code the planet names—Mercury in red, Venus in white, and Earth in green. You can handle these possibilities with <xsl:choose>. Inside this element, you use the <xsl:when> element, setting the test attribute in those elements to the Boolean expression you want to test. For example, Mercury is first in the list, so we can display it in red this way:

```
<xsl:template match="planet">
    <xsl:choose>
        <xsl:when test="name = 'Mercury'">
            <P>
                <FONT COLOR="RED"><B>
                    <xsl:value-of select="name"/>
                </B></FONT>
            </P>
        </xsl:when>
            .
            .
            .
```

We can handle the other two planets using other <xsl:when> elements in the same <xsl:choose>, as you see in ch05_13.xsl in Listing 5.12. Note also that at the end of the group of <xsl:when> element, there's an (optional) <xsl:otherwise> element—if none of the <xsl:when> elements match their test conditions, the <xsl:otherwise> element is chosen.

LISTING 5.12   Using <xsl:choose> (ch05_13.xsl)

```
<?xml version="1.0" encoding="UTF-8"?>
<xsl:stylesheet version="1.0" xmlns:xsl="http://www.w3.org/1999/XSL/Transform">

    <xsl:template match="planets">
        <HTML>
            <HEAD>
                <TITLE>
                    Color Coding the Planets
                </TITLE>
            </HEAD>

            <BODY BGCOLOR="PINK">
                <H1>
                    Color Coding the Planets
                </H1>
                <xsl:apply-templates select="planet"/>
            </BODY>
        </HTML>
    </xsl:template>

    <xsl:template match="planet">
        <xsl:choose>
            <xsl:when test="name = 'Mercury'">
                <P>
                    <FONT COLOR="RED"><B>
                        <xsl:value-of select="name"/>
                    </B></FONT>
                </P>
            </xsl:when>
            <xsl:when test="name = 'Venus'">
                <P>
                    <FONT COLOR="WHITE"><B>
                        <xsl:value-of select="name"/>
                    </B></FONT>
                </P>
            </xsl:when>
            <xsl:when test="name = 'Earth'">
                <P>
                    <FONT COLOR="GREEN"><B>
                        <xsl:value-of select="name"/>
                    </B></FONT>
```

LISTING 5.12   Continued

```
                    </P>
                </xsl:when>
                <xsl:otherwise>
                    <P>
                        <xsl:value-of select="."/>
                    </P>
                </xsl:otherwise>
            </xsl:choose>
        </xsl:template>

</xsl:stylesheet>
```

Here's what you get when you use this stylesheet on our planetary XML document,
ch05_01.xml (note that we're setting the background color to pink to make sure that even the
white text we'll be displaying stands out):

```
<HTML>
    <HEAD>
        <TITLE>
            Color Coding the Planets
        </TITLE>
    </HEAD>

    <BODY BGCOLOR="PINK">
        <H1>
            Color Coding the Planets
        </H1>
        <P>
            <FONT COLOR="RED"><B>Mercury</B></FONT>
        </P>

        <P>
            <FONT COLOR="WHITE"><B>Venus</B></FONT>
        </P>

        <P>
            <FONT COLOR="GREEN"><B>Earth</B></FONT>
        </P>
    </BODY>
</HTML>
```

You can see what this result document looks like in Figure 5.3 in glorious black and white (to see the actual colors for yourself, use `ch05_13.xsl` on `ch05_01.xml` and open the result in a browser).

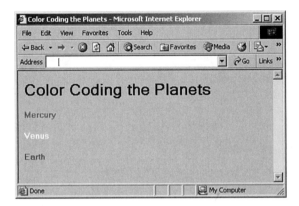

FIGURE 5.3   Making selections with `<xsl:choose>`.

Another important XSLT topic concerns the default template rules that XSLT uses, and that's coming up next.

Understanding the Default Template Rules

XSLT has default rules for each kind of node, which are put into effect if you don't explicitly give a rule for the node. Here are those rules:

- Root node—Call `<xsl:apply-templates/>` by default.

- Element nodes—Call `<xsl:apply-templates/>` by default.

- Attribute nodes—Copy the attribute value to the result document. But copy it as text, not as an attribute.

- Text nodes—Copy the text to the result document.

- Comment nodes—Do no XSLT processing, which means that nothing is copied.

- Processing instruction nodes—Do no XSLT processing, which means that nothing is copied.

- Namespace nodes—Do no XSLT processing, which means that nothing is copied.

Of these, the most important default rule applies to elements, and can be expressed like this:

```
<xsl:template match="*">
    <xsl:apply-templates/>
</xsl:template>
```

As you can see, this rule simply makes sure that every element is processed with `<xsl:apply-templates/>` if you don't supply some other rule. It's important to realize that if you do supply another rule, that new rule overrides the corresponding default rule.

The default rule for text nodes can be expressed like this, where the text of the text node is added to the output document:

```
<xsl:template match="text()">
    <xsl:value-of select="."/>
</xsl:template>
```

In addition, the same kind of default rule applies to attributes, which are added to the output document with a default rule like this:

```
<xsl:template match="@*">
    <xsl:value-of select="."/>
</xsl:template>
```

In addition, by default, processing instructions are not inserted in the output document. That means their default rule can be expressed simply like this:

```
<xsl:template match="processing-instruction()"/>
```

Comments aren't copied over by default either, so their default rule can be expressed this way:

```
<xsl:template match="comment()"/>
```

Now that you know these default rules, it shouldn't surprise you that if you don't supply any rules at all, all the parsed character data (PCDATA in XML terms) in the input document is inserted in the output document by default.

For example, here's what an XSLT stylesheet with no explicit rules looks like:

```
<?xml version="1.0" encoding="UTF-8"?>
<xsl:stylesheet version="1.1" xmlns:xsl="http://www.w3.org/1999/XSL/Transform">
</xsl:stylesheet>
```

Here's what you get when you apply this stylesheet to `ch05_01.xml` (note that the default rule for attributes has not been applied, because they are not considered children of other nodes):

```
<?xml version="1.0" encoding="UTF-8"?>

    Mercury
    .0553
    58.65
    1516
    .983
    43.4

    Venus
    .815
    116.75
    3716
    .943
    66.8

    Earth
    1
    1
    2107
    1
    128.4
```

INTERNET EXPLORER AND DEFAULT RULES

Internet Explorer does not supply any default XSLT rules. You have to supply all the rules yourself that you want to use in templates.

Knowing the default rules is important; if you see this kind of result from your XSLT stylesheets and you're not expecting it, you now know what's causing the problem—the default rules are being applied. If you don't want text stripped from the source document and inserted into the output document in this way, supply an empty rule (one that just matches a node or node-set but doesn't do anything else) or rules to override the applicable default rule or rules. If a rule for a node is empty, the content of the matched node will not be copied to the output document. In this way, you can remove content from the source document when you write the output document.

Displaying Messages While Processing XSLT Stylesheets

Here's another useful XSLT element—you can use the `<xsl:message>` element to make the XSLT processor display a message, and, optionally, end processing a stylesheet. The

`<xsl:message>` element has one attribute: `terminate`, which is optional. You set this attribute to "yes" to terminate processing. The default is "no".

Here's an example. In this case, we'll terminate XSLT processing when the XSLT processor tries to transform a `<radius>` element in `ch05_01.xml`, displaying the message "Sorry, planetary radius data is restricted." You can see how this works in `ch05_14.xsl` in Listing 5.13.

LISTING 5.13   Using `<xsl:choose>` (ch05_14.xsl)

```
<?xml version="1.0" encoding="UTF-8"?>
<xsl:stylesheet version="1.1"
xmlns:xsl="http://www.w3.org/1999/XSL/Transform">

    <xsl:template match="/planets">
        <HTML>
            <HEAD>
                <TITLE>
                    The Planets Table
                </TITLE>
            </HEAD>
            <BODY>
                <H1>
                    The Planets Table
                </H1>
                <TABLE BORDER="2">
                    <TD>Name</TD>
                    <TD>Mass</TD>
                    <TD>Radius</TD>
                    <TD>Day</TD>
                    <xsl:apply-templates/>
                </TABLE>
            </BODY>
        </HTML>
    </xsl:template>

    <xsl:template match="planet">
        <TR>
            <TD><xsl:value-of select="name"/></TD>
            <TD><xsl:apply-templates select="mass"/></TD>
            <TD><xsl:apply-templates select="radius"/></TD>
            <TD><xsl:apply-templates select="day"/></TD>
        </TR>
    </xsl:template>
```

LISTING 5.13   Continued

```xsl
    <xsl:template match="mass">
        <xsl:value-of select="."/>
        <xsl:text> </xsl:text>
        <xsl:value-of select="@units"/>
    </xsl:template>

    <xsl:template match="radius">
        <xsl:message terminate="yes">
            Sorry, planetary radius data is restricted.
        </xsl:message terminate="yes">
    </xsl:template>

    <xsl:template match="day">
        <xsl:value-of select="."/>
        <xsl:text> </xsl:text>
        <xsl:value-of select="@units"/>
    </xsl:template>

</xsl:stylesheet>
```

Here's what you see when you use this stylesheet—the XSLT processor will display this message and quit (note that not all XSLT processors will honor the `terminate` attribute):

```
Sorry, planetary radius data is restricted.
```

Setting Output Document Type

For the most part, we've been creating HTML documents from XML documents with XSLT. You might have noticed that the output documents are HTML, not XML, even though we haven't explicitly told the XSLT processor to make them HTML. That's because there is a special default rule here—if the document node of the output document is <HTML>, XSLT processors are supposed to treat the output document as HTML.

On the other hand, you can specifically specify the type of output document you want, using the XSLT <xsl:output> element. Here are the options:

- XML—This is the default. Makes the output documents start with an <?xml?> declaration.

- HTML—Makes the output document standard HTML 4.0, without an XML declaration.

- Text—Makes the output document simple text.

To select one of these, you set the `<xsl:output>` element's `method` attribute to "xml", "html", or "text". Say that you want to create a plain text document—in that case, you can use this `<xsl:output>` element:

```
<xsl:output method = "text"/>
```

You can also use the `media-type` attribute of `<xsl:output>` to specify the MIME type of the output document yourself. Here's how that might look, where we're creating a rich text format (RTF) document:

```
<xsl:output media-type="text/rtf"/>
```

Besides the `method` and `media-type` attributes, there are some other additional useful `<xsl:output>` attributes that let you control the output document:

- `encoding`—Indicates the value of the XML declaration's `encoding` attribute.

- `indent`—Indicates if the XSLT processor should indent the output (many won't, even if you ask). Set to "yes" or "no".

- `omit-xml-declaration`—Indicates if the processor should omit the XML declaration. Set to "yes" or "no".

- `standalone`—Indicates the value for the XML declaration's `standalone` attribute. Set to "yes" or "no".

- `version`—Indicates the value for the XML declaration's `version` attribute.

- `doctype-system` and `doctype-public` let you specify an external DTD for XML documents. For example, `<xsl:output doctype-system = "planets.dtd"/>` produces `<!DOCTYPE planets SYSTEM "planets.dtd">`.

That finishes our discussion of XSLT in this chapter. There's more that you can do with XSLT than we could cover in this chapter, such as sorting your output results using `<xsl:sort>` or creating new elements with `<xsl:element>` and so on—if you're interested, track down a good XSLT book.

In Brief

- You use XSLT to manipulate, extract, and format data from XML documents. Using XSLT, you don't have to resort to creating your own XML processors. XSLT itself is a specification of W3C, and has been a recommendation since November 16, 1999. You can find the W3C recommendation for XSLT 1.0 at www.w3.org/TR/xslt.

- XSLT has its own syntax, and this chapter's work was dedicated to learning that syntax. You use that syntax in XSLT stylesheets, which starts with an XML declaration and the element `<xsl:stylesheet version="1.0"` `xmlns:xsl="http://www.w3.org/1999/XSL/Transform">`.

- XSLT stylesheets are made up of templates that match the nodes you want to work with. As we saw in this chapter, you use the `match` attribute in the `<xsl:template>` element to match nodes. You can also select the value of nodes using the `<xsl:value-of>` element, setting the select attribute to the XPath expression you want to use. The `<xsl:for-each>` element lets you work with multiple nodes. This element will let you loop over multiple nodes in a node-set.

- There are two different XSLT attributes you use in XSLT elements and can assign XPath expressions to—the `match` and the `select` attributes. Specifically, the `match` attribute appears in the `<xsl:template>` element, and the `select` attribute appears in the `<xsl:apply-templates>`, `<xsl:value-of>`, `<xsl:for-each>`, `<xsl:copy-of>`, and `<xsl:sort>` XSLT elements. The `match` attribute can only handle the `self` or `child` axis (although XPath expressions in the predicate can use any axis), and there is no restriction on the XPath expressions you can assign to the `select` attribute.

- You can use the `<xsl:copy>` element to make a shallow copy of nodes, and the `<xsl:copy-of>` element lets you create deep copies. And the `<xsl:if>` and `<xsl:choose>` elements let you make choices in your XSLT stylesheets.

- Handling whitespace in XSLT and understanding the default XSLT rules are important if you want to create your own templates. In particular, it's important to realize that if you don't provide any rule to the contrary, the parsed character data in the source document will be inserted into the result document.

XPath with XPointer, XLink, and XQuery

6

Data Access Using XPath

In this chapter, we're going to take a look at using XPath with XPointer, XLink, and XQuery. This chapter is also going to help us make the transition between XPath 1.0 and XPath 2.0 because XPointer and XLink both use XPath 1.0, whereas XQuery is integral to XPath 2.0. We're going to see that the demands of data access are growing, and that'll give us a natural introduction to XPath 2.0 in the next chapter.

XLink and XPointer are two XML-related specifications that let you use XPath 1.0 to locate data in XML documents, and as such, we'll discuss them here. Then, as a transition into XPath 2.0—which starts in the next chapter—we'll take a look at one of the newer ways of accessing data in XML documents using XPath—XQuery 1.0. As we're going to see, XQuery is far more powerful than XLink or XPointer, which reflects the fact that handling data is becoming much more sophisticated. In fact, XLink and XPointer can't even be compared directly to XQuery; they're quite simple compared to XQuery's sophistication. And as we're going to see, XQuery 1.0 is actually an extension of XPath 2.0, not just an allied specification (which is true of XPath 1.0 and XLink/XPointer).

Over time, being able to address the particular data you're interested in in an XML document has become more and more important. XLink and XPointer give you a lot of capability, but the need is so great that even more power is needed, and we're seeing the results in XQuery in this chapter. As we're going to see starting in Chapter 7,

"What's New in XPath 2.0," XPath 2.0 and XQuery are integrally connected—in fact, the XQuery working group coleads the XPath 2.0 effort and is a coauthor of the XPath 2.0 specifications. XSLT 2.0 is also integrally connected to XPath 2.0, as we're going to see.

For us in this chapter, the idea of data access begins with simple linking. You already know that HTML supports hyperlinks—for example, if you had a review of the James Bond movie *Goldfinger*, you could create a hyperlink to that review like this:

```
<A HREF="http://www.XPathCorp.com/reviews.xml">Goldfinger</A>
```

So how would this look as an XLink that you could use in an XML document? You can create an XLink with the attribute `xlink:type` like this, where we're creating a simple XLink:

```
<review xmlns:xlink = "http://www.w3.org/1999/xlink"
    xlink:type = "simple"
    xlink:show = "new"
    xlink:href = "http://www.XPathCorp.com/reviews.xml">
    Goldfinger
</review>
```

This is a simple XLink, much like an HTML hyperlink. Here, we're setting the `xlink:type` attribute to "simple" and the `xlink:show` attribute to "new", which means XLink-aware software should open the linked-to document in a new window. The `xlink:href` attribute holds the URI of the linked-to document. That's what a simple XLink looks like, but XLinks can become pretty involved, as we'll see in this chapter. Besides basic unidirectional links like the simple link in this example, you can also create bidirectional links, links between multiple documents and document sets, and much more, including storing your links in link databases called *linkbases*.

XLinks let you link to a particular document, but you often need to be more precise than that. XPointers let you point to specific locations inside a document—without having to modify that document by embedding special tags or markers.

To point to a specific location in a document, the XPointer specification builds on XPath. For example, you can use XPath expressions like `/child::*[5]/child::*[1]` in XPointers. In fact, XPointer 1.0 even extends XPath in ways that we'll see in this chapter.

You can add an XPointer to a document's URI to specify a specific location in a document. For example, you can append # (following the HTML usage for URLs that specify link targets) and then `xpointer()`, placing the XPath expression you want to use in the parentheses. Here's an example:

```
<review xmlns:xlink = "http://www.w3.org/1999/xlink"
    xlink:type = "simple"
    xlink:show = "new"
```

```
   xlink:href =
 "http://www.XPathCorp.com/reviews.xml#xpointer(/child::*[last()])">
    Goldfinger
</review>
```

That's what XLink and XPointer look like in overview—it's time to dig into the details.

Introducing XLinks

The XLink specification is a W3C recommendation, released on June 27, 2001. You can find the most current version of this recommendation at www.w3.org/TR/xlink. Here's what W3C says in the W3C working draft:

"This specification defines the XML Linking Language (XLink), which allows elements to be inserted into XML documents in order to create and describe links between resources. It uses XML syntax to create structures that can describe links similar to the simple unidirectional hyperlinks of today's HTML, as well as more sophisticated links."

XLinks are not restricted to any one element like the <A> element—you can make any XML element into an XLink. XLinks can be quite complex—for example, you might want a link to point to ten mirror sites of a main site and let the browser select the one that's closest, or you can link to an entire set of documents that the browser should search, or you can set up a series of paths that lets the user navigate between a set of documents in various directions but not in others, and so on.

As mentioned, you create an XLink with attributes, not with specific elements. In particular, you use the xlink:type attribute to create an XLink, setting it to one of the allowable types of XLinks: simple, extended, locator, arc, resource, title, or none. Here are the current XLink attributes:

- xlink:arcrole holds the link's role in an *arc* (arcs can contain multiple resources and traversal paths), which may be different for different arcs. More on this later in this chapter.

- xlink:actuate determines when traversal operations occur. You can set this attribute to the official values of onLoad, onRequest, other, none, or other values as required by the software you're using.

- xlink:from defines starting resources.

- xlink:href supplies the data that allows an XLink application to find a remote resource.

- xlink:label holds a human-readable label for the link.

■ `xlink:role` describes the role, or function, of a link's remote resource in a machine-readable fashion. Search engines should be able to read this attribute.

■ `xlink:show` indicates how you want to display the linked-to resource. XLink applications must recognize the following values: `new` (open a new display space, such as a window), `replace` (replace the currently displayed data), `embed` (embed the new resource in the current one), `other` (leaving the `show` function up to the displaying software), or `none` (don't show the resource).

■ `xlink:title` describes the function of a link's remote resource for people to understand.

■ `xlink:to` defines a target of the link.

■ `xlink:type` sets the type of the XLink; can be one of `simple`, `extended`, `locator`, `arc`, `resource`, `title`, or `none`. More on these later in this chapter.

So what does an XLink at work look like? There isn't much software designed to display XLinks, not even simple XLinks, but we can create a mockup that will work in Internet Explorer. In fact, Internet Explorer even supports the `onClick` attribute if you use it with an XML element, so we can use a little JavaScript that will make the browser navigate to a new URI when the XLink is clicked. You can see how this looks in `ch06_01.xml` (Listing 6.1).

LISTING 6.1   A Simple XLink (`ch06_01.xml`)

```
<?xml version="1.0" encoding="UTF-8"?>
<?xml-stylesheet type="text/css" href="ch06_02.css"?>

<document>
    Want to read my review of
    <review xmlns:xlink = "http://www.w3.org/1999/xlink"
        xlink:type = "simple"
        xlink:show = "new"
        xlink:href = "http://www.w3c.org"
        onClick="location.href='http://www.w3c.org'">
        Goldfinger
    </review>?
</document>
```

You can even style this XLink to make it look something like a traditional hyperlink using cascading style sheets (CSS). The style sheet `ch06_02.css`, shown in Listing 6.2, makes this XLink appear in a blue, underlined font, and makes Internet Explorer's cursor change to a hand as the mouse passes over the XLink.

LISTING 6.2   Styling a Simple XLink (ch06_02.css)

```
review {color: #0000FF; text-decoration: underline; cursor: hand}
```

The result appears in Figure 6.1, where the simple XLink functions much like an HTML hyperlink. You can even click this link to make Internet Explorer navigate to a new document.

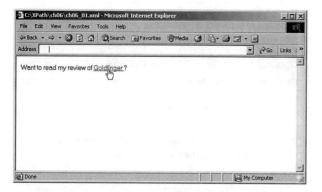

FIGURE 6.1   A mockup of a simple XLink.

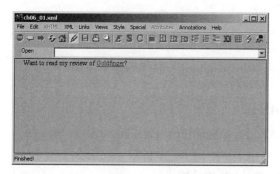

FIGURE 6.2   A simple XLink in Amaya.

There is some software around that will let you work with XLink directly, such as W3C's test browser, Amaya, which you can get for free at http://www.w3.org/Amaya/. You can see our working simple XLink in Amaya in Figure 6.2.

Using XLink Attributes

To create an XLink, you use XLink attributes. So which attributes do you need to create what type of XLink? It all depends on the type of link you're creating, as given by the xlink:type attribute. Depending on link type, some of these attributes are required, and some are optional. You can find the complete rules in Table 6.1, where the rows correspond to the various XLink attributes, and the columns to the various XLink types.

TABLE 6.1

XLink Attributes by `xlink:type`

	SIMPLE	EXTENDED	LOCATOR	ARC	RESOURCE	TITLE
`actuate`	Optional	Omitted	Omitted	Optional	Omitted	Omitted
`arcrole`	Optional	Omitted	Omitted	Optional	Omitted	Omitted
`from`	Omitted	Omitted	Omitted	Optional	Omitted	Omitted
`href`	Optional	Omitted	Required	Omitted	Omitted	Omitted
`label`	Omitted	Omitted	Optional	Omitted	Optional	Omitted
`role`	Optional	Optional	Optional	Optional	Optional	Omitted
`show`	Optional	Omitted	Omitted	Optional	Omitted	Omitted
`title`	Optional	Optional	Optional	Optional	Optional	Omitted
`to`	Omitted	Omitted	Omitted	Optional	Omitted	Omitted
`type`	Required	Required	Required	Required	Required	Required

Each of the attributes in Table 6.1 uses the `xlink` namespace; this namespace always uses the value "http://www.w3.org/1999/xlink", as we saw in our earlier simple link example:

```
<review xmlns:xlink = "http://www.w3.org/1999/xlink"
    xlink:type = "simple"
    xlink:show = "new"
    xlink:href = "http://www.XPathCorp.com/reviews.xml">
    Goldfinger
</review>
```

Because you use these attributes to create XLinks, we'll go over a few of them now.

Using the `xlink:type` Attribute

The `xlink:type` attribute defines the type of XLink you want to create. You can set this attribute to one of these possible values:

- `arc` makes an arc with multiple resources and traversal paths.

- `extended` makes an extended link, which can involve multiple simple links.

- `locator` makes a locator link that points to a resource. This kind of link holds a link to another link.

- `resource` makes a resource link, which indicates a specific resource.

- `simple` makes a simple link, which is like a standard hyperlink.

- `title` makes a title link; such elements are useful, for example, for cases where human-readable label information needs further element markup, or where multiple titles are necessary for internationalization purposes.

Using the `xlink:show` Attribute

The `xlink:show` attribute specifies how you want the linked-to resource displayed when the link is traversed. The `xlink:show` attribute has these predefined values:

- `embed` causes the software to embed the linked-to resource in the current resource, for example, by showing an image in a Web page.

- `new` causes the software to open a new display area, such as a new window, to display the new resource.

- `none` causes the software to *not* show the resource. Although the resource is not specifically displayed, its data is still accessible to implementation-specific software with this kind of link.

- `other` indicates some other setting that those that are predefined.

- `replace` causes the software to replace the current resource, in the same window if there is one.

For example, the default behavior of HTML links is to navigate to a linked-to document, replacing the current document with the new one. You can change that behavior by assigning `xlink:show` a value of `new`, making the software open a new window for the linked-to document:

```
<review xmlns:xlink = "http://www.w3.org/1999/xlink"
    xlink:type = "simple"
    xlink:show = "new"
    xlink:href = "http://www.XPathCorp.com/reviews.xml">
    Goldfinger
</review>
```

Using the `xlink:actuate` Attribute

The `xlink:actuate` attribute indicates when a link should be traversed. The `xlink:actuate` attribute has these predefined values:

- `onRequest` should be traversed only on the user's request.

- `onLoad` should be traversed when the document or resource is loaded.

- `other` means a custom preference as defined by the application.

- `none` means no actuation (or that the behavior of the application is not constrained by the markup).

In addition, you can set your own values for `xlink:actuate`.

If you set the value of `xlink:actuate` to `onLoad`, the link is traversed when the resource containing it is loaded. For example, here's how you'd activate a link only when the user requests it to be activated:

```
<review xmlns:xlink="http://www.w3.org/1999/xlink"
    xlink:type="simple"
    xlink:href="http://www.XPathCorp.com/reviews/goldfinger.xml"
    xlink:actuate="onRequest">
</review>
```

Using the `xlink:href` Attribute

This attribute contains the data which allows an XLink application to find a remote resource, usually a URI, as in this example:

```
<review xmlns:xlink = "http://www.w3.org/1999/xlink"
    xlink:type = "simple"
    xlink:show = "new"
    xlink:href = "http://www.XPathCorp.com/reviews.xml">
    Goldfinger
</review>
```

Introducing XPointers

XPointers are designed to let you point to specific locations inside a document. There isn't much software that supports XPointers currently, although some does. For example, the Adobe Scalable Vector Graphics (SVG) browser plug-in (`http://www.adobe.com/svg/viewer/install/main.html`) does, as well as Amaya (`http://www.w3.org/Amaya/`) and an application named XLip by Fujitsu.

The XPointer specification was split into parts to make it easier to implement. The XPointer specification is now divided into three recommendations and a working draft:

- `http://www.w3.org/TR/xptr-framework/`—The XPointer framework, which gives a general overview and points you to the other three schemes

- `http://www.w3.org/TR/xptr-element/`—The element scheme

- `http://www.w3.org/TR/xptr-xmlns/`—The namespace scheme

- `http://www.w3.org/TR/xptr-xpointer/`—The general XPointer scheme

The XPointer framework specification introduces the idea of XPointers and indicates how you can use *barenames* (that is, simple element names) as XPointers. And it points to the other three parts of the specification that you can use in XPointers—the element scheme, the namespace scheme, and the general XPointer scheme. We'll take a look at four of these ways of creating XPointers here, starting with barenames.

Using Barenames

The XPointer Framework specification (www.w3.org/TR/xptr-framework/) says that you can use barenames—that is, just the names of elements—as XPointers. You can append an XPointer to the end of a URI in an XLink by preceding it with a #, as here, where we're pointing at the <data> element in http://www.XPathCorp.com/jamesbond.xml:

```
<insurance xmlns:xlink = "http://www.w3.org/1999/xlink"
    xlink:type = "simple"
    xlink:show = "new"
    xlink:href = "http://www.XPathCorp.com/jamesbond.xml#data">
    Health Insurance
</insurance>
```

Besides using barenames like this, you can also use the element, namespace, and general XPointer schemes. They're coming up next.

Using the Element Scheme

The element scheme (www.w3.org/TR/xptr-element/) was split out of the general XPointer scheme to make XPointer easier to implement. Here, you use element() to identify elements by ID, not by name. For example, to find the element with the ID data, you could use this expression:

```
<insurance xmlns:xlink = "http://www.w3.org/1999/xlink"
    xlink:type = "simple"
    xlink:show = "new"
    xlink:href = "http://www.XPathCorp.com/jamesbond.xml#element(data)">
    Health Insurance
</insurance>
```

You can also specify child sequences by number; for example, to pick out the <data> element's third child element, and then to identify that element's first child element, you can use this XPath-like expression:

```
<insurance xmlns:xlink = "http://www.w3.org/1999/xlink"
    xlink:type = "simple"
    xlink:show = "new"
```

```
    xlink:href = "http://www.XPathCorp.com/jamesbond.xml#element(data/3/1)">
    Health Insurance
</insurance>
```

In other words, the element scheme lets you specify an element by ID, and you can also add location steps, using numbers, to access child elements.

Using the Namespace Scheme

You can use the namespace scheme (see www.w3.org/TR/xptr-xmlns/) to use namespaces when pointing to data. For example, if the <invoice> element you wanted to access was part of the job namespace, you could specify that element this way:

```
<insurance xmlns:xlink = "http://www.w3.org/1999/xlink"
    xlink:type = "simple"
    xlink:show = "new"
    xlink:href = "http://www.XPathCorp.com/adjunct.xml#xmlns(job=
        "http:/XPathCorp.com/job:invoice">
    Health Insurance
</insurance>
```

This XPointer accesses <job:invoice> in the document
http://www.XPathCorp.com/adjunct.xml.

Using the General XPointer Scheme

Besides using the element and namespace schemes, you can also use the general XPointer scheme. The element and namespace schemes were added to XPointer in an attempt to make XPointer easier to use, but you can still create general XPointers.

The original form of XPointers is still in working draft form as of this writing (see www.w3.org/TR/xptr-xpointer/). This is actually where the real core of XPointer lies, because you can use full XPath expressions to point to exactly what you want. (In fact, as we're going to see, the general XPointer scheme extends XPath.) Here's an example using a general XPointer—note that you use the xpointer() function to contain the XPath expression:

```
<insurance xmlns:xlink = "http://www.w3.org/1999/xlink"
    xlink:type = "simple"
    xlink:show = "new"
    xlink:href = "http://www.XPathCorp.com/invoices.xml#xpointer(
        /child::*[5]/child::*[last()])">
    Health Insurance
</insurance>
```

In this example, we're accessing the last child of the fifth element in www.XPathCorp.com/invoices.xml. That's the way you use full XPath expressions with general XPointers—you pass them to the xpointer function.

You can use the same axes as you use in XPath 1.0 in XPointers, but there are two new node tests. Here are the node tests you can use with XPointers:

- *—Any element

- node()—Any node

- text()—A text node

- comment()—A comment node

- processing-instruction()—A processing instruction node

- point()—A point in a resource

- range()—A range in a resource

Note the point and range node tests. A point represents one specific location in a document, and a range is made up of everything between two points. To support points and ranges, the general XPointer scheme extends the concept of nodes to *locations*. Locations are an XPath node, a point, or a range. Node sets become *location sets* in the XPointer specification. We'll take a look at working with points and ranges next.

Creating XPointer Points

You can create an XPointer point with two items—a node and an index, which can hold a positive integer or zero. The node sets an origin for the point, and the index specifies the distance between the point and that origin. What units are used for the index? There are two different ways of measuring the index: you can measure in terms of characters, or in terms of a number of nodes.

If the starting node can contain *only text*—not child nodes—the index is automatically measured in characters. The points you create this way are called *character-points*. Here, the index must be a positive integer or zero.

For example, you might treat <text> as a container node in this case:

```
<text>
Hello there!
</text>
```

Here, there are twelve character-points, one before every character. The character-point at index zero is right before the first character, "H"; the character-point at index 1 is just before the "e", and so on.

On the other hand, when the start node has *child nodes*—that is, when it's an element node or the root node—the index of a point is measured in child nodes. For example, an index of zero means the point is just before any child nodes. An index of 5 specifies a point immediately after the fifth child node.

How do you actually create points? You can use the `point()` function with an XPath 1.0 predicate like this: `point()[position()=9]`. For example, if you wanted to locate a point right before the "l" in the text "Goldfinger", where that text is in the <name> element of the first <review> element in the <reviews> element, you might do something like this:

```
xpointer(/reviews/review[1]/name/text()/point()[position() = 2])
```

COLLAPSED RANGES

If the start point and the end point are the same point, the range you create is a *collapsed* range.

Creating XPointer Ranges

To create a range, all you need is two points, a start point and an end point. They have to be in the same document, and, as you might expect, the start point must be before or the same as the end point.

There are a few functions that were added to XPointer to create ranges:

- `range(location-set)` takes the locations you pass to it and returns a range that completely covers the locations.

- `range-inside(location-set)` returns a range or ranges covering each location inside the location set; if you pass an element, the result is a range that encloses all that is inside the element.

- `range-to(location-set)` returns a range for each location in the location set.

- `string-range(location_set, string [index [, length]])` returns a range for every match to a search string.

For example, here's how you would use the `string-range` function to return a location set of ranges for all matches to the word "Goldfinger" throughout a document:

```
string-range(/*, "Goldfinger")
```

SHOP TALK

SPLITTING THE XPOINTER SPECIFICATION

Why was the XPointer specification split into four parts—one of which is still in working draft stage? As with some other specifications, I get the feeling that it looks as if it was simply too complex to get much use. In a rather rare disclosure of the inside story on this, take a look at http://www.w3.org/XML/2002/10/LinkingImplementations.html. Here's a quote from that document:

"The XPointer specification entered CR status 2000-06-07, then had a second CR 2001-09-11. During the second CR phase, several implementations were identified. Few, however, implemented the whole XPointer specification. Points and Ranges, the principal extensions beyond XPath, were rarely implemented. In early January of 2002, when it became clear that the XPointer specification would not move to PR, the XML Linking Working Group revisited the specification and began to factor it into separate documents."

In my experience, many people who might have used XPointers were not knowledgeable enough in terms of XPath 1.0 to implement them. It appears that W3C made things easier for such people by allowing for barenames and easier syntax. The general form of XPointers, which allows for the use of XPath 1.0, is still in working draft form, and it's beginning to look like it won't get past that stage.

Introducing XQuery

XLink and XPointer are typical of the XPath 1.0 approach to accessing data—you can embed XPath 1.0 expressions directly in your XLink and XPointer expressions. However, data handling is becoming appreciably more sophisticated in XPath 2.0 and XQuery 1.0. To show how much more sophisticated, we'll take a look at XQuery 1.0. XQuery can't be directly compared to XLink and XPointer because it's an entire language (an extension to XPath 2.0), not just a way of using XPath expressions—and that's the whole point. These days, the relative simplicity of XLink and XPointer is not enough; now we need more power, and that's what a language like XQuery gives us. As you're going to see, XQuery goes far beyond XLink and XPointer, and putting it to work will give us an introduction to XPath 2.0, which starts in the next chapter.

XQuery 1.0 is designed to work with XPath 2.0, and it's designed to treat XML documents much as you'd treat databases. In fact, XQuery does function something like Structured Query Language (SQL) does with relational databases. Here's what W3C says about XQuery:

"XML is a versatile markup language, capable of labeling the information content of diverse data sources including structured and semi-structured documents, relational databases, and object repositories. A query language that uses the structure of XML intelligently can express queries across all these kinds of data, whether physically stored in XML or viewed as XML via middleware. This specification describes a query language called XQuery, which is designed to be broadly applicable across many types of XML data sources."

XQuery 1.0 and XSLT 2.0 both work with XPath 2.0. In particular, XQuery 1.0 is an extension of XPath 2.0, and XPath 2.0 is an embedded language in XSLT 2.0. Although you could replace XPath 2.0 in XSLT 2.0 with another language and it would work as well, XPath 2.0 is completely integral to XQuery 1.0. Another big difference is that XQuery 1.0 and XPath 2.0

are much more strongly typed than XPointer/XLink and XPath 1.0, so we'll have to be more careful about the data types we're working with (strings, integers, and so on) than we were before. XQuery gives you not only a data model to let you interpret XML documents, but also a set of operators and functions to let you extract data from those documents.

The W3C XQuery specification is still subject to change at this time. This specification is divided into several working drafts—the main XQuery 1.0 working draft is at http://www.w3.org/TR/xquery/, but there are also working drafts for XQuery semantics, the data model, and serialization. Here's an overview of what's available online as of this writing:

- The XQuery activity page gives an overview—http://www.w3.org/XML/Query

- The XQuery version 1.0 Working Draft—http://www.w3.org/TR/xquery/

- The XQuery 1.0 and XPath 2.0 Data Model—http://www.w3.org/TR/xpath-datamodel/

- The XQuery 1.0 and XPath 2.0 Formal Semantics—http://www.w3.org/TR/xquery-semantics/

- The XQuery 1.0 and XPath 2.0 Functions and Operators—http://www.w3.org/TR/xquery-operators/

- The XML Query Requirements, an overview of what's going to go into XQuery, in Working Draft form—http://www.w3.org/TR/xquery-requirements/

XQuery is already very popular, and there are a number of implementations of XQuery 1.0 out there. Here's a starter list (check out the XQuery Working Group's Web page at http://www.w3.org/XML/Query for more implementations and to get new URLs if any of these no longer work) :

- The XQuery 1.0 Grammar Test Page—http://www.w3.org/2003/05/applets/xqueryApplet.html

- The XPath 2.0 Grammar Test Page—http://www.w3.org/2003/05/applets/xpathApplet.html

- BEA's Liquid Data—http://edocs.bea.com/liquiddata/docs10/prodover/concepts.html

- Bluestream Database Software Corp.'s—XStreamDBhttp://www.bluestream.com/dr/?page=Home/Products/XStreamDB/

- Cerisent's XQE—http://cerisent.com/cerisent-xqe.html

- Cognetic Systems'—XQuantumhttp://www.cogneticsystems.com/xquery/xquery.html

- Enosys Software's XQuery—Demohttp://xquerydemo.enosyssoftware.com

- eXcelon's eXtensible Information Server (XIS 3.1—SP2)http://www.exln.com/products/xis/

- Stylus Studio 4.5, with XQuery and XML Schema support— http://www.exln.com/products/stylusstudio

- E-XMLMedia's XMLizer— http://www.e-xmlmedia.com/prod/xmlizer.htm

- Fatdog's XQEngine—http://www.fatdog.com/

- GAEL's Derby—http://www.gael.fr/derby/

- GNU's Qexo (Kawa-Query)—http://www.qexo.org/—Compiles XQuery on-the-fly to Java bytecodes

- Ipedo's XML Database v3.0—http://www.ipedo.com

- IPSI's IPSI-XQ—http://ipsi.fhg.de/oasys/projects/ipsi-xq/index_e.html

- Lucent's Galax—http://db.bell-labs.com/galax/. Open-source

- Microsoft's XML Query Language Demo—http://xqueryservices.com

- Neocore's XML management system (XMS)—http://www.neocore.com/products/products.htm

- Nimble Technology's Nimble Integration Suite—http://www.nimble.com/

- OpenLink Software's Virtuoso Universal Server—http://demo.openlinksw.com:8890/xqdemo

- Oracle's XML DB—http://otn.oracle.com/tech/xml/xmldb/htdocs/querying_xml.html

- Politecnico di Milano's XQBE—http://dbgroup.elet.polimi.it/xquery/xqbedownload.html

- QuiLogic's SQL/XML-IMDB—http://www.quilogic.cc/xml.htm

- Software AG's Tamino XML Server—http://www.softwareag.com/tamino/News/tamino_41.htm

- Tamino XML Query Demo—http://tamino.demozone.softwareag.com/demoXQuery/index.html

- SourceForge's Saxon—http://saxon.sourceforge.net/

- SourceForge's XQuench—http://xquench.sourceforge.net/. Open-source

- XQuery Lite—http://sourceforge.net/projects/phpxmlclasses/

- X-Hive's XQuery demo—http://www.x-hive.com/xquery

- XML Global's GoXML DB—http://www.xmlglobal.com/prod/xmlworkbench/

To see XQuery at work, we're going to use it with Lucent's Galax XQuery processor, one of the foremost XQuery implementations. You can download Galax for free at `http://db.bell-labs.com/galax/`. And you can see an online demo at `http://db.bell-labs.com/galax/demo/galax_demo.html`.

To use XQuery, we'll need an XML document, and we'll use the one you see in Listing 6.3 (`ch06_03.xml`). This XML document holds information about a number of meetings set up for two teams of employees. We'll use XQuery to extract information about the meetings and meeting locations from this document.

LISTING 6.3   A Sample XML Document (`ch06_03.xml`)

```xml
<?xml version="1.0" encoding="UTF-8"?>
<employees>
    <title>List of employees</title>
    <employee>John Thompson</employee>
    <employee>Edward Hastings</employee>
    <employee>Traci Franklin</employee>
    <employee>Frank Thomas</employee>
    <meeting ID="Introduction" time="evening" >
        <title>Introduction</title>
        <p>Welcome</p>
        <meeting>
            <title>Team 1</title>
            <p>Team 1 meeting</p>
        </meeting>
        <meeting>
            <title>Team 2</title>
            <p>Team 2 meeting</p>
            <location address="Auditorium">
                <title>Building 1</title>
                <phone number="555-2221"/>
            </location>
            <p>Getting Started</p>
        </meeting>
    </meeting>
    <meeting ID="Leadership" time="morning" >
        <title>Leadership</title>
        <p>Breakfast meeting</p>
        <location address="Meeting Room 5">
            <title>Building 2</title>
                <phone number="555-2222"/>
        </location>
```

LISTING 6.3   Continued

```
            <p>Understanding the Issues</p>
            <meeting>
                <title>Team 1</title>
                <p>Team 1 meeting</p>
            </meeting>
            <meeting>
                <title>Team 2</title>
                <p>Team 2 meeting</p>
                <location address="Auditorium">
                    <title>Building 3</title>
                    <phone number="555-2223"/>
                </location>
            </meeting>
            <meeting>
                <title>Closing Statements</title>
                <p>Wrapping things up</p>
            </meeting>
        </meeting>
</employees>
```

We're going to use XQuery to extract data from `ch06_03.xml` using Galax, and we'll use two XQuery files to do it. The first file will hold XQuery context code, where we'll declare the XML elements in `ch06_03.xml` and the XQuery functions we'll use. The other XQuery file will hold the template we'll use to query our XML document. (Splitting our XQuery code into two parts is not necessary for working with XQuery in general; we're just doing it to work with Galax.)

The XQuery context file, `ch06_04.xq`, will start by defining all the XML elements in our sample XML document so that Galax can check the validity of that document. Defining the XML elements we'll be using can be done with this XML DTD-like syntax, which is specific to Galax:

```
define element employees
{
    element title,
    element employee+,
    element meeting+
}

define element title {xsd:string}
define element employee {xsd:string}
```

```
define element meeting
{
    attribute ID {xsd:string}?,
    attribute time {xsd:string}?,
    element title,
      (element p ¦ element location ¦ element meeting)*
}

define element p {xsd:string}

define element location
{
    attribute address { xsd:string },
    element title,
    element phone
}

define element phone
{
    attribute number {xsd:string}
}
```

Now we need to indicate to Galax what XML document our data can be found in, and that's ch06_03.xml here. In this case, we'll associate that document with an XQuery *variable*, $employeesList, making the data in that document available to our XQuery code. XQuery variable names begin with a $ sign, and the following example shows how we define our global variable named $employeesList to hold the data from ch06_03.xml. (The glx:docu-ment-validate function is specific to Galax that reads in a document and validates it because how a document is validated is implementation-specific; in XPath 2.0, you can read in a document without validating it with the fn:doc function, as we'll see in Chapter 12, "XPath 2.0 Node and Sequence Functions.")

```
define global $employeesList {treat as document employees
(glx:document-validate("ch06_03.xml", "employees"))}
```

XQuery also lets you define your own *functions*. To see how this works, we'll create a function named summation here, which will return a summation of various different types of elements. Here's how we define summation, indicating that we want to pass an XML element to it:

```
define function summation($elem as element) as element*
{
    .
    .
    .
```

```
}
```

We begin our XQuery function by getting the name of the element we're working with using the XQuery `local-name` function, like this:

```
define function summation($elem as element) as element*
{
    let $name := local-name($elem)

            .

            .

            .

}
```

We can check if we've been passed a `<meeting>` element, and if so, return a summation of that element this way:

```
define function summation($elem as element) as element*
{
    let $name := local-name($elem)
    return
        if ($name = "meeting")
        then
            <meeting>
                {$elem/@*}
                {for $item in $elem/* return summation($item)}
            </meeting>

        .

        .

        .

}
```

As far as other elements go, we'll return only `<title>` elements, like this (this function, by the way, points out one of the differences between XSLT and XQuery—in XSLT, you'd need four templates to do this; in XQuery, you only need one function):

```
define function summation($elem as element) as element*
{
    let $name := local-name($elem)
    return
        if ($name = "meeting")
        then
            <meeting>
                {$elem/@*}
                {for $item in $elem/* return summation($item)}
```

```
                </meeting>
            else if ($name = "title")
            then $elem
            else ()
}
```

That's it; now our summation function will return summations for <meeting> and <title> elements. That completes our XQuery context file, ch06_04.xq, which you can see in Listing 6.4.

LISTING 6.4   Our Context XQuery Document (ch06_04.xq)

```
define element employees
{
    element title,
    element employee+,
    element meeting+
}

define element title {xsd:string}
define element employee {xsd:string}

define element meeting
{
    attribute ID {xsd:string}?,
    attribute time {xsd:string}?,
    element title,
      (element p ¦ element location ¦ element meeting)*
}

define element p {xsd:string}

define element location
{
    attribute address { xsd:string },
    element title,
    element phone
}

define element phone
{
    attribute number {xsd:string}
}
```

LISTING 6.4 Continued

```
define element meetingSummary
{
    attribute ID {xsd:string}?,
    attribute time {xsd:string}?,
    element title,
    element locationCount {xsd:int},
    element meetingSummary*
}

define global $employeesList {treat as document employees
    (glx:document-validate("ch06_03.xml", "employees"))}


define function summation($elem as element) as element*
{
    let $name := local-name($elem)
    return
        if ($name = "meeting")
        then
            <meeting>
                {$elem/@*}
                {for $item in $elem/* return summation($item)}
            </meeting>
        else if ($name = "title")
        then $elem
        else ()
}
```

The next step is to create the template file, `ch06_05.xq`, which will use `ch06_03.xml` and `ch06_04.xq` to extract the data we want. In this case, we'll start by creating a `<meetings>` element that holds a summary of the `<meeting>` elements in our XML document. We'll use the summation function to create this summary. Note in particular the XPath syntax here to specify the `<meeting>` child elements of the `<employees>` document element—`$employeesList/employees/meeting`:

```
<meetings>
    {
        for $meeting in $employeesList/employees/meeting return summary($meeting)
    }
</meetings>
;
```

In this case, we're stripping out and displaying a summary of each <meeting> element—including all child <meeting> elements, while also preserving the <title> elements. Here's what the output of our XQuery query looks like so far:

```
<meetings>
  <meeting time="evening"
    ID="Introduction">
    <title>Introduction</title>
    <meeting><title>Team 1</title></meeting>
    <meeting><title>Team 2</title></meeting>
  </meeting>
  <meeting time="morning"
    ID="Leadership">
    <title>Leadership</title>
    <meeting><title>Team 1</title></meeting>
    <meeting><title>Team 2</title></meeting>
    <meeting><title>Closing Statements</title></meeting>
  </meeting>
</meetings>
```

We can also display the locations of the various meetings by selecting <location> elements in the XML document, preserving their attributes and titles, and displaying the results in a <locations> element like this:

```
<locations>
    {
        for $location in $employeesList//location
        return
            <location>
                {$location/@*}
                {$location/title}
            </location>
    }
</locations>
;
```

This code gives us these results in the output, where we're displaying the <location> elements and their attributes, as well as any contained <title> elements:

```
<locations>
  <location address="Auditorium"><title>Building 1</title></location>
  <location address="Meeting Room 5"><title>Building 2</title></location>
  <location address="Auditorium"><title>Building 3</title></location>
</locations>
```

We might also use the XQuery count function to count the number of `<meeting>` elements. To count all `<meeting>` elements, no matter where they are in the input XML document, we can use the expression `$employeesList//meeting`, using the XPath `//` syntax to indicate any descendant:

```
<numberMeetings>{count($employeesList//meeting)}</numberMeetings>
;
```

This gives us this result:

```
<numberMeetings>7</numberMeetings>
```

And we might count the total number of `<location>` elements this way:

```
<numberLocations>{count($employeesList//location)}</numberLocations>
;
```

Here is the result:

```
<numberLocations>3</numberLocations>
```

Finally, we'll count the number of `<meeting>` elements that themselves contain `<meeting>` elements like this:

```
<numberMainMeetings>
    {
        count($employeesList/employees/meeting)
    }
</numberMainMeetings>
;
```

This is what appears in the output:

```
<numberMainMeetings>2</numberMainMeetings>
```

And that's it—you can see the complete XQuery query file, `ch06_05.xq`, in Listing 6.5.

LISTING 6.5 Our XQuery Document (`ch06_05.xq`)

```
<meetings>
    {
        for $meeting in $employeesList/employees/meeting return summation($meeting)
    }
</meetings>
;
```

LISTING 6.5   Continued

```
<locations>
    {
        for $location in $employeesList//location
        return
            <location>
                {$location/@*}
                {$location/title}
            </location>
    }
</locations>
;


<numberMeetings>{count($employeesList//meeting)}</numberMeetings>
;


<numberLocations>{count($employeesList//location)}</numberLocations>
;


<numberMainMeetings>
    {
        count($employeesList/employees/meeting)
    }
</numberMainMeetings>
;
```

Now we're ready to use Galax with our context and template XQuery files. Here's how you do that:

```
%galax -context ch06_04.xq ch06_05.xq
```

Here's what you see when you execute Galax—note that our XQuery results are displayed as XML:

```
%galax -context ch06_04.xq ch06_05.xq
<meetings>
  <meeting time="evening"
    ID="Introduction">
    <title>Introduction</title>
    <meeting><title>Team 1</title></meeting>
    <meeting><title>Team 2</title></meeting>
```

```
    </meeting>
    <meeting time="morning"
      ID="Leadership">
      <title>Leadership</title>
      <meeting><title>Team 1</title></meeting>
      <meeting><title>Team 2</title></meeting>
      <meeting><title>Closing Statements</title></meeting>
    </meeting>
  </meetings>
  <locations>
    <location address="Auditorium"><title>Building 1</title></location>
    <location address="Meeting Room 5"><title>Building 2</title></location>
    <location address="Auditorium"><title>Building 3</title></location>
  </locations>
  <numberMeetings>7</numberMeetings>
  <numberLocations>3</numberLocations>
  <numberMainMeetings>2</numberMainMeetings>
```

You can also write these results to an XML document like this, which creates the document summation.xml:

```
%galax -context ch06_04.xq ch06_05.xq -output-xml summation.xml
```

And that completes our XQuery example.

Variables? Do-it-yourself functions? You can already see in this example how much more detailed and powerful XQuery is than XLink and XPointer. In fact, XQuery is far more sophisticated and can't even be compared directly to XLink and XPointer. Instead, XQuery is better compared to XSLT, although it's even more sophisticated than XSLT is—in XSLT, you're restricted to templates, but in XQuery you can create your own functions and use a flexible programming language that is far more powerful than simple XSLT templates.

As you can see, the trend is towards more and more power and sophistication. And XPath 2.0 is a big part of that. It shouldn't surprise you to learn that XPath 2.0 is much larger than XPath 1.0, and supports many more advanced techniques. XPath 2.0 also supports very strong data typing, and after you've validated an XML document, lets you make use of that data typing information. We're going to see how all this works as we plunge into XPath 2.0, coming up in Chapter 7.

We're done with XPath 1.0 now, and it's time to turn to XPath 2.0. XPath 2.0 is at the heart of the development that's going on in its cospecifications, XSLT 2.0 and XQuery 1.0, and there is a lot of material coming up, as we're going to see.

In Brief

- You use XLinks to create links in XML, like HTML hyperlinks but considerably more extended. Any XML element can be an XLink—all you have to do is to use the correct attributes. The one required attribute, `xlink:type`, sets the type of XLink, and the possible values are `simple`, `extended`, `locator`, `arc`, `resource`, `title`, or `none`.

- XPointers let you narrow down your searches even more, down to specific nodes or even specific characters in text. The XPointer specification is divided into three Recommendations—the XPointer framework, the element scheme, and the namespace scheme—along with the Working Draft for the general XPointer scheme. This division was made to make XPointers easier to implement.

- The XPointer framework shows how you can use element names—referred to as bare-names—as XPointers, the element scheme shows how you can identify elements by ID, and the namespace scheme shows how to use namespaces in XPointers.

- The general XPointer scheme is where the full power of XPointers appears because you can use full XPath 1.0 expressions here. General XPointers are so powerful because they support full XPath expressions, as well as two more data types—points and ranges.

- On the other hand, the other technique we looked at in this chapter—XQuery—is really where the future action is going to be when it comes to data access. Although still just in W3C Working Draft stage, XQuery is generating a lot of excitement, and we got a good introduction to it here. Using the Galax XQuery processor, we were able to create XQuery variables and functions, and used them to successfully query the data in an XML document and extract what we wanted.

Introducing
XPath 2.0

What's New in XPath 2.0?

As of this writing, XPath 2.0 is still in Working Draft form, but it's now stabilized, giving us the chance to work with it. XPath 2.0 is described this way by W3C—just as you'd describe XPath 1.0, in fact:

"The primary purpose of XPath is to address parts of an XML document. XPath uses a compact, non-XML syntax to facilitate use of XPath within URIs and XML attribute values. XPath gets its name from its use of a path notation as in URLs for navigating through the hierarchical structure of an XML document."

Although the primary purpose of XPath hasn't changed in this new version, much of the actual specification has. You'll still be able to use the familiar path steps, each made up of an axis (XPath 2.0 uses the same axes as XPath 1.0), followed by a node test, followed by a predicate. However, much of the terminology has changed, along with some basic concepts—for example, XPath supports *sequences* instead of node-sets. We're going to see how all this works in detail over the next few chapters.

XPath 2.0, XQuery 1.0, and XSLT 2.0 are all tied together, and XPath 2.0 is the common denominator. The W3C groups working on these standards have been working together closely. One way of looking at what's been going on is that XSLT 2.0 and XQuery 1.0 are designed to share as much as possible—and that what they share is in fact XPath 2.0.

So why XPath 2.0? What's it got that XPath 1.0 doesn't have? There are many answers, but one of the main ones is support for new data types. As you know, XPath 1.0 supports only these data types:

- `string`
- `boolean`
- `node-set`
- `number`

That was okay long ago, but things have changed—in particular, W3C has been moving toward XML schema for its data types. Supporting new data types based on XML schema means that XPath 2.0 supports all the simple primitive types built into XML schema. There are 19 such types in all, including many that XPath 1.0 doesn't support, such as data types for dates, URIs, and so on.

The XPath 2.0 data model also supports data types that you can derive from these data types in your own XML schema. We're going to see how to work with these various types ourselves.

XML SCHEMA

If you're not familiar with XML schema, you can get all the details at `http://www.w3.org/TR/xmlschema-0/`, `http://www.w3.org/TR/xmlschema-1/`, and `http://www.w3.org/TR/xmlschema-2/`. Another good resource is the book *Sams Teach Yourself XML in 21 Days* (ISBN: 0672325764).

XPath 2.0 also gives you tremendously more power than XPath 1.0 did. There are dozens of new built-in functions that you can use now, and many more operators. These functions and operators are far more type-aware than what we've seen in XPath 1.0. We'll take a look in this chapter at how these new operators and functions can simplify tasks that were difficult in XPath 1.0.

Also new in XPath 2.0 are *sequences*, which replace the familiar node-sets from XPath 1.0. In fact, all XPath 2.0 expressions evaluate to sequences, as we're going to see. And you can also use variables in XPath 2.0.

The current working draft for XPath 2.0 is at `http://www.w3.org/TR/xpath20/`. This document tells you about XPath 2.0 in some detail, but it doesn't provide the whole story. In addition, there are documents outlining the XPath 2.0 data model—which tells you how XPath 2.0 sees an XML document—the data types used in XPath 2.0, and the functions and operators available. Here's the list:

- The XPath 2.0 specification is at `http://www.w3.org/TR/xpath20/`.
- The XPath data model defines the information in an XML document that is available to an XPath processor. The data model is defined in the XQuery 1.0 and XPath 2.0 Data Model document at `http://www.w3.org/TR/xpath-datamodel/`.

- The library of functions and operators supported by XPath 2.0 is defined in the XQuery 1.0 and XPath 2.0 Functions and Operators document, which is at `http://www.w3.org/TR/xquery-operators/`.

- The type system used in XPath 2.0 is based on XML Schema, which you can read all about at `www.w3.org/TR/xmlschema-0/`, `www.w3.org/TR/xmlschema-1/`, and `www.w3.org/TR/xmlschema-2/`. The types defined in XML schema can be found in `www.w3.org/TR/xmlschema-2/`.

- The formal semantics of XPath 2.0 are defined in the XQuery 1.0 and XPath 2.0 Formal Semantics document. This document is useful for programmers creating XPath processors, and you can find it at `http://www.w3.org/TR/xquery-semantics/`.

You still create location paths in XPath 2.0, of course, and build them from location steps. A location step, as in XPath 1.0, can contain an axis, a node test, and a predicate. The allowable axes are the same as in XPath 1.0. However, there are differences already—the namespace axis is considered *deprecated* in XPath 2.0, which means it's considered obsolete. It's included for backward compatibility, but is not available at all in XQuery 1.0.

Handling Nodes

Although the data types have changed, the node kinds are more or less the same in XPath 2.0 compared to XPath 1.0. As you recall, you can have these kinds of nodes in XPath 1.0: root nodes, element nodes, attribute nodes, processing instruction nodes, comment nodes, text nodes, and namespace nodes. There is one difference in XPath 2.0, however—root nodes are now called document nodes instead, ending a long-standing confusion.

Handling Data Types

As also mentioned, one of the main motivations behind XPath 2.0 was to expand the data types available. XPath 1.0 supported Booleans, node-sets, strings, and numbers, but that was pretty basic. XPath 2.0 supports all the primitive simple types built into XML schema, as well as the types you can derive by restriction from the primitive simple types, which gives you a great deal more control over data typing. Here are the simple primitive types—the xs namespace corresponds to "http://www.w3.org/2001/XMLSchema":

- xs:string
- xs:boolean
- xs:decimal
- xs:float
- xs:double
- xs:duration
- xs:dateTime
- xs:time
- xs:date
- xs:gYearMonth
- xs:gYear
- xs:gMonthDay

- `xs:gDay`
- `xs:gMonth`
- `xs:hexBinary`
- `xs:base64Binary`

- `xs:anyURI`
- `xs:QName`
- `xs:NOTATION`

Besides these types, you can also use types derived from primitive simple types by restriction, as we'll see when we discuss the data model in depth in this chapter, after this overview. Collectively, these simple primitive types and the types derived from primitive simple types by restriction are called *atomic types*. And XPath 2.0 sequences can contain both atomic types and nodes.

Working with Sequences

Every XPath 2.0 expression (that is, anything an XPath processor can evaluate, including expressions that return nodes from a document or string values and so on) evaluates to a sequence. Here's the XPath 2.0 definition of a sequence:

- A *sequence* is an ordered collection of zero or more items.

- An *item* is either an atomic value or a node.

- An *atomic value* is a value in the value space of an XML Schema atomic type, as defined in the XML Schema specification. Atomic values can either be simple primitive types, or be derived by restriction from these types, as we'll discuss in this chapter.

- A *node* is one of the seven node kinds described in the XQuery 1.0 and XPath 2.0 Data Model document.

- A sequence containing exactly one item is called a *singleton sequence*. An item is identical to a singleton sequence containing that item.

- A sequence containing zero items is called an *empty sequence*.

Sequences can contain nodes or atomic values. As we've seen, an atomic value is a value of one of the 19 built-in simple primitive data types defined in the XML schema specification, or a type derived from them by restriction.

Sequences are the successor to node-sets—besides nodes, they also let you work with simple data items. The term "sequence" is really a catch-all way to refer to data you can work with in XPath 2.0, either an atomic value or a node, or a collection of such items. Sequences can be made up of a single item or multiple items; it's all the same to XPath 2.0. Giving them one name, sequence is an easy way to let you handle single or multiple items (even though the term "sequence" is not very apt for single items).

Sequences can be constructed with this kind of syntax: (1, 2, 3), which is a sequence of the atomic values 1, 2, and 3. In fact, the comma is an operator in XPath 2.0—the sequence construction operator. You can also extract items from a sequence using the [] operator. Here's an example:

```
(4, 5, 6)[2]
```

This expression returns the value 5. You can also use the range operator, to, to create sequences, as in this example:

```
(1 to 1000)
```

Note that you cannot nest sequences—that is, if you have a sequence (1, 2) and then try to nest that in another sequence as ((1, 2), 3), the result is simply the sequence (1, 2, 3).

Sequences are also *ordered*, which is different from node-sets in XPath 1.0. For example, take a look at this sequence:

```
(//planet/mass, //planet/name)
```

Here, we're creating a sequence in which <mass> elements from our planetary data XML document come before <name> elements—which is the opposite of the way these elements appear in actual document order. But the order of these elements as we've specified them is preserved in the sequence we're creating here.

Here's another way in which XPath 2.0 differs from 1.0—sequences, unlike node-sets, can have duplicate items. For example, take a look at this sequence:

```
(//planet/mass, //planet/name,
//planet/mass)
```

Here, we're creating a sequence of all <mass> elements, followed by all <name> elements—followed by all <mass> elements again. This is legal in sequences, but not in node-sets. (In fact, the very definition of XPath 1.0 node-sets precludes duplicate items.)

So that's what sequences are all about in general—instead of only supporting one multiple-item construct, the node-set, XPath 2.0 supports sequences, which can contain multiple simple-typed data items as well as nodes.

ORDERED VERSUS UNORDERED SEQUENCES

Here's something to know behind the scenes about sequences versus node-sets. W3C wanted to make life a little easier for people moving from XPath 1.0 to 2.0, so the way sequences are constructed is designed to be somewhat node-set friendly.

Although node-sets are unordered, node-sets are usually constructed in document order. XSLT 2.0 is designed to work on sequences in sequence order, but in order to be compatible with XPath 1.0, path expressions are designed to always return their results using document order by default.

Also, duplicates are removed from the results by default, which means the sequence you get from a path expression is usually going to be the same as the node-set you'd get.

The `for` Expression

Sequences are more than just a new concept—XPath 2.0 is really centered around them. There are whole new expressions designed to work with sequences, such as the `for` expression. This expression is designed to let you handle sequences by looping, or iterating, over all items in a sequence.

We'll meet the `for` expression in Chapter 8, "XPath 2.0 Expressions and Operators," but here's a preview that also puts XPath 2.0 variables to work. Say that you wanted to find the average planetary mass in our planets example. Doing that with the `for` expression is easy— here's what that might look like:

```
for $variable in /planets/planet return $variable/mass
```

Notice what we're doing here—we're using the `for` expression to loop over all <mass> values. We do that with a variable, something new for us in XPath, named $variable. Variables in XPath 2.0 start with a $ preceding a normal XML-legal name, so you can use any legal XML name here, like $var, $numberProducts, $name, and so on.

We're using the path expression /planets/planet to return a sequence holding all <planet> elements in the document. How do we return the <mass> elements of these <planet> elements in a sequence? We can use the `return` keyword, as you see here. In this case, the expression we want to return each time through the loop is $variable/mass, and because $variable holds a new <planet> element each time through the loop, we'll get a sequence of all <mass> elements this way.

To get the average mass of the planets, you could use the `avg` function this way:

```
avg(for $variable in /planets/planet return $variable/mass)
```

Note that you could also write our `for` expression as

```
for $variable in /planets/planet/mass return $variable
```

This does the same thing that the expression /planets/planet/mass does—it returns a sequence of <mass> elements. Here's another example, where we're multiplying the miles per gallon of a number of cars by their fuel capacity to get their total operating ranges:

```
for $variable in /cars return $variable/milesPerGallon * $variable/gasCapacity
```

That's how the `for` expression works in general, like this:

```
for variable in sequence return expression
```

The if Expression

Besides the for expression, you can now use the conditional if expression in XPath 2.0. Being able to use conditional expressions like if and loop expressions like for in XPath adds a lot of the programming power of true programming languages to XPath 2.0.

Here's an example of an if expression, which finds the minimum of two temperatures (which you can also do with the XPath 2.0 min function):

```
if ($temperature1 < $temperature2) then $temperature1 else $temperature2
```

Here, we're comparing the value in $temperature1 to the value in $temperature2. If $temperature1 holds a value that is less than the value in $temperature2, this if expression returns the value in $temperature1; otherwise, it returns to the value in $temperature2.

This has the feel of a true programming language, and there's a lot more power here than in XPath 1.0. Now, you're allowed to branch to different expressions based on a test expression. More on the if statement in Chapter 8.

The some and every Expressions

You can use a rudimentary form of a conditional expression in XPath 1.0—for example, this expression, as used in a predicate:

```
/planets/planet[1]/name = "Mars"
```

would be true if *any* <name> element in the first <planet> element had the text "Mars".

XPath 2.0 extends this kind of checking. You can either perform the same test in XPath 2.0 using the same syntax, or you can use the some expression. Using the some expression means that at least one item in a sequence satisfies an expression given with a satisifies predicate, like this:

```
some $variable in /planets/planet[1]/name satisfies $variable = "Mars"
```

In this case, this expression returns true if at least one <name> element in the first <planet> element has the text "Mars".

You can also perform other kinds of tests here, such as this expression, which is true if any <radius> element in the first <planet> element contains a value greater than 2000:

```
some $variable in /planets/planet[1]/radius satisfies $variable > 2000
```

You can also insist that *every* <radius> element in the first <planet> element contains a value greater than 2000 if you use the every expression instead of some, like this:

```
every $variable in /planets/planet[1]/radius satisfies $variable > 2000
```

More about some and every in Chapter 8.

Unions, Intersections, and Differences

In XPath 1.0, you could use the ¦ operator to create the *union* (that is, the combination) of two sets, as in this case, where we're matching attributes and nodes in an XSLT template:

```
<?xml version="1.0" encoding="utf-8"?>
<xsl:stylesheet version="1.1"
xmlns:xsl="http://www.w3.org/1999/XSL/Transform">
<xsl:output method="xml"/>

  <xsl:template match="distance[preceding::*/name='Mercury']">
    <distance>This planet is farther than Mercury from the sun.</distance>
  </xsl:template>

  <xsl:template match="@*¦node()">
    <xsl:copy>
      <xsl:apply-templates select="@*¦node()"/>
    </xsl:copy>
  </xsl:template>

</xsl:stylesheet>
```

In XPath 2.0, you can create not only unions like this, but also *intersections*, which contain all the items two sequences have in common, and *differences*, which contain all the items that two sequences have that are *not* in common.

Let's take a look at how this works. For example, to get the same result as the previous XPath 1.0 example, we can use the union operator in XPath 2.0:

```
<?xml version="1.0" encoding="utf-8"?>
<xsl:stylesheet version="2.0"
xmlns:xsl="http://www.w3.org/1999/XSL/Transform">
<xsl:output method="xml"/>

  <xsl:template match="distance[preceding::*/name='Mercury']">
    <distance>This planet is farther than Mercury from the sun.</distance>
  </xsl:template>

  <xsl:template match="@* union node()">
    <xsl:copy>
      <xsl:apply-templates select="@* union node()"/>
    </xsl:copy>
  </xsl:template>

</xsl:stylesheet>
```

In addition, XPath 2.0 introduces the `intersect` operator, which returns the intersection of two sequences (that is, all those items they have in common). For example, if the variable `$planets` holds a sequence of `<planet>` elements, we could create a sequence of `<planet>` elements that `$variable` has in common with the planets in our planetary data document, like this:

```
$planets intersect /planets/planet
```

To find the difference between two sequences, you can use the `except` operator. For example, if you wanted to find all items in `$planets` that were not also in the sequence returned by `/planets/planet`, you could use `except` this way:

```
$planets except /planets/planet
```

Here's something else that's new in XPath 2.0—you can now specify multiple node tests in location steps. Here's an example:

```
planets/(mass¦day)/text()
```

Here's what that would look like in XPath 1.0:

```
planets/mass/text() ¦ planets/day/text()
```

And, as already mentioned, there are many new functions coming up in XPath 2.0, and we're going to see them in the final four chapters of this book. One of the specific tasks that W3C undertook in XPath 2.0 was to augment its string-processing capabilities. Accordingly, you'll find more string functions in XPath 2.0, including `upper-case`, `lower-case`, `string-pad`, `matches`, `replace`, and `tokenize`.

Note in particular the `matches`, `replace`, and `tokenize` functions—these functions use *regular expressions*, a powerful new addition to XPath. As we'll discuss in Chapter 10, "XPath 2.0 String Functions," regular expressions let you create *patterns* to use in matching text. Regular expression patterns use their own syntax—for example, the pattern `\d{3}-\d{3}-\d{4}` matches U.S. phone numbers, like 888-555-1111. Being able to use regular expressions like this is very powerful because you can match the text in a node to the patterns you're searching for.

Comments

You can also create XPath 2.0 comments using the delimiters (`:` and `:`). Here's an example:

```
(: Check for at least one planet with the name Mars :)
some $variable in /planets/planet[1]/name satisfies $variable = "Mars"
```

Comments may be nested.

That completes our XPath 2.0 overview—now you've gotten an idea of the kinds of things that are different in XPath 2.0. Besides what we've seen in these few examples, there are plenty of additional new expressions coming up, such as `cast`, `treat`, and `instance of`. We'll get all the details in the coming chapters. In the meantime, how about a few working examples?

Creating Some XPath 2.0 Examples

There is relatively little software out there that supports XPath 2.0—in fact, besides XQuery processors like Galax, the only real XPath 2.0-enabled processor in popular use today is the Saxon XSLT application, which you can get for free at `http://saxon.sourceforge.net`. Because Saxon supports some XPath 2.0—as well as some XSLT 2.0—we'll use it in examples in our XPath 2.0 discussions.

If you want to follow along in these examples, you should download Saxon and unzip it. For our purposes, the important file is `saxon7.jar`, the Java Archive file which holds the Saxon implementation. Saxon is written in Java, so you'll need to have Java installed on your computer as well. Java is free and you can get the latest version at `http://java.sun.com/j2se/`.

Saxon supports a good deal of XSLT 2.0 as well as XPath 2.0, which is handy for use because we'll be able to put XPath 2.0 to work in XSLT 2.0 examples. For instance, take a look at the XML document in Listing 7.1, `ch07_01.xml`. This document contains data on several cities, as you can see.

LISTING 7.1   City Data in an XML Document (`ch07_01.xml`)

```
<?xml version="1.0" encoding="UTF-8"?>
<document>

    <data
        city="Glendale"
        people="194973"
        state="California"
    />

    <data
        city="Fresno"
        people="457652"
        state="California"
    />

    <data
```

LISTING 7.1   Continued

```
            city="Sacramento"
            people="407018"
            state="California"
        />

        <data
            city="Oakland"
            people="399484"
            state="California"
        />

        <data
            city="Boston"
            people="589141"
            state="Massachusetts"
        />

        <data
            city="Cambridge"
            people="101359"
            state="Massachusetts"
        />

        <data
            city="Pittsburgh"
            people="334563"
            state="Pennsylvania"
        />

        <data
            city="Erie"
            people="103707"
            state="Pennsylvania"
        />

        <data
            city="Allentown"
            people="106632"
            state="Pennsylvania"
        />

</document>
```

We might want to use the new capabilities of XSLT 2.0 to process the data you see in ch07_01.xml. Although this is not a book on XSLT 2.0, and although XSLT 2.0 is still in flux, we'll put Saxon to work here to show off some of the new power available in XSLT 2.0. For example, we can use the new <xsl:for-each-group> element to group the data on the various cities you see in ch07_01.xml by state, displaying the sum of the people in all the cities in a particular state in an HTML table.

We start the XSLT 2.0 style sheet we'll use here this way—note that the version is 2.0:

```
<xsl:stylesheet version="2.0" xmlns:xsl="http://www.w3.org/1999/XSL/Transform">
    .
    .
    .
```

Here's how we group our data by state and loop over each group:

```
<xsl:for-each-group select="data" group-by="@state">
    .
    .
    .
</xsl:for-each-group>
```

Inside this loop, we can refer to the current group of cities in a particular state with the XSLT 2.0 current-group function like this, where we're summing up the people of the cities in each group state:

```
<xsl:for-each-group select="data" group-by="@state">
    <TR>
        <TD>
            <xsl:value-of select="@state"/>
        </TD>
        <TD>
            Cities People:
            <xsl:value-of
                select="sum(current-group()/@people)"/>
        </TD>
        .
        .
        .
</xsl:for-each-group>
```

We'll also display the names of the cities in each group with <xsl:value-of>, as you see in ch07_02.xsl (Listing 7.2).

LISTING 7.2   An XSLT 2.0 Style Sheet (ch07_02.xsl)

```
<xsl:stylesheet version="2.0" xmlns:xsl="http://www.w3.org/1999/XSL/Transform">

    <xsl:template match="document">
    <HTML>

        <HEAD>
            <TITLE>City Data</TITLE>
        </HEAD>

        <BODY>

            <H1>City Data</H1>

            <TABLE BORDER="1" CELLPADDING="5">

<xsl:for-each-group select="data" group-by="@state">
    <TR>
        <TD>
            <xsl:value-of select="@state"/>
        </TD>
        <TD>
            Number of People:
            <xsl:value-of
                select="sum(current-group()/@people)"/>
        </TD>
        <TD>
            Cities Used:
            <xsl:value-of select="current-group()/@city"
                separator=" "/>
        </TD>
    </TR>
</xsl:for-each-group>

            </TABLE>

        </BODY>

    </HTML>
    </xsl:template>

</xsl:stylesheet>
```

To make this example work with Saxon, you need to set the `classpath` environment variable to include the `saxon7.jar` file. To do that, move to the directory that contains `ch07_01.xml` and `ch07_02.xsl` and enter this line at the command prompt (in Windows, open a DOS command-prompt window to do this):

```
%set classpath=.;saxon7.jar
```

Next, to let Saxon convert `ch07_01.xml` using `ch07_02.xsl`, you can enter this line at the command prompt if you're in the same directory as `ch07_01.xml` using `ch07_02.xsl`:

```
%java net.sf.saxon.Transform ch07_01.xml ch07_02.xsl
```

This assumes that the Java `bin` directory is in your machine's path; if not, you need to qualify "java" with the path to the Java `bin` directory, like this (in this case, the Java `bin` directory is `C:\java\bin`):

```
%C:\java\bin\java net.sf.saxon.Transform ch07_01.xml ch07_02.xsl
```

When you execute this command line, this HTML will appear in the command-prompt window as the output from the Saxon XSLT processor:

```
<HTML>
   <HEAD>
      <meta http-equiv="Content-Type" content="text/html; charset=UTF-8">

      <TITLE>City Data</TITLE>
   </HEAD>
   <BODY>
      <H1>City Data</H1>
      <TABLE BORDER="1" CELLPADDING="5">
         <TR>
            <TD>California</TD>
            <TD>
               Number of People:
               1459127
            </TD>
            <TD>
               Cities Used:
               Glendale Fresno Sacramento Oakland
            </TD>
         </TR>
         <TR>
            <TD>Massachusetts</TD>
            <TD>
```

```
                    Number of People:
                    690500
                </TD>
                <TD>
                    Cities Used:
                    Boston Cambridge
                </TD>
            </TR>
            <TR>
                <TD>Pennsylvania</TD>
                <TD>
                    Number of People:
                    544902
                </TD>
                <TD>
                    Cities Used:
                    Pittsburgh Erie Allentown
                </TD>
            </TR>
        </TABLE>
    </BODY>
</HTML>
```

To capture this HTML in an HTML document named `results.html`, you can use this command line:

```
%java net.sf.saxon.Transform ch07_01.xml ch07_02.xsl > results.html
```

And you can see what this HTML looks like in a browser in Figure 7.1.

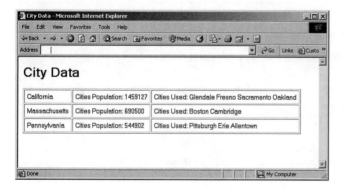

FIGURE 7.1   Using XSLT 2.0 and Saxon.

Here's an example that uses the new XPath 2.0 max function to determine the maximum radius of any of the three planets in our planetary data XML document, `ch01_01.xml`. You can see how that works in the XSLT 2.0 style sheet `ch07_03.xsl` in Listing 7.3.

LISTING 7.3   An XSLT 2.0 Style Sheet Using the max Function (`ch07_03.xsl`)

```
<xsl:stylesheet version="2.0" xmlns:xsl="http://www.w3.org/1999/XSL/Transform">

    <xsl:template match="planets">
        <HTML>
            <HEAD>
                <TITLE>
                    The Largest Planetary Radius
                </TITLE>
            </HEAD>

            <BODY>
                <H1>
                    The Largest Planetary Radius
                </H1>
                <BR/>
                The largest planetary radius is
                <xsl:value-of select="max(//planet/radius)"/>
                miles.
            </BODY>

        </HTML>
    </xsl:template>

</xsl:stylesheet>
```

Here's how you use this style sheet with Saxon:

```
%java net.sf.saxon.Transform ch01_01.xml ch07_03.xsl > results.html
```

And here's the HTML created—as you can see, the XPath 2.0 max function was indeed able to determine the maximum radius of the three planets:

```
<HTML>
    <HEAD>
        <meta http-equiv="Content-Type" content="text/html; charset=UTF-8">

        <TITLE>
            The Largest Planetary Radius
```

```
      </TITLE>
   </HEAD>
   <BODY>
      <H1>
         The Largest Planetary Radius

      </H1><BR>
      The largest planetary radius is
      3716
      miles.

   </BODY>
</HTML>
```

You can see what this HTML looks like in Figure 7.2.

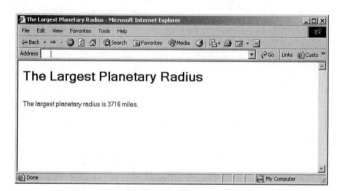

FIGURE 7.2   Using the max function.

In Saxon, you have a tool that's useful in letting you test your XPath 2.0 expressions—even before XPath 2.0 becomes an official recommendation. Each version of Saxon includes documentation showing what parts of XPath 2.0 and XSLT 2.0 are supported.

Understanding the XPath Data Model

The XPath 2.0 data model is based on an XML document's *infoset*. A document's infoset contains all the document's data reduced to a standard form in a set of properties; you can read all about infosets at www.w3.org/TR/xml-infoset/.

For example, if you're working with a processing instruction, the infoset will contain a number of properties for that processing instruction, including target, content, base-uri, and parent. These properties are then translated into XPath 2.0 data model properties.

The details of how this works are not directly important to us because they're handled by the software, and the XPath 2.0 properties for a node aren't directly available to us anyway (these properties are accessed by the XPath 2.0 processor when you use the XPath 2.0 language). However, it's good to know how the process works in overview.

In general, an XML document is first reduced to its infoset, which may be validated by an XML schema (although XPath 2.0 makes provisions for DTD validation, it's clear they're focusing on schemas), resulting in a Post Schema Validated Infoset (PSVI). The PSVI's properties are then converted to the corresponding XPath 2.0 data model properties and made available to XPath processors.

All the data from the PSVI is represented in sequences (single items, like single nodes, are represented as singleton sequences). As you know, sequences can contain nodes or atomic values, or a mix of the two. The XPath 2.0 data model uses the same seven node kinds as the XPath 1.0 data model does (except that root nodes are now called document nodes):

- Document nodes
- Element nodes
- Attribute nodes
- Processing instruction nodes
- Comment nodes
- Text nodes
- Namespace nodes

Note that in the XPath 2.0 data model, each node has two types of values—its *string value* and its *typed value*. The string value is just the string value of the node. Its typed value, on the other hand, is of the type the node has been declared to be. For example, if you've declared an element to contain decimal data, and if it holds the string "1.0", its type value will be the decimal value 1.0. As a result of schema validation, every element and attribute node has a *type annotation*, which is the name of the type against which the node was successfully validated. For attribute nodes, the type annotation is always the name of a simple type. For element nodes, the type annotation may be the name of a simple or a complex type. Now that there is more type data in the type annotation, nodes also have an associated typed value.

Typed values of attributes and elements based on simple types are just sequences of atomic values corresponding to the node's content after validation. The typed value of an element based on a complex type, on the other hand, is considered undefined.

Atomic values, on the other hand, correspond to the primitive simple types defined by the XML Schema specification, or values whose types are derived from those types by restriction in a schema.

That's what the picture looks like in overview. Now we'll take a closer look at the various legal items in the XPath 2.0 data model—nodes and atomic values—starting with the kinds of nodes allowed.

The first node kind we'll take a look at is the document node in XPath 2.0.

Document Nodes

The document node (the same as XPath 1.0 root nodes) encapsulates the entire XML document—it's the starting point in the tree that describes the XML document. In the XPath 2.0 data model, document nodes have a number of properties derived from the PSVI. You don't access these properties directly (the software you're using does)—but they give you an idea of the data that is available for a document node:

- `base-uri`

- `children`

- `unparsed-entities`

- `document-uri`

Every document node must have a unique identity and must be distinct from all other nodes. If there are children, they must consist only of element, processing instruction, comment, and text nodes. You cannot have attribute, namespace, and document nodes as direct children of a document node.

Note also that the sequence of nodes in the `children` property is ordered (those nodes will be in document order), and the `children` property must not contain two consecutive text nodes (they must be merged to normalize that text). In well-formed XML documents, the children of the document node must not be empty and must consist only of element nodes, processing-instruction nodes, and comment nodes. Exactly one of these children, the document element, is an element node. (Don't confuse the document element with the document node—the document element contains all the other elements in the document.)

Included in the information available to XPath 2.0 software about a document node is: the base URI, the kind of node the node is (which returns "document" in this case), the string value of the node (which is all the string values of all text node descendants concatenated together), the typed value of this node (which is its string value), the node's children, and the URI of the document itself.

Element Nodes

Element nodes encapsulate XML elements. In the XPath 2.0 data model, elements have these properties:

- `base-uri`

- `node-name`

- `parent`

- `type`

- `children`

- `attributes`

- `namespaces`

In addition, element nodes must have a type annotation, which indicates what type of element they are. (As mentioned earlier, exactly how the type annotation works is implementation-specific at this point, and is not defined by XPath 2.0.) Element nodes must also have a unique identity, distinct from all other nodes. If there are children, the children of an element must be only element, processing instruction, comment, and text nodes. Attribute, namespace, and document nodes cannot be element node children.

ELEMENT AND ATTRIBUTE NODES THAT DO NOT HAVE PARENTS

The XPath 2.0 data model supports element and attribute nodes that do not have parents. It does this to let you work with partial results during expression processing. However, as you'd expect, these elements or attributes may not be children of any other node.

Also, the `children` property may not contain two consecutive text nodes, and the sequence of nodes in the `children` property is ordered (in document order). The attributes of elements must have distinct names, as well as the namespace modes of an element, if there are any. And no namespace node may have the name "xmlns".

Included in the PSVI for element nodes is this kind of information:

- The element's base URI

- The node kind (which returns "element" here)

- The node name (which is the qualified name of the element)

- The parent of the element

- Its string value

- Its typed value

- The children of the element if there are any

- Its attributes

- Its namespaces, if there are any

Attribute Nodes

In the XPath 2.0 data model, attribute nodes encapsulate XML attributes. Attributes have these properties:

- `node-name`
- `string-value`
- `parent`
- `type`

In XPath 2.0, attribute nodes must have a type annotation, which indicates what type of element they are. Attribute nodes must also have a unique identity, distinct from all other nodes. Note that in XPath 2.0, the element node that owns an attribute is often called its parent. However, an attribute node is *not* considered a child of its parent element.

Included in the information about an attribute in the PSVI are its base URI, node kind (which is "attribute" here), its node name (which is the qualified name of the attribute), its parent element, its string value, its typed value, and its type.

Namespace Nodes

In XPath 2.0, namespace nodes encapsulate XML namespaces. Namespaces have these properties in the XPath 2.0 data model:

- `prefix`
- `uri`
- `parent`

Namespace nodes must have a unique identity, distinct from all other nodes. Namespace prefixes may be an empty sequence. In fact, if the namespace URI is an empty string, the prefix must be an empty sequence.

The information in the data model stored for namespace nodes includes its base URI,

USING THE NAMESPACE AXIS

Because the namespace axis is deprecated in XPath 2.0, the information held in namespace nodes is instead made available to applications using two functions: `get-in-scope-namespaces` and `get-namespace-uri-for-prefix`.

its node kind (which returns "namespace" here), its node name (which returns a qualified name with the namespace prefix and an empty URI), its parent node, and its string value (which is the namespace URI of the node).

Processing Instruction Nodes

In XPath 2.0, processing instruction nodes encapsulate XML processing instructions. Processing instructions have these properties:

- `target`

- `content`

- `base-uri`

- `parent`

Included in the information the XPath 2.0 data model stores for processing instructions is its base URI, node kind (returns "processing-instruction"), node name (returns a qualified name with the processing-instruction target in the local-name and an empty URI), its parent, its string value (the content of the processing-instruction), and its typed value (which is the string value of the processing-instruction).

Comment Nodes

Comment nodes encapsulate XML comments. Comments have these properties:

- `content`

- `parent`

Included in the information the XPath 2.0 data model stores for comments is the base URI of the comment's parent, its node kind (which returns "comment" here), its parent, its string value, and its typed value (which is just the string value of the comment).

Text Nodes

Text nodes encapsulate XML character content. Text nodes have these properties in the XPath 2.0 data model:

- `content`

- `parent`

In XPath 2.0, text nodes cannot contain the empty string as its content, and document and element nodes impose the constraint that two consecutive text nodes can never occur as adjacent siblings.

Included in the information the XPath 2.0 data model stores for text nodes are the base URI of the node's parent, the node kind (which returns "text") here, the parent element or document node, and its string value (which is just the content of the text node).

Atomic Values

As opposed to nodes, atomic values correspond to the primitive simple types defined by the XML Schema specification, or values whose types are derived from them by restriction in a schema. Here are the primitive simple types as predefined in the XML schema specification—the xs namespace corresponds to "http://www.w3.org/2001/XMLSchema":

- `xs:string`
- `xs:boolean`
- `xs:decimal`
- `xs:float`
- `xs:double`
- `xs:duration`
- `xs:dateTime`
- `xs:time`
- `xs:date`
- `xs:gYearMonth`
- `xs:gYear`
- `xs:gMonthDay`
- `xs:gDay`
- `xs:gMonth`
- `xs:hexBinary`
- `xs:base64Binary`
- `xs:anyURI`
- `xs:QName`
- `xs:NOTATION`

Along with the primitive simple types, types that are derived from them (including by the user) by restriction are considered atomic types in the XPath 2.0 data model. You use the `<restriction>` element in an XML schema to derive this kind of a type and restrict the types of values it can take.

> **MORE ON PRIMITIVE TYPES**
>
> For more on the primitive simple types built into XML schema, see `http://www.w3.org/TR/xmlschema-2`.

In the following example, we're declaring a derived and restricted type named StateAbbreviation, and using a `<pattern>` element to restrict it to two-character strings like AZ or CA:

```
<simpleType name='StateAbbreviation'>
    <restriction base='xs:string'>
      <pattern value='[A-Z]{2}'/>
    </restriction>
</simpleType>
```

There are some types built into XPath 2.0 that have already been derived by restriction from the XML schema `xs:duration` type. These types are in the namespace `http://www.w3.org/2003/05/xpath-datatypes`, which is represented by the prefix xdt:

- `xdt:dayTimeDuration` is a subtype of `xs:duration`, which contains only day, hour, minute, and second components. In XPath 2.0, if you subtract two date values, the result is of the `xdt:dayTimeDuration` type.

- `xdt:yearMonthDuration` is a subtype of `xs:duration`, which is restricted to only year and month components.

In addition, there are three *abstract* types, `xdt:anyAtomicType`, `xdt:untypedAtomic`, and `xdt:untypedAny`, which are now built into XPath 2.0. Because they're abstract, you can't create variables of these types directly, but you can use them in certain places as we'll see in the next chapter (for example, see the discussion of the `instance of` expression in the next chapter, where we can use `xdt:anyAtomicType` to indicate that we want to match any atomic type) :

- `xdt:anyAtomicType` is an abstract type that is the base type of all atomic values. All atomic types, such as `xs:integer`, `xs:string`, and `xdt:untypedAtomic`, are subtypes of `xdt:anyAtomicType`.

- `xdt:untypedAtomic` is an atomic type used for untyped data, such as text that is not given a specific type by schema validation. `xdt:untypedAtomic` is the type used to annotate unvalidated attribute nodes, for example, attribute nodes in well-formed documents. `xdt:untypedAny` is the type used to annotate unvalidated element nodes, for example, elements in well-formed documents.

- `xdt:untypedAny` is a type that annotates an element whose type is unknown (such as might occur in a schemaless document).

As in XPath 1.0, you often don't deal with the various data types directly. Instead, you might use functions or expressions that return items of the various data types. For example, say that you wanted to use the XPath 2.0 `current-dateTime` function, which returns a value of the `xs:dateTime` type. Here's how we might assign an XSLT variable named `rightNow` the `xs:dateTime` value returned by `current-dateTime`:

```
<xsl:stylesheet version="2.0" xmlns:xsl="http://www.w3.org/1999/XSL/Transform">

<xsl:variable name="rightNow" select="current-dateTime()" />
        .
        .
        .
</xsl:stylesheet>
```

Now we can use this new variable as a valid XPath 2.0 expression, because its type, `xs:dateTime`, is valid in XPath 2.0. Here's how that might work in a style sheet that just displays the current date and time (replacing the document node of whatever document you use it with that data) :

```
<xsl:stylesheet version="2.0" xmlns:xsl="http://www.w3.org/1999/XSL/Transform">

<xsl:variable name="rightNow" select="current-dateTime()" />

    <xsl:template match="/">
        The date and time is:
        <xsl:value-of select="$rightNow"/>
    </xsl:template>

</xsl:stylesheet>
```

And here's what you get when you use the style sheet with Saxon—as you can see, our xs:dateTime variable was indeed supported:

```
<?xml version="1.0" encoding="UTF-8"?>
        The date and time is:
        2003-08-29T19:38:01.787Z
```

However, sometimes you do want to work with the supported data types explicitly. Here's an example, where we're using the xs:date *constructor* to create an xs:date value:

```
<xsl:stylesheet version="2.0"
    xmlns:xsl="http://www.w3.org/1999/XSL/Transform"
    xmlns:xs="http://www.w3.org/2001/XMLSchema">

    <xsl:template match="/">
        <xsl:value-of
select="xs:date('2004-09-02')"/>
    </xsl:template>

</xsl:stylesheet>
```

Now that we've created our xs:date value, Saxon is able to display its value to us this way:

```
<?xml version="1.0" encoding="UTF-8"?>
    2004-09-02
```

TYPES DERIVED BY LIST OR UNION

What about types you may derive in XML schema that are not restricted, such as types derived by list or union? Items of these types are converted into sequences in XPath 2.0—it's easy to see how list types are converted into sequences, but union types are more troublesome. When you derive a type from the union of other types, that union is converted into a simple sequence of the types in the union, one after the other. The actual type defined by union is not preserved, although its components are. Only the type of each individual item in the union is kept in this case.

In Brief

- XPath 2.0 builds on top of XPath 1.0 and adds much more power, including expressions like `if`, `for`, `some`, and others that we'll see in depth in the upcoming chapters.

- Sequences are new in XPath 2.0, and they are ordered collections of zero or more items. And an item is either an atomic value or a node.

- XPath 1.0 supported only four data types, XPath 2.0 extends that to support not only the node kinds supported in XPath 1.0, but also many atomic types, which include the primitive simple types defined by the XML Schema specification and values whose types are derived from them by restriction in a schema.

XPath 2.0 Expressions and Operators

8

Creating Primary Expressions

The most basic expression type is the primary expression type. This type can be one of these:

- A literal

- A variable

- A function call

- A context item

- A parenthesized expression, which is used to control precedence of operators

- A comment

To understand these in detail, we'll take a look at them one by one.

Literals

A literal is just a value that is of an atomic type. As we saw in Chapter 7, "What's New in XPath 2.0," this means a value of a primitive simple type defined by the XML Schema specification, or a value of a type derived from them by restriction in a schema.

XPath 2.0 has built-in support for two types of literals—numeric literals and string literals. You can create a string literal simply by enclosing a string of characters in quotes, and numeric literals simply by writing the numeric value. You can see a simple example in ch08_01.xsl (Listing 8.1), which uses a string literal as an XPath expression.

LISTING 8.1   An XSLT Example Using an XPath Literal (ch08_01.xsl)

```
<xsl:stylesheet version="2.0" xmlns:xsl="http://www.w3.org/1999/XSL/Transform"
    xmlns:xs="http://www.w3.org/2001/XMLSchema">

    <xsl:template match="/">
        <xsl:value-of select="'No worries!'"/>
    </xsl:template>

</xsl:stylesheet>
```

A string literal's value is an xs:string atomic type. You can simply enclose a string of characters in quotes, but be careful about nested quotes. For example, this literal is okay: "This is fine." You can also use single quotes like this: 'This is also fine.' But what if you want to use quotation marks inside a string literal? In that case, you can nest single and double quotes, like this:

```
"I said, 'This literal is OK.'"
```

You can also use double quotation marks to indicate quoted text. For example, this string literal works just as the previous one did, except that the internal quoted text is delimited by two double quotes:

```
"I said, ""This literal is OK."""
```

Doubling single quotation marks works the same way:

```
'I said, ''This literal is OK.'''
```

By default, numeric literals that don't contain a "." and contain no "e" or "E" (used to specify exponents), are of type xs:integer. For example, here are some integer numeric literals:

```
345
1
-9999
```

On the other hand, if your numeric value includes a ".", but no "e" or "E", XPath 2.0 assumes the literal is of the xs:decimal data type. Here are a few examples:

```
3.14159
-1.000
2.7128
```

If you include an "e" or an "E" character, XPath 2.0 assumes your numeric literal is an `xs:double` type. Here are a few examples:

```
3.14159E10
55.00e45
1.9e-5
```

Besides string and numeric literals, you can also use Boolean values, representing them with the built-in functions `true()` and `false()`.

You can also create literals of any of the XML schema types using their constructors. We saw an example of how that works in Chapter 7, where we created an `xs:date` literal:

```
<xsl:stylesheet version="2.0" xmlns:xsl="http://www.w3.org/1999/XSL/Transform"
    xmlns:xs="http://www.w3.org/2001/XMLSchema">

    <xsl:template match="/">
        <xsl:value-of select="xs:date('2004-09-02')"/>
    </xsl:template>

</xsl:stylesheet>
```

Here are a few other examples of creating literals based on XML schema types using the appropriate constructors:

```
xs:integer(45)
xs:decimal(3.14159)
xs:string("No worries!")
```

> ### USING THE cast EXPRESSION
>
> You can also create literals of a desired data type using the `cast` expression, which we'll see later in this chapter.

Variables

Variables are also expressions in XPath 2.0—the value of the expression is the value stored in the variable. In XPath 2.0, variables are valid XML names (that is, an XML QName), preceded by a $.

There are two sources of variables in XPath 2.0—the host language (such as XSLT), and those variables that you can define in XPath itself. For example, we've seen in Chapter 7 that you can create variables in XSLT using the `<xsl:variable>` element, and use them in XPath 2.0 like this:

```
<xsl:stylesheet version="2.0" xmlns:xsl="http://www.w3.org/1999/XSL/Transform">

<xsl:variable name="rightNow" select="current-dateTime()" />

    <xsl:template match="/">
```

```
    The date and time is:
        <xsl:value-of select="$rightNow"/>
    </xsl:template>

</xsl:stylesheet>
```

You can also use support for variables in XPath 2.0, as in these for and some expressions:

```
for $variable in /planets/planet return $variable/mass
some $variable in /planets/planet[1]/name satisfies $variable = "Mars"
```

Parenthesized Expressions

UNDERSTANDING SCOPE

As in various programming languages, variables in XPath 2.0 also have *scope*, which is the region in which the XPath processor can access them. For example, in the for expression in the preceding code, the variable named $variable is in scope only inside the body of the return clause—outside that body, you can't use this variable. In the some expression in the preceding code, $variable is in scope in the satisifies clause's body.

When you're using multiple operators, such as multiple arithmetic operators, there can be some confusion about which operator is applied first. For example, what does 1 + 2 * 3 equal—3 * 3 or 1 + 6? It turns out that the multiplication operator is evaluated first, so 1 + 2 * 3 = 1 + 6 = 7.

On the other hand, if you wanted to add the 1 and 2 before multiplying the result by 3, you could use parentheses to indicate the order of execution you want:

```
(1 + 2) * 3
```

In XPath 2.0, parenthesized expressions like these are valid. (And don't forget that you can use an empty set of parentheses—( )—to represent an empty sequence.)

Function Calls

Function calls are also considered expressions in XPath 2.0, and their value is simply the value returned by the function. For example, we took a look at the XPath 2.0 built-in max function in Chapter 7:

```
<xsl:stylesheet version="2.0" xmlns:xsl="http://www.w3.org/1999/XSL/Transform">

    <xsl:template match="planets">
        <HTML>
            <HEAD>
                <TITLE>
                    The Largest Planetary Radius
```

```
            </TITLE>
        </HEAD>

        <BODY>
            <H1>
                The Largest Planetary Radius
            </H1>
            <BR/>
            The largest planetary radius is
            <xsl:value-of select="max(//planet/radius)"/>
            miles.
        </BODY>

    </HTML>
</xsl:template>

</xsl:stylesheet>
```

Here, the value of the function call is the sequence it returns.

Note that you can pass not only atomic values to functions, but also sequences. For example, this function call passes the values 4, 5, and 6 to a function:

```
function(4, 5, 6)
```

But this example passes a sequence consisting of 4 and 5, and then a value of 6:

```
function((4, 5), 6)
```

Context Item Expressions

The context item expression is simply a dot, ".", and as in XPath 1.0, it stands for the current context item. This can be a context node (the node from which evaluation of an expression starts), as in the path expression `//planet[count(./name) > 1]`.

In XPath 2.0, context items can also be atomic values, as in this expression: `(1 to 100)[.
mod 10 eq 0]`, which returns the sequence (10, 20, 30, 40, 50, 60, 70, 80, 90, 100) .

Creating Arithmetic Expressions

Besides primary expressions, XPath 2.0 also supports arithmetic operators for addition, subtraction, multiplication, division, and modulus. These operators are represented this way (note that instead of using the / symbol for division, which can be interpreted as markup, XPath 2.0 uses the `div` operator):

USING THE SUBTRACTION OPERATOR

In XPath 2.0, you must precede a subtraction operator with a space, because "-" is a legal name character. In other words, x-y can be interpreted as a name, whereas x - y is an expression involving a subtraction operation.

- +—Addition

- -—Subtraction and Negation

- *—Multiplication

- div—Division

- idiv—Integer division

- mod—Modulus

The idiv operator requires its operands to be of type xs:integer and returns a result of type xs:integer, rounded toward zero. And the mod operator returns the remainder after a division (for example, 16 mod 3 is 1) .

Here are some examples of arithmetic expressions:

SUBTRACTING DATE VALUES

In XPath 2.0, if you subtract two date values, the result is of the xdt:dayTimeDuration type.

- 4 * 2 returns 8

- 33 + 11 returns 44

- -5 div 2 returns –2.5

- -5 idiv 2 returns –2

- $temp + 12 returns 72 if $temp holds 60

- -(20 + 6) returns –26

Creating Path Expressions

As in XPath 1.0, you can use a path expression to locate nodes. In fact, XPath 2.0 carries over just about all the same syntax for path expressions from XPath 1.0, although, of course, node-sets are now called sequences and there are other changes, such as deprecating (making obsolete) the namespace axis.

As in XPath 1.0, path expressions are made up of location steps. In turn, location steps are made up of an axis, a node test, and zero or more predicates:

axis :: node-test [predicate]*

If you start a location path with / or //, the location path is an absolute location path because you're a specifying the path from the root node of the XML document. Otherwise, the location path is relative, starting with the context node.

XPath 2.0 Axes

Each XPath 2.0 path expression must specify an axis (or use the default `child` axis), as in this location path: `/library/book/title[2]/text`. The XPath 2.0 axes are the same as the XPath 1.0 axes.

Note in particular that the `namespace` axis is now deprecated in XPath 2.0. That means that it's in a kind of limbo, preparatory to being phased out. Whether or not the software package you're using supports the namespace axis is now up to the package itself—it no longer has to.

XPath 2.0 Node Tests

When you use an axis in a location step, you're telling XPath 2.0 where to look and identify-ing a set of nodes. As in XPath 1.0, a node test tells XPath 2.0 which of the nodes in that set you're interested in.

There are two ways of creating node tests in XPath 2.0. You can use node names as node tests, along with a wildcard character, `*`, as in XPath 1.0. Or you can use "kind" tests like `comment()`, `text()`, and so on, as also in XPath 1.0. Here's an overview of the kinds of node tests you can use in XPath 2.0—note that `element()`, `attribute()`, and `document-node()` are new in XPath 2.0:

- A name matches a node with that name (for example, `planet` will match a `<planet>` element).

- The `*` wildcard character matches any node of the principal node kind—elements, attributes, or namespaces. For example, `child::*` will select all element children of the context node, and `attribute::*` will select all attributes of the context node. You can also use `*` with the namespace axis.

- The `comment()` node test selects comment nodes.

- The `node()` node test selects any type of node.

- The `processing-instruction()` node test selects a processing instruction node. You can specify the name of the processing instruction to select in the parentheses.

- The `text()` node test selects a text node.

- The `element()` node test selects elements.

- The `attribute()` node test selects attributes.

In XPath 2.0, you can pass parameters to the kind node tests `element()` and `attribute()`. Here are some examples (for more on type annotations, see the discussion on them in Chapter 7):

- `element(planet)` matches any element node whose name is planet and whose type annotation conforms to the schema declaration for a `<planet>` element.

- `element(planet, *)` matches any element node whose name is planet without any restriction on type annotation.

- `element(planet, giant)` matches any element node whose name is planet, and whose type annotation is giant or is derived from giant.

- `element(*, giant)` matches any element node whose type annotation is giant, regardless of its name.

- `element(solarsystem/planet)` matches any element node whose name and type annotation conform to the schema declaration of a `<planet>` element in a `<solarsystem>` element.

- `attribute()` matches any attribute node.

- `attribute(language, *)` matches any attribute whose name is language, regardless of its type annotation.

- `attribute(*, xs:decimal)` matches any attribute whose type annotation is xs:decimal or derived from xs:decimal.

- `document-node()` matches any document node.

- `document-node(element(planet))` matches any document node whose content consists of a single element node that satisfies the element(planet) node test.

XPath 2.0 Predicates

As in XPath 1.0, the next part of a location step, which follows the node text, is the predicate. A location step doesn't need a predicate, but using predicates, you can filter the nodes you want to locate even more.

Predicates are where you use the many XPath 2.0 functions when you want to use them in path expressions. This works as it does in XPath 1.0; for example, in the location step `child::planet[position() = 2]`, the predicate is `position() = 2`. This means that the value the built-in XPath function `position()` returns must indicate that this is the second `<planet>` child in order for the location step to match. As in XPath 1.0, this location step can also be abbreviated as `planet[2]`.

XPath 2.0 Abbreviated Syntax

The rules for abbreviated syntax in XPath 2.0 are the same as in XPath 1.0 (technically speaking, . is not actually an abbreviation—it's the context node item, as discussed earlier.):

- `self::node()` can be abbreviated as .

- `parent::node()` can be abbreviated as ..

- `child::`*nodename* can be abbreviated as *nodename*

- `attribute::`*nodename* can be abbreviated as @*nodename*

- `/descendant-or-self::node()/` can be abbreviated as `//`

As you know from XPath 1.0, you can also abbreviate position expressions like `[position() = 6]` as `[6]`. That's all there is to abbreviated syntax. The next type of XPath 2.0 expression we'll take a look at is sequence expressions.

Creating Sequence Expressions

As we've seen in Chapter 7, you can create sequence expressions with the comma (,) operator. In XPath 2.0, the comma operator evaluates each of its operands and joins the results into a sequence.

You can use empty parentheses to indicate an empty sequence. Also note that sequences can never be nested—for example, combining the values 4, (5, 6), into a single sequence results in the sequence (4, 5, 6). Sequences can contain nodes or atomic values, or a mix.

Sequences may contain duplicate values or nodes. When you create a new sequence by concatenating two or more input sequences, the new sequence contains all the items in the original sequences.

We'll start our work on sequence expressions by seeing how to create sequences with them.

Creating Sequences

Here are a few examples; this sequence expression creates a sequence of six integers:

```
(9, 10, 11, 12, 13, 14)
```

In this case, we're creating a new sequence from the sequences 1, (2, 3), ()—that is, an empty sequence—and (4, 5, 6):

```
(1, (2, 3), (), 4, 5, 6))
```

This expression gives you the following sequence:

```
1, 2, 3, 4, 5, 6
```

Here's how you could create a sequence made up of all the <name> children of the context node, followed by all the <mass> children:

```
(name, mass)
```

You can also use variables or other expressions when creating sequences, like this:

```
($temperature, 3 * 6)
```

If $temperature holds 68, this example gives you this sequence:

```
(68, 18)
```

You can also use the range operator, as mentioned in Chapter 7, to create a sequence of integers. Here's an example:

```
(1 to 5)
```

This sequence expression creates the following sequence:

```
(1, 2, 3, 4, 5)
```

You can also use the range operator inside a sequence expression, like this:

```
(1, 2 to 5)
```

Here's the result:

```
1, 2, 3, 4, 5
```

What if you were to make the start and end of the range the same value by mistake? For example, how is XPath 2.0 supposed to handle this?:

```
9999 to 9999
```

In this case, the result is a singleton sequence with just one item, 9999.

Combining Sequences

EXCLUDING DUPLICATES

The union, intersect, and except operators return their results as sequences in document order, without any duplicate items in those sequences.

XPath 2.0 also gives you a set of operators to work with sequences, as we saw in the overview in Chapter 7. We'll take a look at these operators—union, intersect, and except—which create sequence expressions, next.

The union **Operator**

The union operator takes two node sequences as operands and returns a sequence containing all the nodes that occur in either of the original sequences. This operator works something like the logical or operator in other languages. The union operator is identical to the ¦ operator.

Here are a few examples, where a, b, c, d, and e are nodes:

```
a, b, union c, d, e
```

This expression gives you

```
a, b, c, d, e
```

On the other hand, duplicate items do not appear in the resulting sequence. This expression

```
a, b, c union c, d, e
```

gives you

```
a, b, c, d, e
```

The intersect **Operator**

The intersect operator takes two node sequences as operands and returns a sequence containing all the nodes that occur in *both* operands. This operator works like the logical and operator in other languages.

Here are a few examples; in this expression, both the nodes b and c are common to both sequence operands:

```
a, b, c intersect b, c, d
```

And here's the result:

```
b, c
```

This sequence combination expression

```
d, e, f intersect b, c, d
```

gives you just a singleton sequence:

```
d
```

If you try to find the intersection of two sequences that have no items in common, like this:

```
a, b intersect c, d
```

the result will be an empty sequence, ( ).

The except **Operator**

The except operator takes two node sequences as operands and returns a sequence containing all the nodes that occur in the first operand but not in the second operand.

Here's an example:

a, b, c except c

gives you

a, b

Here's another example:

a, b, c, d except c, d, e

gives you

a, b

FUNCTIONS THAT SUPPORT INDEXED ACCESS

Besides the sequence operators we're discussing here that are evaluated as XPath expressions, there's also a set of functions that support indexed access to items or subsequences of a sequence, indexed insertion or removal of items in a sequence, and removal of duplicate values or nodes from a sequence. They're coming up in Chapter 12, "XPath 2.0 Node and Sequence Functions."

This expression

a, b, c except d, e, f

gives you

a, b, c

And this expression

a, b, c except a, b, c, d, e

gives you an empty sequence, ().

Creating Comparison Expressions

Comparison expressions return the result of comparing two values. XPath 2.0 actually supports four kinds of comparison expressions: value comparisons, general comparisons, node comparisons, and order comparisons.

We'll take a look at them all here, starting with value and general comparisons. These two types of comparisons have been added so that XPath 2.0 can support comparisons with both single values and with sequences.

Value Comparisons

You use the value comparison operators when you're working with atomic values. Here they are:

- eq—Equals

- ne—Not equals

- lt—Less than

- le—Less than or equal to

- gt—Greater than

- ge—Greater than or equal to

These operators give you a result of true or false. Here's an example—say that $temperature holds the value 68; in that case, this expression would evaluate to true:

```
$temperature lt 72
```

This comparison is true only if $planet has a single <name> child element and its value is "Venus":

```
$planet/name eq "Venus"
```

SHOP TALK

DATA TYPES AND TYPE ERRORS

Here's something to note—if $planet/name evaluates to more than one name node, or $planet/name evaluates to one name node, which contains more than one validated string, a type error is raised.

It's important to realize that type errors are the most significant difference between XPath 1.0 and XPath 2.0. If the XPath processor determines that there's been a type error, even a relatively innocent one like this one, a type error occurs.

Strong typing like this is at the very heart of XPath 2.0. In my work with XPath 2.0, that is by far the biggest difference between XPath 1.0 and 2.0.

However, how type errors are handled is up to the implementation. So far, all that usually happens is that XPath or XQuery processors simply stop and display an error message.

That's not what you want to have happen when someone else is using your XPath or XQuery expressions, of course, so be careful. I always spend some time trying to think of type problems that could break XPath expressions, and try to make sure that such problems won't arise. Until XPath processors come up with some way of handling type errors as recoverable errors, the strong data typing in XPath 2.0 is something I recommend you pay special attention to.

General Comparisons

You can use general comparisons on sequences (including singleton sequences). Here are the general comparisons:

- =—Equals
- !=—Not equals
- <—Less than
- <=—Less than or equal to
- >—Greater than
- >=—Greater than or equal to

You use these operators on sequences. (What actually happens is that a value comparison operator, eq, ne, lt, le, gt, or ge—depending on which corresponding general comparison operator was used—is used to compare individual items in the sequence.) The software evaluating a general comparison usually will return a value of true as soon as it finds an item in the first operand and an item in the second operand for which the value comparison is true.

Here's an example pointing out how these operators deal with sequences, not just individual values. In this case, we're comparing two sequences, (1, 2) and (2, 3) with the general equality operator:

```
(1, 2) = (2, 3)
```

In this case, the result is true because the value 2 appears in both sequences.

Here, however, the result is false, because there is no value in the first sequence that is equal to a value in the second:

```
(1, 2) = (3, 4)
```

As with value comparisons, this comparison is true only if $planet has a single <name> child element and its value is "Venus":

```
$planet/name = "Venus"
```

Node Comparisons

You can use node comparison expressions to compare nodes using the is operator.

A comparison expression with the is operator is true if the two operands are nodes that are identical; otherwise it is false.

For example, this comparison is true only if the left and right sides each evaluate to exactly the same single node:

```
//planet[name="Venus"] is //planet[days=116.75]
```

Order Comparisons

You use order comparison expressions to compare the order of nodes; both operands here must be either a single node or an empty sequence (if either operand is an empty sequence, the result of the comparison is an empty sequence). Here are the order comparison operators:

- <<—Earlier than

- >>—Later than

Using the << operator returns `true` if the first operand node is earlier than the second operand node in document order; otherwise it returns `false`. Using the >> operator returns `true` if the first operand node is later than the second operand node in document order; otherwise it returns `false`.

Here's an example:

```
//planet[name="Venus"] << //planet[days=116.75]
```

This example returns true if the node matched by `//planet[name="Venus"]` comes earlier in document order than the node matched by `//planet[days=116.75]` .

Creating Logical Expressions

A logical expression uses logical operators and is a compound expression. Unless there's an error, its value is always either `true` or `false`. Here are the logical operators:

- and—Performs a logical and operation

- or—Performs a logical or operation

The and operator lets you connect two Boolean operands and returns `true` if *both* operands are true, and `false` otherwise. The or operator lets you connect two logical operands and returns `true` if *either* operand is true, and `false` otherwise.

Here's an example. Say that $temperature holds a value of 72; in that case, this example returns a value of `true`:

```
$temperature < 80 and $temperature > 60
```

THE not FUNCTION

XPath 2.0 also has a function named not(), which reverses the Boolean value of the value you pass to it. For example, if $temperature holds a value of 72, then $temperature = 72 is true, and not($temperature = 72) is false. More on this function is coming up in Chapter 11, "XPath 2.0 Boolean, QName, and Date Functions."

And this expression also returns true, because one logical operand ($temperature > 60) is true:

```
$temperature > 80 or $temperature > 60
```

This expression returns false:

```
$temperature > 80 and $temperature > 60
```

Creating for Expressions

XPath provides the for expression so that you can iterate over data. Here's how the for expression works in general:

```
for variable in sequence return expression
```

Here, the variable is called the *range variable*, the value of the expression that follows the in keyword is called the *input sequence*, and the expression that follows the return keyword is called the *return expression*.

The result of the for expression is obtained by evaluating the return expression once for each item in the input sequence. The resulting sequence is returned (if multiple sequences are generated, they are concatenated).

You can see an example in ch08_02.xsl, where we're using a for expression to create a sequence of all the planet names in our planetary data XML document:

```
for $variable in //planet return $variable/name
```

To display our results using an XPath 2.0 style sheet, we'll use the <xsl:value-of> element to insert the result sequence of names into the output. That means we have to use this element's separator attribute to indicate what text we want inserted between items in the sequence—if you don't use this attribute, you'll only get the first item in the sequence. You can see what the XSLT 2.0 style sheet looks like in ch08_02.xsl (Listing 8.2).

LISTING 8.2   An XSLT Example Using the for Expression (ch08_02.xsl)

```
<xsl:stylesheet version="2.0"
    xmlns:xsl="http://www.w3.org/1999/XSL/Transform"
    xmlns:xs="http://www.w3.org/2001/XMLSchema">

    <xsl:template match="/">
        <xsl:value-of select="for $variable in //planet return $variable/name"
```

LISTING 8.2   Continued

```
                    separator=", "/>
    </xsl:template>


</xsl:stylesheet>
```

And here's the result when we use Saxon to apply the `ch08_02.xsl` style sheet to our planetary data document:

```
C:\Saxon>java net.sf.saxon.Transform ch02_01.xml ch08_02.xsl
<?xml version="1.0" encoding="UTF-8"?>
Mercury, Venus, Earth
```

As you can see, we do indeed get all three planetary names this way. A `for` expression can also use multiple variables. For example, this expression uses two variables at once:

```
for $x in (1, 2)
    $y in (3, 4)
return ($x * $y)
```

The result of this `for` expression is the sequence (3, 4, 6, 8).

Creating Conditional Expressions

As we saw in the overview in Chapter 7, XPath 2.0 supports a conditional expression that uses the keywords `if`, `then`, and `else`. Here's what this expression, also called the `if` expression, looks like in its general form:

```
if expression then then-expression else else-expression
```

The expression following the `if` keyword is called the *test expression*, and the expressions following the `then` and `else` keywords are called the *then-expression* and *else-expression*, respectively.

If the value of the test expression is true, the value of the *then-expression* is returned. If the Boolean value of the test expression is false, the value of the *else-expression* is returned.

Here's an example using a conditional expression in an XSLT 2.0 stylesheet. In this case, we'll declare an XSLT variable named `$temperature` that holds the value 80:

```
<xsl:variable name="temperature" select="80" />
```

Now we'll test that new variable's value in a conditional expression, evaluating to the text "Too hot" if the temperature is above 72, and "OK" otherwise:

```
if ($temperature > 72) then 'Too hot' else 'OK'
```

You can see what the complete XSLT 2.0 stylesheet looks like in ch08_03.xsl (Listing 8.3).

LISTING 8.3   An XSLT Example Using the if Expression (ch08_03.xsl)

```
<xsl:stylesheet version="2.0"
    xmlns:xsl="http://www.w3.org/1999/XSL/Transform"
    xmlns:xs="http://www.w3.org/2001/XMLSchema">
<xsl:variable name="temperature" select="80" />

    <xsl:template match="/">
        <xsl:value-of select="if ($temperature > 72) then 'Too hot' else 'OK'"/>
    </xsl:template>

</xsl:stylesheet>
```

And here's the result you get when you use Saxon:

```
<?xml version="1.0" encoding="UTF-8"?>
Too hot
```

You can use any kind of a test expression, as long as it evaluates to a true/false value. For example, in this case, we're checking which of two planets has the greater mass, and returning the one that does:

```
if (//planet[1]/mass > //planet[2]/mass)
    then //planet[1]
    else //planet[2]
```

You don't have to compare values either; you can simply test for the existence of an item, as here, where we're testing if a <planet> element has a <name> child element:

```
if (//planet[1]/name)
    then //planet[1]/name
    else //planet[2]/name
```

You can also nest if expressions, as in this example:

```
if ($fruit eq "apple")
then "It's an apple."
else if ($fruit eq "orange")
then "It's an orange."
else "I have no idea what this is."
```

Creating Quantified Expressions

Quantified expressions use the some and every keywords to perform checks on the items in a sequence. You can use the some keyword to ensure that at least one of the items in the sequence satisfies a particular criterion, and the every keyword to make sure that every item in the sequence satisfies some criterion.

Using the some Expression

Here's how you use the some quantified expression:

```
some in-claus(es) statisfies test-expression
```

A quantified expression like this starts with the some keyword, followed by one or more *in-clauses*, followed by the keyword satisfies, followed by a *test-expression*. What this expression does is to let you test if at least one item in the in-clause(s) satisfies the test expression.

Let's take a look at a few examples to make this clear. This expression is true if at least one of the <planet> elements in the document has a <name> child element:

```
some $planet in //planet satisfies $planet/name
```

Here's an example that tests if at least one <planet> element has a language attribute:

```
some $planet in //planet satisfies $planet/@language
```

In this way, you can use quantified expressions to test for the existence of items like elements and attributes.

You can also test logical conditions, as here, where we're making sure that at least one planet has a mass greater than 1.5:

```
some $planet in //planet satisfies ($planet/mass > 1.5)
```

Here's another example:

```
some $planet in //planet satisfies ($planet/name = "Mars")
```

You can also use multiple in-clauses in a some expression. Here's an example, where we're testing the product of numbers:

```
some $operand1 in (4, 5, 6), $operand2 in
(7, 8, 9)
    satisfies $operand1 * $operand2 = 40
```

TERMINATING A some EXPRESSION

Although this is implementation-specific, the software may terminate a some expression as soon as it is able to satisfy the test expression, without evaluating all possible values.

In this case, all possible combinations of the items in the in-clauses are tested—nine combinations in all. That is, 4 * 7 is tested, then 4 * 8, 4 * 9, then 5 * 7, 5 * 8, and so on.

Using the `every` Keyword

Here's how you use the every quantified expression:

```
every in-claus(es) statifies test-expression
```

This quantified expression starts with the `every` keyword, followed by one or more *in-clauses*, followed by the keyword `satisfies`, followed by a *test-expression*. This expression lets you test if *every* item in the in-clause(s) satisfies the test expression.

Here are a few examples. This expression is true if every one of the <planet> elements in a document has a <name> child element:

```
every $planet in //planet satisfies $planet/name
```

As with the some expression, you can either test for the existence of an item this way, or you can test a logical condition. This every expression tests whether planet's <day> value is greater than or equal to one:

```
every $planet in //planet satisfies ($planet/day ge 1)
```

And you can also use multiple in-clauses with the every expression, just as you can with some, as in this example:

```
every $operand1 in (4, 5, 6), $operand2 in (7, 8, 9)
    satisfies $operand1 * $operand2 > 27
```

You can see an example where we're using every in an XSLT 2.0 stylesheet in `ch08_04.xsl` (Listing 8.4). In this case, we're testing three temperatures to see if they're all above 72, and if so, we'll display the message "Too hot".

LISTING 8.4   An XSLT example Using the every Expression (ch08_04.xsl)

```
<xsl:stylesheet version="2.0"
    xmlns:xsl="http://www.w3.org/1999/XSL/Transform"
    xmlns:xs="http://www.w3.org/2001/XMLSchema">
<xsl:variable name="t1" select="80" />
<xsl:variable name="t2" select="90" />
<xsl:variable name="t3" select="100" />

    <xsl:template match="/">
        <xsl:value-of select="if (every $temperature in ($t1, $t2, $t3)
```

LISTING 8.4   Continued

```
                satisfies $temperature > 72) then 'Too hot' else 'OK'"/>
  </xsl:template>
</xsl:stylesheet>
```

Here's the result:

```
<?xml version="1.0" encoding="UTF-8"?>
Too hot
```

Creating Expressions That Work on Types

XPath 2.0 emphasizes data types, and you can create XPath 2.0 expressions that work expressly with types using these keywords:

- `instance of`—Check an item's data type (works with any simple or complex type).

- `cast`—Change an item's data type.

- `castable`—Check whether an item's data type may be cast.

- `treat`—Treat an item as if it were a new data type for the purposes of evaluation (but don't actually change the item's data type). (The `treat` expression works with any simple or complex type.)

We'll take a look at how these expressions work now.

instance of

The `instance of` operator is a Boolean operator that lets you test the type of an operand. Here's how you use it in an expression, where `operand2` is a simple or complex type:

operand1 `instance of` *operand2*

This expression returns `true` if `operand1` is of the data type `operand2`, and `false` otherwise. The type you give in `operand2` can be fairly general—it can be an atomic type like `xs:integer`, a kind test like `element()` or `node()`, the keyword `empty`, or an empty sequence like this: `()`. It can also be the `xdt:anyAtomicType` type, which, as noted in Chapter 7, is an abstract type that you can't create variables of directly. If you use the `xdt:anyAtomicType` type with the `instance of` operator, you're saying that you're testing for any of the atomic types.

Using the `instance of` expression, you can test the data type of various items; for example, this expression returns `true` because 26 is an integer:

```
26 instance of xs:integer
```

Actually, testing an xs:integer value against the xs:decimal type will return true because in XML schemas, the xs:integer type is derived by restriction from xs:decimal.

Similarly, if $variable contains an integer value, this expression will return true:

```
$variable instance of xs:integer
```

Here's an example that checks if 3.1415 is of type xs:decimal:

```
3.1415 instance of xs:decimal
```

Here's an example that lets you test the context item to see if it's an element:

```
. instance of element()
```

Instance of is very useful when you are working with schema-validated nodes and need to examine their runtime type.

cast

Because XPath 2.0 implements strong typing, it's sometimes necessary to convert values from one data type to another. You can use a cast expression to change an item's data type to another data type. You can use a cast expression like this:

```
source cast as target-type
```

Bear in mind that you can also use the constructor functions that come with various types to cast data from one type to another. For example, to cast an xs:string into an xs:date, you can use the xs:date constructor function to create a new xs:date value like this: xs:date("2005-03-02").

Here, *source* is cast to a new data type, the *target-type*. In this case, the data type of *source* is actually changed to the *target-type*, if that cast is possible.

Here are a few examples showing how to use cast:

```
"2004-09-02" cast as xs:date
$variable cast as xs:integer
$temperature cast as xs:decimal
```

When can you use cast? Here's the list:

- cast expressions are supported for the combinations of input type and target type listed in the table at http://www.w3.org/TR/xquery-operators/#casting. This is the definitive place to look for cast operations. For example, you can find there that you can cast from xs:double to xs:decimal.

- cast expressions are supported if the input type is a derived atomic type and the target type is a supertype of the input type. For example, if the zipcode type is derived by restriction from xs:integer, a value of type zipcode can be cast into the type xs:integer.

- cast expressions are supported if the target type is a derived atomic type and the input type is xs:string or xdt:untypedAtomic.

- cast expressions are supported if the target type is a derived atomic type and the input type is a supertype of the target type. The resulting value is the same as the input value, but with a different type.

These rules can get pretty involved—how can you be sure the cast you're about to attempt is legal? Luckily, there's a fairly easy answer to that—you can use a castable expression to check if a cast is legal.

castable

The castable expression lets you test if an item may be cast to a specific type, and it returns a true/false answer. Here's how you use this expression:

```
source castable as target-type
```

This expression is true if *source* may be cast to *target-type*. Here's an example where we're checking whether $fruit may be cast to the type apple, and if not, whether it can be cast to the type orange:

```
if ($fruit castable as apple)
then $fruit cast as apple
else if ($fruit castable as orange)
then $fruit cast as orange
else $fruit cast as xs:string
```

treat

The treat expression is much like the cast expression, except that, unlike cast, it doesn't change the type of its operand. It acts like an assertion, checking the type of an expression. Here's how you use the treat operator in an expression:

```
source treat as target-type
```

This expression asserts that *source* is of the *target-type* data type. Otherwise, this expression returns an error.

Here's an example. In this case, the original type of $number might be number. Say that another type, ZIP, is derived from that type; in that case, this expression will be of the ZIP type when evaluated:

```
$number treat as ZIP
```

This expression also succeeds if the type of $number is ZIP. In other words, the treat expression acts much like an assertion, which succeeds if $number is of type ZIP or of a type derived from ZIP.

In Brief

- Primary expressions can be a literal, a variable, a function call, a context item, a comment, or a parenthesized expression.

- Besides the primary expressions, you can also use the arithmetic operators +, -, *, div, idiv, and mod. These operators perform addition, subtraction, multiplication, division, integer division, and modulus, respectively.

- You can also create path expressions in XPath 2.0. XPath 2.0 path expressions are much the same as they are in XPath 1.0, with some exceptions, such as the deprecation of the namespace axis, and some additions, such as new node tests.

- You can also create sequence expressions in XPath 2.0 that return sequences using the comma operator, and combine sequences with the union, intersect, and except operators.

- XPath 2.0 also supports a number of comparison operators: eq, ne, lt, le, gt, and ge for comparisons of single values, and =, !=, <, <=, >, and >= to work with sequences. Node comparisons with is let you compare nodes. And the order comparisons << and >> let you determine the order of nodes.

- XPath 2.0 logical expressions are supported with the and and or logical operators. These operators let you connect logical operands.

- The for expression lets you create a loop to iterate over your data. This expression works much like the for statement in various programming languages, and supports the use of variables. The if expression lets you create conditional statements that let you test an expression's value and branch accordingly.

- The quantified expressions, some and every, let you perform tests on the items in a sequence. The some expression tests whether at least one item in a sequence or sequences satisfies a particular expression, and the every expression tests whether every item in the sequence or sequences satisfies a test expression.

- XPath 2.0 also contains expressions that deal with types—instance of to check an item's type, cast to change an item's data type, castable to check whether an item may be cast to a particular new type, and treat to treat an item as if it were of a different data type without actually changing the item's data type.

The XPath 2.0 Numeric, Constructor, and Context Functions

Introducing the XPath 2.0 Functions

This chapter starts our coverage of the many functions built into XPath 2.0. Although we've seen structural changes in XPath 2.0 compared to XPath 1.0 in the preceding two chapters, on a sheer size basis, there's no question that all the new functions added to XPath 2.0 are the biggest change.

The specification for the XPath 2.0 functions appears in the document XQuery 1.0 and XPath 2.0 Functions and Operators, which is at http://www.w3.org/TR/xquery-operators.

This document is an integral part of the XPath 2.0 specification. Not only are these functions now built into XPath 2.0, but they're also built into XML Query 1.0 and XSLT 2.0. The functions we're going to discuss in this and the following chapters were specifically designed to work on the XPath 2.0 data types, which we covered in Chapter 7, "Introducing XPath 2.0?"

Formally, each function is given by its *signature*, which shows you how to use the function. A signature shows what parameters you pass to a function, and the type of return value, if there is one:

```
function-name($parameter-name as parameter-type, ...) as return-type
```

For example, the signature of the node-name function, which returns the name of the node you pass to it as a string, looks like this:

```
node-name($srcval as node) as xs:string
```

Function Namespaces

The function name itself for all the functions we'll be taking a look at is an XML QName, followed by parentheses. The functions and operators in the XQuery 1.0 and XPath 2.0 Functions and Operators document use various namespaces, which you should know about.

For data types, the xs namespace is used for standard XML-schema types, as before; this namespace corresponds to "http://www.w3.org/2001/XMLSchema". And the xdt namespace, which corresponds to "http://www.w3.org/2003/05/xpath-datatypes", is the namespace for the data types specifically added for XPath 2.0.

The namespace for functions is identified by the fn prefix. Its value is "http://www.w3.org/2003/05/xpath-functions". You can call functions with this namespace prefix; for example, the node-name function is referred to as fn:node-name in the XQuery 1.0 and XPath 2.0 Functions and Operators document:

```
fn:node-name($srcval as node) as xs:string
```

Saxon supports many of the XPath 2.0 functions we're going to see, but you do *not* use the fn prefix when calling these functions in Saxon.

SHOP TALK

IMPLEMENTATION DEFINITIONS VERSUS SPECIFICATION DEFINITIONS

The fn: prefix, used in the XPath 2.0 functions specification, is not used in Saxon. Technically, the XPath 2.0 functions should be in the "http://www.w3.org/2003/05/xpath-functions" namespace, but the current versions of Saxon don't do things that way in order to retain compatibility with XPath 1.0.

This brings up an interesting point—much in the XPath 2.0 specifications is still defined by the implementation, not by XPath 2.0. As you go through the XPath 2.0 specifications, you'll often find the terms "implementation-defined" and "implementation-dependent," and those are items to be aware of.

SHOP TALK

For example, the precision of numbers returned by the numeric XPath 2.0 functions is actually defined by the implementation, not by XPath 2.0 (except for those functions that let you actually set the precision yourself).

And the expanded names returned by functions like `fn:node-name` consist of a pair of values, a namespace URI, and a local name. The way this return value is actually handled is also being left up to the implementation.

And there are many other such issues as well—how non-XML media types are handled, for example, whether the implementation uses DTD or schema validation to check a document's syntax, the order of nodes returned in some functions, and so on.

Some of these issues—such as whether or not you need to preface function names with `fn:`—make a big difference to you before you use a particular XPath processor. Some, such as which of two identical maximum values in a sequence are returned by the `fn:max` function, probably won't. It's going to be interesting to see how these issues shake out in the long run.

There's also a fourth prefix defined in the XQuery 1.0 and XPath 2.0 Functions and Operators document—the op prefix, which corresponds to the namespace "http://www.w3.org/2003/05/xpath-operators for operators", and which you use with operators. The operator functions are included in the XQuery 1.0 and XPath 2.0 Functions and Operators document to make clear how the various XPath 2.0 operators work on various data types, and they're there to back up the standard operators, which we saw in Chapter 8, "XPath 2.0 Expressions, Sequences, and Operators." For example, the * operator on numeric values has a corresponding function named op:numeric-multiply:

```
op:multiply($operand1 as numeric, $operand2 as numeric) as numeric
```

The op functions are *not* directly accessible in XPath 2.0, so you cannot call them directly (some software may make them accessible, but Saxon does not). They're in the specification to make it clear how the operators we covered in Chapter 8 work on various data types— we've already covered those operators, so we won't give much coverage to the op functions here. However, if you need to know exactly how, say, xs:date values work when you subtract one from another, you can get all the details by looking at how op:subtract-dates is defined for xs:date values in the XQuery 1.0 and XPath 2.0 Functions and Operators document.

The XQuery 1.0 and XPath 2.0 Functions and Operators document starts off with the specification for the *accessor functions*, which work on nodes, and we'll start there too.

Using Accessor Functions

The XPath 2.0 Data Model describes a set of accessor functions for use with different types of nodes, and some of those accessor functions are made available through general functions. Here they are:

- `fn:node-name` returns the name of a node.

- `fn:string` returns the string value of the argument.

- `fn:data` takes a sequence of items and returns a sequence of atomic values.

- `fn:base-uri` returns a node's base URI.

- `fn:document-uri` returns the document's URI.

We'll take a closer look at these functions here.

The `fn:node-name` Function

The `fn:node-name` function returns the expanded name of nodes that can have names (for other node kinds, it returns the empty sequence). Here is the signature for this function—the question mark at the end of the return type indicates in XPath 2.0 that the empty sequence can be returned:

```
fn:node-name($srcval as node) as xs:QName?
```

Expanded names consist of a pair of values, a namespace URI, and a local name. In consequence, the way this function actually returns its values is implementation-specific.

The `fn:string` Function

The `fn:string` function returns the string value of a node. Here's how you use this function—this function can take one argument or an empty sequence, which XPath represents by adding a question mark after the argument type:

```
fn:string($srcval as item?) as xs:string
```

Here, `fn:string` returns the value of *$srcval* represented as a `xs:string`. If you don't pass an argument to this function, *$srcval* defaults to the context item (which is represented by a dot, .). If you pass an empty sequence, you'll get an empty string, "", back.

String representations in XPath 2.0 are nearly the same as in XPath 1.0, with some small differences—for example, the representations of positive and negative infinity are now `'INF'` and `'-INF'` rather than `'Infinity'` and `'-Infinity'`. You can see an example in `ch09_01.xsl`, Listing 9.1—in this case, we're displaying the string value of the `<planet>` elements in our planetary data document.

LISTING 9.1   An XSLT Example Using the XPath Function `fn:string` (ch09_01.xsl)

```
<xsl:stylesheet version="2.0" xmlns:xsl="http://www.w3.org/1999/XSL/Transform"
xmlns:xs="http://www.w3.org/2001/XMLSchema">

    <xsl:template match="//planet">
        <xsl:value-of select="string(.)"/>
    </xsl:template>

</xsl:stylesheet>
```

You can see the results when you apply this stylesheet to our planetary data document, including the string value of each <planet> element:

```
C:\Saxon>java net.sf.saxon.Transform ch02_01.xml ch09_02.xsl
<?xml version="1.0" encoding="UTF-8"?>

        Mercury
        .0553
        58.65
        1516
        .983
        43.4

        Venus
        .815
        116.75
        3716
        .943
        66.8

        Earth
        1
        1
        2107
        1
        128.4
```

This function is handy for turning data of various types into strings. Because of XPath 2.0's reliance on strong data typing, this is an important function—for example, if you want to pass a non-string variable's value to a string function like `fn:concat`, you should convert that value to a string using the `fn:string` function first.

The `fn:data` Function

The `fn:data` function converts a sequence of items (which can include nodes and atomic values) into a sequence of atomic values. Here's how you use this function in general—the `*` symbol here means "zero or more of," which is how you represent a sequence in function signatures:

```
fn:data($srcval as item*) as xdt:anyAtomicType*
```

If an item in the passed sequence is already an atomic value, it's returned in the returned sequence. On the other hand, if an item in the passed sequence is a node, its typed value is returned (see `http://www.w3.org/TR/xpath-datamodel/#dm-typed-value` for a description of exactly how typed values for nodes are calculated). If the node has not been validated, its typed value is simply its string value, given the type `xdt:untypedAtomic`.

The `fn:base-uri` Function

This accessor function returns the base URI for a node. Here's how you use this function:

```
fn:base-uri($srcval as node) as xs:string?
```

In XML documents, you set a base URI with the XML `xml:base` attribute. You can see an example in `ch09_03.xml`, where we're setting a base URI for our planetary data document in a new version, `ch09_02.xml` (Listing 9.2).

LISTING 9.2   Setting a Base URI (ch09_02.xml)

```xml
<?xml version="1.0"?>
<?xml-stylesheet type="text/xsl" href="ch01_02.xsl"?>
<planets xml:base="http://www.XPathCorp.com">

    <planet>
        <name>Mercury</name>
        <mass units="(Earth = 1)">.0553</mass>
        <day units="days">58.65</day>
        <radius units="miles">1516</radius>
        <density units="(Earth = 1)">.983</density>
        <distance units="million miles">43.4</distance>
        <!--At perihelion-->
    </planet>

    <planet>
        <name>Venus</name>
        <mass units="(Earth = 1)">.815</mass>
```

LISTING 9.2 Continued

```
            <day units="days">116.75</day>
            <radius units="miles">3716</radius>
            <density units="(Earth = 1)">.943</density>
            <distance units="million miles">66.8</distance>
            <!--At perihelion-->
        </planet>

        <planet>
            <name>Earth</name>
            <mass units="(Earth = 1)">1</mass>
            <day units="days">1</day>
            <radius units="miles">2107</radius>
            <density units="(Earth = 1)">1</density>
            <distance units="million miles">128.4</distance>
            <!--At perihelion-->
        </planet>

</planets>
```

Now we can determine the base URI of each `<planet>` element in a new XSLT 2.0 stylesheet, as you see in `ch09_03.xsl` (Listing 9.3).

LISTING 9.3 Reading a Base URI (`ch09_03.xsl`)

```
<xsl:stylesheet version="2.0" xmlns:xsl="http://www.w3.org/1999/XSL/Transform"
xmlns:xs="http://www.w3.org/2001/XMLSchema">

    <xsl:template match="//planet">
        <xsl:value-of select="base-uri(.)"/>
    </xsl:template>

</xsl:stylesheet>
```

And here's the result when you apply this stylesheet to our new XML document—you can see the base URI of the `<planet>` elements in this example:

```
C:\Saxon>java net.sf.saxon.Transform ch09_03.xml ch09_04.xsl
<?xml version="1.0" encoding="UTF-8"?>
    http://www.XPathCorp.com
    http://www.XPathCorp.com
    http://www.XPathCorp.com
```

The `fn:document-uri` Function

When you pass it a node, the `fn:document-uri` function returns the URI of the document that contains the node, which is useful, for example, if you want to display an error that lists the current document's name. Here's how you use this function:

```
fn:document-uri($srcval as node) as xs:string?
```

You can see an example putting `fn:document-uri` to work in `ch09_04.xsl` (Listing 9.4). Here, we're simply displaying the URI of the current document to test this function.

LISTING 9.4   Using the `fn:document-uri` Function (`ch09_04.xsl`)

```
<xsl:stylesheet version="2.0" xmlns:xsl="http://www.w3.org/1999/XSL/Transform"
xmlns:xs="http://www.w3.org/2001/XMLSchema">

    <xsl:template match="/">
        <xsl:value-of select="document-uri(.)"/>
    </xsl:template>

</xsl:stylesheet>
```

And here's the result you get when apply this stylesheet to `ch09_02.xml`—in this case the result is the location on disk of `ch09_02.xml`:

```
C:\Saxon>java net.sf.saxon.Transform ch09_03.xml ch09_04.xsl
<?xml version="1.0" encoding="UTF-8"?>
file:/C:/Saxon/ch09_02.xml
```

Using the `fn:error` Function

The `fn:error` function makes the XPath processor display an error message and stop processing. You can pass the error message you want displayed to this function like this—there is no return type, which XPath indicates with a return type of "none" ("none" is a special type defined in XPath 2.0, and it's not actually usable in the XPath language with XPath processors—it's just to indicate there is no return type):

```
fn:error($srcval as item?) as none
```

You can see an example in `ch09_05.xsl` (Listing 9.5). In this case, we're checking the number of a particular item we have in stock and reporting the results.

LISTING 9.5   Using the fn:error Function (ch09_05.xsl)

```
<xsl:stylesheet version="2.0"
    xmlns:xsl="http://www.w3.org/1999/XSL/Transform"
    xmlns:xs="http://www.w3.org/2001/XMLSchema">
    <xsl:variable name="inStock" select="80" />

    <xsl:template match="/">
        <xsl:value-of select="if ($inStock > 0)
            then concat('Number in stock: ', string($inStock))
            else error('Invalid argument')"/>
    </xsl:template>

</xsl:stylesheet>
```

Here's the result using Saxon as the example is written:

```
<?xml version="1.0" encoding="UTF-8"?>
Number in stock: 80
```

However, if we change the number in stock to –20 like this:

```
<xsl:stylesheet version="2.0"
    xmlns:xsl="http://www.w3.org/1999/XSL/Transform"
    xmlns:xs="http://www.w3.org/2001/XMLSchema">
    <xsl:variable name="inStock" select="-20" />

    <xsl:template match="/">
        <xsl:value-of select="if ($inStock > 0)
            then concat('Number in stock: ', string($inStock))
            else error('Invalid argument')"/>
    </xsl:template>

</xsl:stylesheet>
```

Then running Saxon on this example raises this error and makes Saxon quit:

```
C:\Saxon>java net.sf.saxon.Transform ch09_02.xml ch09_05.xsl
Error at xsl:value-of on line 7 of file:/C:/Saxon/ch09_05.xsl:
  Invalid argument
Transformation failed: Run-time errors were reported
```

In this way, you can cause an error and make the XPath processor report that error—the string we passed to the fn:error function is displayed by Saxon.

Constructor Functions

You can use constructor functions to create typed values in XPath 2.0. There is a constructor function for every built-in atomic type except `xs:NOTATION`. Here's what they look like:

pref:*type*(*$srcval* as xdt:anyAtomicType) as *pref*:*type*

Here, *pref* is the prefix of the type you want to create, either xs or xdt. A constructor function has the same name as the type you want to create—for example, to create an `xs:double` with a value of 3.1415, you can use the `xs:double` constructor function like this:

xs:double("3.1415")

This expression returns an `xs:double` value of 3.1415. Here are the legal constructor functions that are supported for the built-in types:

- `xdt:untypedAtomic($srcval as xdt:anyAtomicType) as xdt:untypedAtomic`

- `xdt:dayTimeDuration($srcval as xdt:anyAtomicType) as xdt:dayTimeDuration`

- `xdt:yearMonthDuration($srcval as xdt:anyAtomicType) as xdt:yearMonthDuration`

- `xs:anyURI($srcval as xdt:anyAtomicType) as xs:anyURI`

- `xs:QName($srcval as xdt:anyAtomicType) as xs:QName`

- `xs:base64Binary($srcval as xdt:anyAtomicType) as xs:base64Binary`

- `xs:boolean($srcval as xdt:anyAtomicType) as xs:boolean`

- `xs:byte($srcval as xdt:anyAtomicType) as xs:byte`

- `xs:date($srcval as xdt:anyAtomicType) as (xs:date, xdt:dayTimeDuration)`

- `xs:dateTime($srcval as xdt:anyAtomicType) as (xs:dateTime, xdt:dayTimeDuration)`

- `xs:decimal($srcval as xdt:anyAtomicType) as xs:decimal`

- `xs:double($srcval as xdt:anyAtomicType) as xs:double`

- `xs:duration($srcval as xdt:anyAtomicType) as xs:duration`

- `xs:ENTITY($srcval as xdt:anyAtomicType) as xs:ENTITY`

- `xs:float($srcval as xdt:anyAtomicType) as xs:float`

- `xs:gDay($srcval as xdt:anyAtomicType) as xs:gDay`

- `xs:gMonth($srcval as xdt:anyAtomicType) as xs:gMonth`

- `xs:gMonthDay($srcval as xdt:anyAtomicType) as xs:gMonthDay`

- xs:gYear(*$srcval* as xdt:anyAtomicType) as xs:gYear

- xs:gYearMonth(*$srcval* as xdt:anyAtomicType) as xs:gYearMonth

- xs:hexBinary(*$srcval* as xdt:anyAtomicType) as xs:hexBinary

- xs:ID(*$srcval* as xdt:anyAtomicType) as xs:ID

- xs:IDREF(*$srcval* as xdt:anyAtomicType) as xs:IDREF

- xs:int(*$srcval* as xdt:anyAtomicType) as xs:int

- xs:integer(*$srcval* as xdt:anyAtomicType) as xs:integer

- xs:language(*$srcval* as xdt:anyAtomicType) as xs:language

- xs:long(*$srcval* as xdt:anyAtomicType) as xs:long

- xs:Name(*$srcval* as xdt:anyAtomicType) as xs:Name

- xs:NCName(*$srcval* as xdt:anyAtomicType) as xs:NCName

- xs:negativeInteger(*$srcval* as xdt:anyAtomicType) as xs:negativeInteger

- xs:NMTOKEN(*$srcval* as xdt:anyAtomicType) as xs:NMTOKEN

- xs:nonNegativeInteger(*$srcval* as xdt:anyAtomicType) as xs:nonNegativeInteger

- xs:nonPositiveInteger(*$srcval* as xdt:anyAtomicType) as xs:nonPositiveInteger

- xs:normalizedString(*$srcval* as xdt:anyAtomicType) as xs:normalizedString

- xs:positiveInteger(*$srcval* as xdt:anyAtomicType) as xs:positiveInteger

- xs:short(*$srcval* as xdt:anyAtomicType) as xs:short

- xs:string(*$srcval* as xdt:anyAtomicType) as xs:string

- xs:time(*$srcval* as xdt:anyAtomicType) as (xs:time, xdt:dayTimeDuration)

- xs:token(*$srcval* as xdt:anyAtomicType) as xs:token

- xs:unsignedByte(*$srcval* as xdt:anyAtomicType) as xs:unsignedByte

- xs:unsignedInt(*$srcval* as xdt:anyAtomicType) as xs:unsignedInt

- xs:unsignedLong(*$srcval* as xdt:anyAtomicType) as xs:unsignedLong

- xs:unsignedShort(*$srcval* as xdt:anyAtomicType) as xs:unsignedShort

We saw an example in Chapter 7, where we created an xs:date value like this:

```
<xsl:stylesheet version="2.0" xmlns:xsl="http://www.w3.org/1999/XSL/Transform"
xmlns:xs="http://www.w3.org/2001/XMLSchema">
```

```
<xsl:template match="/">
    <xsl:value-of select="xs:date('2004-09-02')"/>
</xsl:template>
```

```
</xsl:stylesheet>
```

You can also have constructor functions for user-defined types if you derive them by restriction from primitive types. For example, in Chapter 7, we declared a derived type by restriction from the xs:string type named StateAbbreviation like this, restricting it to two-character strings like AZ or CA:

```
<simpleType name='xdat:StateAbbreviation'>
    <restriction base='xs:string'>
      <pattern value='[A-Z]{2}'/>
    </restriction>
</simpleType>
```

After you declare a user-defined type like this, a constructor function is made available to users:

```
xdat:StateAbbreviation($srcval as xdt:anyAtomicType) as xdat:StateAbbreviation
```

Using Context Functions

There is also a set of functions designed to get information about the evaluation context. Here are those functions, some of which we've seen in XPath 1.0:

- fn:position returns the position of the context item within the sequence of items currently being processed.

- fn:last returns the number of items in the sequence of items currently being processed.

- fn:current-dateTime returns the current xs:dateTime.

- fn:current-date returns the current xs:date.

- fn:current-time returns the current xs:time.

- fn:default-collation returns the value of the default collation property from the static context.

- fn:implicit-timezone returns the value of the implicit timezone property from the evaluation context.

We'll take a closer look at these functions here, starting with fn:position.

The `fn:position` Function

XPath 2.0 supports our old friend from XPath 1.0, the `fn:position()` function. In XPath 2.0, this function returns an `xs:integer` value holding the position of the context item among its siblings:

```
fn:position() as xs:integer?
```

Here's an example; say that you wanted to format the names of the planets in our planetary data document like this (note the extra annotation for Venus):

```
1 Mercury.
2 Venus (the planet of love).
3 Earth.
```

To make this happen, we'll loop over all the `<planet>` elements using an `<xsl:for-each>` element:

```
<xsl:template match="planets">
    <xsl:for-each select="planet">
            .
            .
            .
    </xsl:for-each>
</xsl:template>
```

We can number each planet's name using the `position` function like this:

```
    <xsl:template match="planets">
        <xsl:for-each select="planet">
            <xsl:value-of select="position()"/>
            <xsl:text> </xsl:text>
            <xsl:value-of select="name"/>
                .
                .
                .
            <br/>
        </xsl:for-each>
    </xsl:template>
```

And we can also add the annotation for Venus like this:

```
    <xsl:template match="planets">
        <xsl:for-each select="planet">
            <xsl:value-of select="position()"/>
            <xsl:text> </xsl:text>
```

```
        <xsl:value-of select="name"/>
        <xsl:value-of select="if (position() = 2) then
            ' (the planet of love).' else '.'"/>
        .
        .
        .
        <br/>
    </xsl:for-each>
</xsl:template>
```

All that's left is to separate each planet's entry onto a different line, and we'll use a `<br/>` element for that, as you can see in this example's code, ch09_06.xsl, which appears in Listing 9.6.

LISTING 9.6   Using the `fn:position` Function (ch09_06.xsl)

```
<xsl:stylesheet version="2.0"
    xmlns:xsl="http://www.w3.org/1999/XSL/Transform">

    <xsl:template match="planets">
        <xsl:for-each select="planet">
            <xsl:value-of select="position()"/>
            <xsl:text> </xsl:text>
            <xsl:value-of select="name"/>
            <xsl:value-of select="if (position() = 2) then
                ' (the planet of love).' else '.'"/>
            <br/>
            <br/>
        </xsl:for-each>
    </xsl:template>

</xsl:stylesheet>
```

Here's what you get when you apply this stylesheet to our planetary data document:

```
C:\Saxon>java net.sf.saxon.Transform ch02_01.xml ch09_06.xsl
<?xml version="1.0" encoding="UTF-8"?>
1 Mercury.
<br/>
2 Venus (the planet of love).
<br/>
3 Earth.
<br/>
```

The `fn:last` Function

The `last()` function in XPath 1.0 appears in XPath 2.0 as `fn:last()`, which returns an `xs:integer` indicating the number of items in the sequence of items currently being processed. Here's its signature:

`fn:last() as xs:integer?`

Here's an example using the `last()` function. Say that we want to adapt our previous XSLT example to create an HTML document in which we enclose the planetary list with horizontal rule, `<hr/>`, elements. To convert the output of our XSLT stylesheet from XML to HTML, we only need to make the document element of the output document `<html>`, which causes the XSLT processor to assume the output document is HTML:

```
<xsl:template match="planets">
    <html>
        .
        .
        .
    </html>
</xsl:template>
```

Then we just add the other HTML we need, and add an `<xsl:if>` element to check for the beginning of the list, where we add the first `<hr/>` element:

```
<xsl:template match="planets">
    <html>
        <head>
            <title>
                The Planets
            </title>
        </head>

        <body>
            <h1>
                The Planets
            </h1>
            <xsl:for-each select="planet">
                <xsl:if test="position() = 1"><hr/></xsl:if>
                <xsl:value-of select="position()"/>
                <xsl:text> </xsl:text>
                <xsl:value-of select="name"/>
```

```
                    <xsl:value-of select="if (position() = 2)
                        then ' (the planet of love).'
                        else '.'"/>
                        .
                        .
                        .
                    <br/>
                </xsl:for-each>
            </body>
        </html>
    </xsl:template>
```

All that's left is to add the final `<hr/>` element at the end of the list, and that works as you can see in ch09_07.xsl (Listing 9.7) .

LISTING 9.7   Using the `fn:last` Function (ch09_07.xsl)

```
<xsl:stylesheet version="2.0"
    xmlns:xsl="http://www.w3.org/1999/XSL/Transform">

    <xsl:template match="planets">
        <html>
            <head>
                <title>
                    The Planets
                </title>
            </head>

            <body>
                <h1>
                    The Planets
                </h1>
                <xsl:for-each select="planet">
                    <xsl:if test="position() = 1"><hr/></xsl:if>
                    <xsl:value-of select="position()"/>
                    <xsl:text> </xsl:text>
                    <xsl:value-of select="name"/>
                    <xsl:value-of select="if (position() = 2)
                        then ' (the planet of love).'
                        else '.'"/>
                    <xsl:if test="position() = last()"><hr/></xsl:if>
                    <br/>
```

LISTING 9.7 Continued

```
            </xsl:for-each>
        </body>
    </html>
  </xsl:template>

</xsl:stylesheet>
```

To store our results in an HTML document named `results.html`, you can use this command with Saxon:

```
C:\Saxon>java net.sf.saxon.Transform ch02_01.xml ch09_07.xsl > results.html
```

And you can see the result in Figure 9.1.

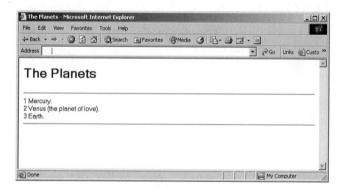

FIGURE 9.1 Using the `last()` function.

The `fn:current-dateTime` Function

This function returns the current date and time, with timezone. Here's the signature of this function:

```
fn:current-dateTime() as dateTime
```

This function returns an `xs:dateTime` value, and you can see an example in `ch09_08.xsl`, Listing 9.8, where we're just displaying the current time and date.

LISTING 9.8   Using the fn:current-dateTime Function (ch09_08.xsl)

```
<xsl:stylesheet version="2.0"
    xmlns:xsl="http://www.w3.org/1999/XSL/Transform">

    <xsl:template match="/">
        <xsl:value-of select="current-dateTime()"/>
    </xsl:template>

</xsl:stylesheet>
```

Here's the kind of result you get when you run this example through Saxon:

```
<?xml version="1.0" encoding="UTF-8"?>
2003-09-19T17:00:25.255Z
```

The fn:current-date Function

The fn:current-date() function just returns an xs:date object, with timezone information, that holds the current date. Here's how you use this function:

```
fn:current-date() as xs:date
```

You can see an example in ch09_09.xsl, Listing 9.9, where we're displaying the current date.

LISTING 9.9   Using the fn:current-date Function (ch09_09.xsl)

```
<xsl:stylesheet version="2.0"
    xmlns:xsl="http://www.w3.org/1999/XSL/Transform">

    <xsl:template match="/">
        <xsl:value-of select="current-date()"/>
    </xsl:template>

</xsl:stylesheet>
```

Here's the kind of result you get from Saxon using this example:

```
<?xml version="1.0" encoding="UTF-8"?>
2003-09-19
```

The `fn:current-time` Function

As you can gather from its name, the `fn:current-time()` function returns the current time. Here's how you use it:

```
fn:current-time() as time
```

The return value is an `xs:time` value, including timezone. You can see an example in `ch09_10.xsl` (Listing 9.10).

LISTING 9.10 Using the `fn:current-time` Function (`ch09_10.xsl`)

```
<xsl:stylesheet version="2.0"
    xmlns:xsl="http://www.w3.org/1999/XSL/Transform">

    <xsl:template match="/">
        <xsl:value-of select="current-time()"/>
    </xsl:template>

</xsl:stylesheet>
```

And here's what you might see when you run this example:

```
<?xml version="1.0" encoding="UTF-8"?>
17:24:23.503Z
```

Using Numeric Functions

XPath 2.0 also has a number of numeric functions, designed to work with these numeric types:

- `xs:decimal`
- `xs:integer`
- `xs:float`
- `xs:double`

These functions also apply to types derived by restriction from these types.

The XQuery 1.0 and XPath 2.0 Functions and Operators document lists a large number of op functions that specify how various numeric operators work on different data types. Here are some of the op functions described—you can tell what operator each function is describing by its name:

- op:numeric-add—Addition (+)

- op:numeric-subtract—Subtraction (–)

- op:numeric-multiply—Multiplication (*)

- op:numeric-divide—Division (div)

- op:numeric-integer-divide—Integer division (idiv)

- op:numeric-mod—Modulus (mod)

- op:numeric-unary-plus—Unary plus (+)

- op:numeric-unary-minus—Unary minus (negation) (–)

These functions are not callable from XPath 2.0 expressions; they underpin the operators in the language. However, you can work with a set of numeric functions in the fn namespace. Each of the fn functions returns a value of the same type as the type of its argument. If the argument is the empty sequence, the empty sequence is returned, and if the argument is xdt:untypedAtomic, it is converted to xs:double.

Here's an overview of the callable numeric functions:

- fn:floor returns the largest number with no fractional part that is less than or equal to the value you pass.

- fn:ceiling returns the smallest number with no fractional part that is greater than or equal to the value you pass.

- fn:round rounds to the nearest number with no fractional part.

- fn:round-half-to-even accepts a number and a rounding precision value and returns a number rounded to the precision you've requested. Note that if the fractional part of the value you pass is .5, the result is the number whose least significant digit is even.

We'll take a look at them here.

The fn:floor Function

The fn:floor function returns the largest number—that is, the closest to positive infinity—that has no fractional part, such that the returned number is not greater than the value you pass to this function. Here's the signature of this function:

```
fn:floor($srcval as numeric?) as numeric?
```

Here are some examples:

```
fn:floor(2.3) returns 2
fn:floor(1.5) returns 1
fn:floor(-9.5) returns -10
```

And here's an example putting this function to work in an XSLT 2.0 stylesheet. In this example, we'll determine whether a number is an integer, and we start by assigning that number to a variable named $number:

```
<xsl:stylesheet version="2.0"
    xmlns:xsl="http://www.w3.org/1999/XSL/Transform">
    <xsl:variable name="number" select="1.5" />
        .
        .
        .
```

If floor($number) = $number, the number is indeed an integer, and we can insert the message "That number is an integer." in the result document like this:

```
<xsl:stylesheet version="2.0"
    xmlns:xsl="http://www.w3.org/1999/XSL/Transform">
    <xsl:variable name="number" select="1.5" />
        .
        .
        .

    <xsl:template match="/">
        <xsl:value-of select="if (floor($number) = $number)
            then 'That number is an integer.'
            .
            .
            .
</xsl:template>
```

On the other hand, if floor($number) != $number, we can insert the message "That number is not an integer." in the result document, as you see in ch09_11.xsl (Listing 9.11).

LISTING 9.11   Using the fn:floor Function (ch09_11.xsl)

```
<xsl:stylesheet version="2.0"
    xmlns:xsl="http://www.w3.org/1999/XSL/Transform">
    <xsl:variable name="number" select="1.5" />

    <xsl:template match="/">
```

LISTING 9.11   Continued

```
        <xsl:value-of select="if (floor($number) = $number)
            then 'That number is an integer.'
            else 'That number is not an integer.'"/>
    </xsl:template>

</xsl:stylesheet>
```

And here's the result when you use Saxon on this stylesheet—as you can see, this code knows that 1.5 is not an integer:

```
<?xml version="1.0" encoding="UTF-8"?>
That number is not an integer.
```

The `fn:ceiling` Function

The `fn:ceiling` function returns the smallest—that is, closest to negative infinity—number with no fractional part, such that the returned number is not less than the value you pass this function. Here's what this function's signature looks like:

```
fn:ceiling($srcval as numeric?) as numeric?
```

Here are some examples:

```
fn:ceiling(9.3) returns 10.
fn:ceiling(1.5) returns 2.
fn:ceiling(-4.5) returns -4.
```

Here's an example using `fn:ceiling`. In this case, say you have one and a half truckloads of iron ore to move and want to know how many trucks you'll need. We start by setting up a variable, $numberofTruckLoads:

```
<xsl:stylesheet version="2.0"
    xmlns:xsl="http://www.w3.org/1999/XSL/Transform">
    <xsl:variable name="numberofTruckLoads" select="1.5" />
        .
        .
        .
```

And passing this variable to the `fn:ceiling` function tells us how many trucks we'll need to transport the load; you can see the XPath code in `ch09_12.xsl` (Listing 9.12).

LISTING 9.12   Using the `fn:ceiling` Function (ch09_12.xsl)

```
<xsl:stylesheet version="2.0"
    xmlns:xsl="http://www.w3.org/1999/XSL/Transform">
    <xsl:variable name="numberofTruckLoads" select="1.5" />

    <xsl:template match="/">
        <xsl:value-of select="concat('You will need ',
            string(ceiling($numberofTruckLoads)), ' trucks.')"/>
    </xsl:template>

</xsl:stylesheet>
```

Here's the result:

```
<?xml version="1.0" encoding="UTF-8"?>
You will need 2 trucks.
```

The `fn:round` Function

The `fn:round` function is XPath 2.0's main rounding function. The `fn:round` function returns the number with no fractional part that is closest to the value you pass. If there are two such numbers, this function returns the one closest to positive infinity. Here's what the signature of this function looks like:

```
fn:round($srcval as numeric?) as numeric?
```

Here are some examples—note in particular that `fn:round(-9.5)` returns –9, not –10:

```
fn:round(1.2) returns 1.
fn:round(6.5) returns 7.
fn:round(6.4999999) returns 6.
fn:round(-9.5) returns -9.
```

> **USING `fn:round` AND `fn:floor`**
>
> `fn:round($srcval)` returns the same value as `fn:floor($srcval + 0.5)`.

Here's an example using this function in XSLT 2.0; say you're in charge of the movie reviews of a newspaper and have to multiply the average number of stars awarded to a movie, like 3.73, by your reviewers and come up with a whole number. You can use the `fn:round` function to do that, as you see in ch09_13.xsl (Listing 9.13).

LISTING 9.13   Using the `fn:round` Function (ch09_13.xsl)

```
<xsl:stylesheet version="2.0"
    xmlns:xsl="http://www.w3.org/1999/XSL/Transform">
    <xsl:variable name="movieName" select="Casablanca" />
    <xsl:variable name="numberOfStars" select="3.73" />

    <xsl:template match="/">
        <xsl:value-of select="concat('Casablanca got ',
            string(round($numberOfStars)), ' stars.')"/>
    </xsl:template>

</xsl:stylesheet>
```

And here's the result:

```
<?xml version="1.0" encoding="UTF-8"?>
Casablanca got 4 stars.
```

The `fn:round-half-to-even` Function

The `fn:round-half-to-even` function gives you a chance to specify the rounding precision yourself. There are two ways to use it—passing it a value, and passing a value and precision:

```
fn:round-half-to-even($srcval as numeric?) as numeric?
fn:round-half-to-even($srcval as numeric?, $precision as integer) as numeric?
```

The first version of this function returns the nearest value to the value you pass that has no fractional part. If two values are equally close—that is, the fractional part of the value you pass is exactly .5—the value returned is the one whose least significant digit is even.

If you pass a *$precision* value to this function, you can set the precision yourself. In this case, the value returned is the nearest value to *$srcval* that is a multiple of 1/10 to the power of *$precision*. As with the other form of this function, if two values are equally close—that is, the fractional part of the value you pass is exactly .5—the value returned is the one whose least significant digit is even.

Here is an example:

```
fn:round-half-to-even(3.5) returns 4.
```

On the other hand, the next example also returns 4:

```
fn:round-half-to-even(4.5) returns 4.
```

Here's an example that uses a precision of 2 (here we're using the standard exponentiation syntax you use in XPath 2.0; note that 1E+3 = 1000, 1E-1 = 1/10, and so on):

`fn:round-half-to-even(9.477512E+3, 2) returns 9477.51E0.`

You can also round to positive powers of 10 if you pass a negative value as the precision you want. For example, here's how you can round to the nearest 100:

`fn:round-half-to-even(12312.63, -2) returns 12300.`

AGGREGATE FUNCTIONS

There are also some numeric functions that are specifically designed to work on sequences, called aggregate functions, such as max, min, count, avg, and sum, that are coming up in Chapter 12, "XPath 2.0 Node and Sequence Functions."

In Brief

- The specification for the XPath 2.0 functions is in the document named XQuery 1.0 and XPath 2.0 Functions and Operators, which you can find at `http://www.w3.org/TR/xquery-operators`.

- The namespace for functions is tied to the fn prefix. Its URL is `http://www.w3.org/2003/05/xpath-functions`, and you can call these functions directly (although when you use Saxon, you omit the fn: prefix). The other prefix defined in the XQuery 1.0 and XPath 2.0 Functions and Operators document is the op prefix, which identifies the operator functions. These functions are not directly callable; these functions are designed to indicate how the XPath 2.0 operators work with various data types.

- The XPath 2.0 functions fn:node-name, fn:string, fn:data, fn:base-uri, and fn:document-uri are generic functions that you use with nodes.

- The fn:error function gives you some control over the processing of XSLT stylesheets—calling this function lets you display an error message and halt the XSLT processor.

- The context functions return information about the current context. These functions are fn:position, fn:last, fn:current-dateTime, fn:current-date, fn:current-time, fn:default-collation, and fn:implicit-timezone.

- The numeric functions in this chapter. These functions are fn:floor, fn:ceiling, fn:round, and fn:round-half-to-even.

XPath 2.0 String Functions

Working on Strings

This chapter is all about the XPath 2.0 string functions. XPath 2.0 now includes support for *regular expressions*, which let you match strings and work with the text in them, as we'll see in this chapter.

The functions in this chapter work on operands of type xs:string and types derived from xs:string. There are a number of general-purpose functions that work on strings in XPath 2.0, and we'll begin with them:

- fn:compare compares two or more strings.

- fn:concat joins two or more strings.

- fn:string-join joins strings using an optional separator.

- fn:starts-with returns true if a string begins with a specified start string.

- fn:ends-with returns true if a string ends with a specified end string.

- fn:contains returns true if one string contains a specified string.

- fn:substring extracts the substring located at a specified location in a string.

- fn:string-length returns the length of a string.

- fn:substring-before returns the characters of one string that come before a match with another string.

- fn:substring-after returns the characters of one string that come after a match with another string.

- fn:normalize-space returns the whitespace-normalized value of a string.

- fn:normalize-unicode returns the normalized value of a string using a specified Unicode normalization form.

- fn:upper-case returns the value of an uppercased string.

- fn:lower-case returns the value of a lowercased string.

- fn:translate returns a string with occurrences of characters in a map string replaced by the character at the corresponding position in a translate string.

- fn:escape-uri returns the xs:anyURI value represented as a string with certain characters escaped.

We'll take a look at these functions now.

The fn:compare Function

You can use the fn:compare function to compare two xs:strings; here are the two possible ways to use this function:

```
fn:compare($operand1 as xs:string?, $operand2 as xs:string?) as xs:integer?

fn:compare($operand1  as xs:string?, $operand2  as xs:string?,
    $collation  as xs:string) as xs:integer?
```

This function returns –1, 0, or 1, depending on whether the value of $operand1 is less than, equal to, or greater than the value of $operand2:

- – $operand1 is less than $operand2.

- 0 $operand1 is equal to $operand2.

- 1 $operand1 is greater than $operand2.

If the value of $operand2 begins with a string that is equal to the value of $operand1 and has additional characters following that beginning string, the result is –1. If the value of $operand1 begins with a string that is equal to the value of $operand2 and has additional characters following that beginning string, the result is 1. As you might expect, if either argument is the empty sequence, the result is the empty sequence.

Here's an example; in this case, we'll compare two strings, "bcdef" and "abcdef"; the first of these is greater than the second in string terms. If the comparison yields a value greater than 0, we know that string 1 is greater than string 2:

```
<xsl:value-of select="if(compare('bcdef', 'abcdef') > 0)
    then 'String 1 is greater than String 2'
```
.
.
.

Otherwise, we know that string 2 is less than or equal to string 1, as you can see in ch10_01.xsl (Listing 10.1).

LISTING 10.1 An XSLT Example Using the XPath Function fn:compare (ch10_01.xsl)

```
<xsl:stylesheet version="2.0"
    xmlns:xsl="http://www.w3.org/1999/XSL/Transform">

    <xsl:template match="/">
        <xsl:value-of select="if(compare('bcdef', 'abcdef') > 0)
            then 'String 1 is greater than String 2'
            else 'String 2 is less than or equal to String 1' "/>
    </xsl:template>

</xsl:stylesheet>
```

And here's the result you get when you use this stylesheet:

```
<?xml version="1.0" encoding="UTF-8"?>
String 1 is greater than String 2
```

The second form of the fn:compare function introduces us to the idea of *collations*, which let you specify the order in which comparisons are made—note the $collation value:

```
fn:compare($operand1  as xs:string?, $operand2  as xs:string?,
    $collation  as xs:string) as xs:integer?
```

$collation holds the name of a collation, which indicates the collation you want to use to compare the strings. That's as far as the XPath 2.0 specification goes in letting you indicate what collation to use. Connecting a named collation to the code that implements it is up to the implementation.

Collations are useful when you need a different comparison order, as might be

MORE ON COLLATIONS

Some programming languages let you define your own collations using functions. XPath 2.0 does not support that, although some such provision might be made in the future. At this point, XPath 2.0 only supports implementation-dependent named collations. Collations are named by URIs; that is, functions that allow specification of a collation use an argument whose type is xs:string but whose lexical representation is xs:anyURI.

needed in different languages. For example, in some collations, the words "Jaeger" and "Jäger" might be treated as equal. If you don't specify a collation to be used, the standard default collation is used, called the Unicode codepoint collation, whose name is "http://www.w3.org/2003/05/xpath-functions/collation/codepoint".

Here's an example that uses a fictitious collation named "http://XPathCorp/german" that may be supported by some XPath 2.0 implementation that will consider the words "Musse" and "Muße" as equal (in German, ß is a special character that corresponds to using two *s* characters). Here's how you might make that comparison:

```
\fn:compare("Musse", "Muße", "http://XPathCorp/german")
```

In this case, this comparison would yield 0. Only default comparisons are supported in Saxon at this time, so we won't deal with special named collations here.

The fn:concat Function

You use the fn:concat function to concatenate strings; here is the signature:

```
fn:concat($operand1 as xs:string?, $operand2 as xs:string?, ...) as xs:string
```

This function is designed to accept two or more xs:string values as arguments, and returns the concatenation of the arguments you pass to it as an xs:string. In other words, you can pass this function an arbitrary number of string arguments, and it will join them together for you.

Here are some examples:

```
fn:concat('Now is ', 'the time.') returns "Now is the time.".
fn:concat('Now ', 'is ', 'the ', 'time.') returns "Now is the time.".
```

We've already used this function in both XPath 1.0 and 2.0; here's an example from the preceding chapter, ch09_12.xsl, where we used this function to assemble a string:

```
<xsl:stylesheet version="2.0"
    xmlns:xsl="http://www.w3.org/1999/XSL/Transform">
    <xsl:variable name="numberofTruckLoads" select="1.5" />
```

```
<xsl:template match="/">
    <xsl:value-of select="concat('You will need ',
        string(ceiling($numberofTruckLoads)), ' trucks.')"/>
</xsl:template>

</xsl:stylesheet>
```

This is a good one to know, and it's handy because it allows you to pass multiple strings to it. As in XPath 1.0, you'll probably find yourself working with this one a lot.

The `fn:string-join` Function

This function is much like `fn:concat`, except that it joins strings using a separator that you specify. Here's what its signature looks like (recall that the * symbol indicates a sequence):

```
fn:string-join($operand1 as xs:string*, $operand2 as xs:string) as xs:string
```

For instance, we just saw this example in the preceding section—note that we had to explicitly include spaces in each string to be concatenated to make the final string come out right:

```
fn:concat('Now ', 'is ', 'the ', 'time.') returns "Now is the time.".
```

On the other hand, if you use a space character, " ", as a separator, you don't need to add that space to each string to be concatenated:

```
fn:string-join(('Now', 'is', 'the', 'time.'), " ") returns "Now is the time.".
```

This function is useful if you want to create comma-separated lists, as you can see in `ch10_02.xsl` (Listing 10.2), where we're creating such a list of the planets in our planetary data document.

> **PASSING AN EMPTY STRING**
>
> If you pass an empty string, "", as the separator to this function, this function works much the same as the `fn:concat` function.

LISTING 10.2 An XSLT Example Using the XPath Function `fn:string-join` (ch10_02.xsl)

```
<xsl:stylesheet version="2.0"
    xmlns:xsl="http://www.w3.org/1999/XSL/Transform">

    <xsl:template match="/">
        <xsl:value-of select="string-join(//planet/name, ', ')"/>
    </xsl:template>

</xsl:stylesheet>
```

Here's what you see when you run this example through Saxon:

```
C:\Saxon>java net.sf.saxon.Transform ch02_01.xml ch10_02.xsl
<?xml version="1.0" encoding="UTF-8"?>
Mercury, Venus, Earth
```

The fn:starts-with Function

As you can guess from its name, the fn:starts-with function lets you check whether one string starts with another. Here are the possible signatures for this function:

```
fn:starts-with($operand1 as xs:string?, $operand2 as xs:string?) as xs:boolean?

fn:starts-with( $operand1 as xs:string?, $operand2 as xs:string?,
    $collation as xs:string) as xs:boolean?
```

This function returns an xs:boolean value indicating whether or not the value of $operand1 starts with a string that is equal to the value of $operand2 according to the collation that is used.

You can see an example in ch10_03.xsl (Listing 10.3), where we're confirming that the string "Steven" does indeed start with the string "Steve".

LISTING 10.3   An XSLT Example Using the XPath Function fn:starts-with (ch10_03.xsl)

```
<xsl:stylesheet version="2.0"
    xmlns:xsl="http://www.w3.org/1999/XSL/Transform"
    xmlns:xs="http://www.w3.org/2001/XMLSchema">

    <xsl:template match="/">
        <xsl:value-of select="if(starts-with('Steve', 'Steve'))
            then 'Hi Steve!'
            else 'Hi there.'"/>
    </xsl:template>

</xsl:stylesheet>
```

Here is the result you get from Saxon:

```
<?xml version="1.0" encoding="UTF-8"?>
Hi Steve!
```

Here are a few more examples:

```
fn:starts-with("lemonade", "lemon") returns true.
fn:starts-with("lemonade", "onade") returns false.
fn:starts-with("lemonade", "") returns true.
```

The fn:ends-with Function

This function is the counterpart of fn:starts-with, but this one tests whether one string ends with another string. Here are the two ways to use this function:

```
fn:ends-with($operand1 as xs:string?, $operand2 as xs:string?) as xs:boolean?

fn:ends-with( $operand1 as xs:string?, $operand2 as xs:string?,
    $collation as xs:string) as xs:boolean?
```

This function returns an xs:boolean value indicating whether or not the value of $operand1 ends with a string that is equal to the value of $operand2.

You can see an example in ch10_04.xsl (Listing 10.4), where we're confirming that the string "Red car" ends with the string "car".

LISTING 10.4 An XSLT Example Using the XPath Function fn:ends-with (ch10_04.xsl)

```
<xsl:stylesheet version="2.0"
    xmlns:xsl="http://www.w3.org/1999/XSL/Transform"
    xmlns:xs="http://www.w3.org/2001/XMLSchema">

    <xsl:template match="/">
        <xsl:value-of select="if(ends-with('Red car', 'car'))
            then 'That is a car.'
            else 'That is not a car.'"/>
    </xsl:template>

</xsl:stylesheet>
```

Here are the results you get when you run this example through Saxon:

```
<?xml version="1.0" encoding="UTF-8"?>
That is a car.
```

And here are a few more examples:

```
fn:ends-with("Cary Grant", "ant") returns true.
fn:ends-with("Cary Grant", "ent") returns false.
```

The `fn:contains` Function

This function checks to see whether one string contains another. The two forms of this function look like this:

```
fn:contains($operand1 as xs:string?, $operand2 as xs:string?) as xs:boolean?

fn:contains( $operand1 as xs:string?, $operand2 as xs:string?,
    $collation as xs:string) as xs:boolean?
```

The `fn:contains` function returns true if $operand1 contains $operand2, and false otherwise.

Here's an example; in this case, we're scanning some text for nasty words, as you can see in ch10_05.xsl (Listing 10.5).

LISTING 10.5 An XSLT Example Using the XPath Function `fn:contains` (ch10_05.xsl)

```
<xsl:stylesheet version="2.0"
    xmlns:xsl="http://www.w3.org/1999/XSL/Transform"
    xmlns:xs="http://www.w3.org/2001/XMLSchema">

    <xsl:template match="/">
        <xsl:value-of select="if(contains('That darn George!', 'darn'))
            then 'Don''t use nasty words!'
            else 'That text was OK.'"/>
    </xsl:template>

</xsl:stylesheet>
```

And here's what you get when you run this example through Saxon:

```
<?xml version="1.0" encoding="UTF-8"?>
Don't use nasty words!
```

The `fn:substring` Function

The `fn:substring` function lets you extract a substring from another string. Here are the two ways to use this function:

```
fn:substring($sourceString as xs:string?,
    $startPosition as xs:double) as xs:string?
```

```
fn:substring($sourceString as xs:string?, $startPosition as xs:double,
    $length as xs:double) as xs:string?
```

The first version of this function lets you pass a string to it and a starting position (the beginning of the string corresponds to position 1), and it returns the substring that starts at the starting position in the string and ends at the end of the string.

The second version of this function accepts a string, a starting position, and a length, and returns the same string as the first version of the function, except that the returned string is truncated to be the specified length.

Here are a few examples—note that the numbers you pass to this function are rounded if they are not integers:

```
fn:substring("Now is the time", 2) returns "ow is the time".
fn:substring("This is Chapter 10.", 2, 3) returns "his".
fn:substring("This is Chapter 10.", 1.6, 2.9) returns "his".
```

You can see an example in an XSLT 2.0 stylesheet in ch10_06.xsl (as shown in Listing 10.6), where we're extracting a string from the string "Now is the time." using XSLT variables. In this case, we just want to extract the substring "time".

LISTING 10.6   An XSLT Example Using the XPath Function fn:substring (ch10_06.xsl)

```
<xsl:stylesheet version="2.0"
    xmlns:xsl="http://www.w3.org/1999/XSL/Transform"
    xmlns:xs="http://www.w3.org/2001/XMLSchema">
    <xsl:variable name="start" select="12" />
    <xsl:variable name="length" select="4" />

    <xsl:template match="/">
        <xsl:value-of select="substring('Now is the time', $start, $length)"/>
    </xsl:template>

</xsl:stylesheet>
```

And here's what you see when you run this through Saxon:

```
<?xml version="1.0" encoding="UTF-8"?>
time
```

This function is a good one to use when the data in an XML document you're using contains text that you have to extract substrings from, for example, when what should be single records are stored together in longer strings.

The `fn:string-length` Function

As you can guess from this function's name, it returns the length of a string. There are two ways to use this function, as you can see here:

```
fn:string-length($operand as xs:string?) as xs:integer?
```

```
fn:string-length() as xs:integer?
```

Usually, you pass a string to this function, which returns the string's length in characters. If you don't pass a string to this function, it returns the string length of the context item (that is, .).

Here's an example; in this case, we're checking the relative lengths of two strings, "Now is the time!" and "No worries!". First, we store those lengths in two XSLT variables:

```
<xsl:stylesheet version="2.0"
    xmlns:xsl="http://www.w3.org/1999/XSL/Transform"
    xmlns:xs="http://www.w3.org/2001/XMLSchema">
    <xsl:variable name="length1" select="string-length('Now is the time!')" />
    <xsl:variable name="length2" select="string-length('No worries!')" />
        .
        .
        .
```

Then we compare those lengths using two nested XPath 2.0 `if` expressions, as you can see in `ch10_07.xsl` (Listing 10.7). These `if` expressions return various messages depending on the comparison: "The first string is longer.", "The second string is longer.", or "The strings have the same length."

LISTING 10.7   An XSLT Example Using the XPath Function `fn:string-length` (ch10_07.xsl)

```
<xsl:stylesheet version="2.0"
    xmlns:xsl="http://www.w3.org/1999/XSL/Transform"
    xmlns:xs="http://www.w3.org/2001/XMLSchema">
    <xsl:variable name="length1" select="string-length('Now is the time!')" />
    <xsl:variable name="length2" select="string-length('No worries!')" />

    <xsl:template match="/">
        <xsl:value-of select="if($length1 > $length2)
```

LISTING 10.7 Continued

```
         then 'The first string is longer.'
         else if ($length2 > $length1)
         then 'The second string is longer.'
         else 'The strings have the same length.'"/>
   </xsl:template>

</xsl:stylesheet>
```

In this case, we're comparing "Now is the time!" and "No worries!", so as you'd expect, you get this result from Saxon:

```
<?xml version="1.0" encoding="UTF-8"?>
The first string is longer.
```

The fn:substring-before Function

This function returns the substring that comes before a matched substring in another string. Here are the two ways to use this function:

```
fn:substring-before($operand1 as xs:string?,
    $operand2 as xs:string?) as xs:string?

fn:substring-before($operand1 as xs:string?, $operand2 as xs:string?,
    $collation as xs:string) as xs:string?
```

Here, $operand1 is the string you want to work with, and $operand2 holds the substring you want to match in $operand1. This function returns the substring in $operand1 that precedes the first complete match to the text in $operand2. Note that if $operand1 does not contain $operand2, this function returns an empty string, " ".

Here are a few examples:

```
fn:substring-before("No worries","wo") returns "No ".
fn:substring-before("No worries","o") returns "N".
fn:substring-before("No worries","") returns "No worries".
```

The fn:substring-after Function

The fn:substring-after function works just as the fn:substring-before function works, except that it returns the substring that comes after the match, not before. Here are the two ways to use this function:

```
fn:substring-after($operand1 as xs:string?,
    $operand2 as xs:string?) as xs:string?
```

```
fn:substring-after($operand1 as xs:string?, $operand2  as xs:string?,
    $collation as xs:string) as xs:string?
```

As with the `fn:substring-before` function, *$operand1* is the string you want to work with, and *$operand2* holds the substring you want to match in *$operand1*. In this case, this function returns the text in *$operand1* that follows the first complete match to the text in *$operand2*. If *$operand1* does not contain *$operand2*, this function returns an empty string, "".

You can see an example in `ch10_08.xml` (Listing 10.8), where we're extracting the substring that follows the first space in the string "No worries!".

LISTING 10.8   An XSLT Example Using the XPath Function `fn:substring-after` (ch10_08.xsl)

```
<xsl:stylesheet version="2.0"
    xmlns:xsl="http://www.w3.org/1999/XSL/Transform"
    xmlns:xs="http://www.w3.org/2001/XMLSchema">

    <xsl:template match="/">
        <xsl:value-of select="substring-after('No worries!', ' ')"/>
    </xsl:template>

</xsl:stylesheet>
```

And here's the result when you use Saxon:

```
<?xml version="1.0" encoding="UTF-8"?>
worries!
```

Here are a few more examples:

```
fn:substring-after("No worries!", "w") returns "orries!".
fn:substring-after("No worries!", "lorries") returns "".
fn:substring-after("No worries!", "") returns "".
```

The `fn:normalize-space` Function

The `fn:normalize-space` function lets you normalize—in XML terms—the whitespace in a string. Here are the two ways to use this function:

```
fn:normalize-space($srcval as xs:string?) as xs:string?
```

```
fn:normalize-space() as xs:string?
```

This function is designed to return $srcval with whitespace normalized by stripping leading and trailing whitespace and replacing sequences of more than one whitespace character by a single space. (In XML, whitespace includes not just spaces, but carriage returns, tabs, line feeds, and so on.) Note that if you don't pass an argument, this function uses the string value of the context item (.).

In this example, ch10_09.xsl, we'll normalize the text "No   worries!", which should result in the text "No worries!". You can see how this works in Listing 10.9.

LISTING 10.9 An XSLT Example Using the XPath Function `fn:normalize-space` (ch10_09.xsl)

```
<xsl:stylesheet version="2.0"
    xmlns:xsl="http://www.w3.org/1999/XSL/Transform"
    xmlns:xs="http://www.w3.org/2001/XMLSchema">

    <xsl:template match="/">
        <xsl:value-of select="normalize-space('No     worries!')"/>
    </xsl:template>

</xsl:stylesheet>
```

And here's what Saxon gives you when you run this example:

```
<?xml version="1.0" encoding="UTF-8"?>
No worries!
```

SHOP TALK

NORMALIZED OR NOT?

Normalization is a somewhat tricky issue in XPath 2.0. Ideally, W3C says that strings should be normalized before you work on them. However, they acknowledge that it's not possible to guarantee that all strings in the postvalidation stage are normalized.

In my experience, whether or not strings are normalized depends on the XML processor you're using—some normalize strings automatically, some don't.

How various collations work with unnormalized strings is not defined—it's implementation-defined. XPath 2.0 allows collations that operate on unnormalized strings, and you can also have collations that cause errors when unnormalized strings are used.

For that reason, I always watch out for this issue when working with a new XML processor. If you're working with an XSLT processor, it's easy to display the results of any validation, and you can see whether string normalization has occurred.

The XPath 2.0 specifications even allow for collations that normalize strings for the purposes of collating them, although there are no implementations that I know of yet.

The `fn:normalize-unicode` Function

This function lets you normalize text according to Unicode normalization forms; you can read all about these forms at `http://www.unicode.org/reports/tr15/`. Here are the two ways to use this function:

```
fn:normalize-unicode($srcval as xs:string?) as xs:string?
```

```
fn:normalize-unicode($srcval as xs:string?,
    $normalizationForm as xs:string) as xs:string?
```

This function returns the value of *$srcval* normalized according to the normalization form identified by the value of *$normalizationForm*. Here are the possibilities:

- "NFC" means the function will use Unicode Normalization Form C (NFC).

- "NFD" means the function will use Unicode Normalization Form D (NFD).

- "NFKC" means the function will use Unicode Normalization Form KC (NFKC).

- "NFKD" means the function will use Unicode Normalization Form KD (NFKD).

- "Fully normalized" means that the value returned by the function is the value of *$srcval* in the fully normalized form.

- If no normalization form is specified, it will be assumed to be "NFC".

The `fn:upper-case` Function

The `fn:upper-case` function, as you can tell from its name, converts strings to uppercase. Here's how you use it:

```
fn:upper-case($srcval as xs:string?) as xs:string?
```

This function converts the string you send to it to uppercase. Note that not every character has an uppercase version (for example, "2"), and those that don't are returned in their original version.

You can see a quick example in `ch10_10.xsl` (Listing 10.10), where we're capitalizing the text "I said, 'No thanks.'" using this function.

LISTING 10.10   An XSLT Example Using the XPath Function `fn:upper-case` (`ch10_10.xsl`)

```
<xsl:stylesheet version="2.0"
    xmlns:xsl="http://www.w3.org/1999/XSL/Transform"
    xmlns:xs="http://www.w3.org/2001/XMLSchema">
```

LISTING 10.10 Continued

```
    <xsl:template match="/">
        <xsl:value-of select="upper-case('I said, ''No thanks.''')"/>
    </xsl:template>

</xsl:stylesheet>
```

And here are the results:

```
<?xml version="1.0" encoding="UTF-8"?>
I SAID, 'NO THANKS.'
```

The `fn:lower-case` Function

This function is the counterpart of the `fn:upper-case` function, and it converts a string to lowercase. Here's how you use this function:

```
fn:lower-case($srcval as xs:string?) as xs:string?
```

Not all characters have a lowercase version; if a character does not, the original version of the character is returned.

Here are a few examples:

```
fn:lower-case("This is an example!") returns "this is an example!"
fn:lower-case("This is NOT a test. 1-2-3-4-5.") returns
    "this is not a test. 1-2-3-4-5."
```

The `fn:translate` Function

The `fn:translate` function lets you translate text, character by character, into other text. Here's how you use this function:

```
fn:translate($srcval as xs:string?, $mapString as xs:string?,
    $translationString as xs:string?) as xs:string?
```

This function performs a character-by-character translation. You pass it a source string to translate, a string of characters to match, and a string of characters to translate the matched characters to. Each character in the source string that matches a character in the match string is replaced by the character in the same position in the translation string.

For example, say you want to convert the text "hello!" to uppercase, and had temporarily forgotten about the `fn:upper-case` function. In this case, you start by passing this text to the `fn:translate` function:

```
<xsl:template match="/">
    <xsl:value-of select="translate('hello!',
        .
        .
        .

</xsl:template>
```

For every lowercase character, you want to supply an uppercase equivalent, so you start by matching every lowercase character this way:

```
<xsl:template match="/">
    <xsl:value-of select="translate('hello!',
        'abcdefghijklmnopqrstuvwxyz',
        .
        .
        .

</xsl:template>
```

When a lowercase character is matched, you can translate it to the corresponding character in the translation string you pass to this function, as you see in ch10_11.xsl in Listing 10.11.

LISTING 10.11   An XSLT Example Using the XPath Function fn:translate (ch10_11.xsl)

```
<xsl:stylesheet version="2.0"
    xmlns:xsl="http://www.w3.org/1999/XSL/Transform"
    xmlns:xs="http://www.w3.org/2001/XMLSchema">

    <xsl:template match="/">
        <xsl:value-of select="translate('hello!',
            'abcdefghijklmnopqrstuvwxyz',
            'ABCDEFGHIJKLMNOPQRSTUVWXYZ')"/>
    </xsl:template>

</xsl:stylesheet>
```

Now when a lowercase character is found in the string you're translating, the corresponding uppercase character will be used instead. Here's the result:

```
<?xml version="1.0" encoding="UTF-8"?>
HELLO!
```

As you can see, this function works on text character by character, so it's not as useful as, say, a text-replacing function.

Note also that if you don't provide a translated version of a character in the translation string, that character is omitted in the result. Here's an example:

```
fn:translate("xyz", "xyz", "XY") returns "XY".
```

If the translation string doesn't include a translation character for a character in the input string (that is, if the translation string is too short to include all characters you're translating), that character is simply omitted in the output.

The `fn:escape-uri` Function

This function is designed to "escape" URIs to convert the characters in them to a form more palatable to XML and browsers by converting sensitive characters to their simplified Unicode (UTF-8) equivalents. Here's this function's signature:

```
fn:escape-uri($uri as string, $escape-reserved as xs:boolean) as xs:string
```

To use this function, you pass the URI to escape and an `xs:boolean` value named `$escape-reserved`.

If `$escape-reserved` is true, all characters are escaped except for lowercase letters, a–z; uppercase letters, A–Z; the digits 0–9; and the characters "-", "_", ".", "!", "~", "*", "'", "(", and ")". The "%" character is also escaped if it is not followed by two hexadecimal digits.

On the other hand, if `$escape-reserved` is false, only these characters are escaped: " ", ";", "?", ":", "@", "&", "=", "+", "$", ",", "#", "[", "]".

For example, say that you have the URI `http://www.XPathCorp/My Web Page.html`, which has spaces in it that are problematic to use in a Web browser. You can escape the space characters in the URI with %20 character sequences using `fn:escape-uri`.

In this case, we don't want every possible character to be escaped, so we set `$escape-reserved` to `false` (using the Boolean function `fn:false()`). You can see what this looks like in `ch10_12.xsl` (Listing 10.12).

LISTING 10.12   An XSLT Example Using the XPath Function `fn:escape-uri` (ch10_12.xsl)

```
<xsl:stylesheet version="2.0"
    xmlns:xsl="http://www.w3.org/1999/XSL/Transform"
    xmlns:xs="http://www.w3.org/2001/XMLSchema">

    <xsl:template match="/">
        <xsl:value-of select="escape-uri(
            'http://www.XPathCorp/My Web Page.html', false())"/>
    </xsl:template>

</xsl:stylesheet>
```

And here's the result, where you see that the URI was properly escaped and is ready to be used in a browser:

```
<?xml version="1.0" encoding="UTF-8"?>
http://www.XPathCorp/My%20Web%20Page.html
```

Unicode Code Point Functions

There are two functions in XPath 2.0 designed to work with Unicode *code points*, which refers to Unicode equivalent of characters. These functions are `fn:codepoints-to-string` and `fn:string-to-codepoints`. They're coming up next.

The `fn:codepoints-to-string` Function

You pass this function a sequence of Unicode code points, and it converts them to a string. Here's how you use this function:

```
fn:codepoints-to-string($srcval as xs:integer*) as xs:string
```

For example, to convert the Unicode code point sequence (65, 66, 67) into the corresponding string, "ABC", we can use this function as you see in `ch10_13.xsl` (Listing 10.13).

LISTING 10.13 An XSLT Example Using the XPath Function `fn:codepoints-to-string` (ch10_13.xsl)

```
<xsl:stylesheet version="2.0"
    xmlns:xsl="http://www.w3.org/1999/XSL/Transform"
    xmlns:xs="http://www.w3.org/2001/XMLSchema">

    <xsl:template match="/">
        <xsl:value-of select="codepoints-to-string((65, 66, 67))"/>
    </xsl:template>

</xsl:stylesheet>
```

And here is the result:

```
<?xml version="1.0" encoding="UTF-8"?>
ABC
```

The `fn:string-to-codepoints` Function

This function lets you create a sequence of Unicode code points from a string. Here's how you use this function:

```
fn:string-to-codepoints($srcval as xs:string) as xs:integer*
```

You can see an example in `ch10_14.xsl` in Listing 10.14, where we're converting the string "ABC" to a sequence of code points, and displaying that sequence by using the separator attribute in the `<xsl:value-of>` element.

LISTING 10.14   An XSLT Example Using the XPath Function `fn:string-to-codepoints` (`ch10_14.xsl`)

```
<xsl:stylesheet version="2.0"
    xmlns:xsl="http://www.w3.org/1999/XSL/Transform"
    xmlns:xs="http://www.w3.org/2001/XMLSchema">

    <xsl:template match="/">
        <xsl:value-of select="string-to-codepoints('ABC')" separator=", "/>
    </xsl:template>

</xsl:stylesheet>
```

And here's the result—as you can see, we've been able to convert "ABC" into a sequence of code points:

```
<?xml version="1.0" encoding="UTF-8"?>
65, 66, 67
```

Using Pattern Matching

A big addition to XPath in version 2.0 are the pattern-matching functions. These functions let you use regular expression syntax:

- `fn:matches` returns `true` if a string is matched by a supplied regular expression.
- `fn:replace` replaces every occurrence of a match to a regular expression with a replacement string.
- `fn:tokenize` returns a sequence of substrings of a given string.

All of these functions use regular expressions. The regular expressions used in XPath 2.0 are the same as those used in XML schema, with some additions.

Understanding Regular Expressions

MORE ON REGULAR EXPRESSIONS

You can find the XML schema support for regular expressions discussed in http://www.w3.org/TR/xmlschema-2/. This support is a subset of the regular expressions used in the Perl programming language, and you can find the complete documentation for Perl regular expressions at the Comprehensive Perl Archive Network (CPAN) Web site: www.cpan.org/doc/manual/html/pod/perlre.html.

Now that regular expressions are supported by XML schema, books on XML discuss how to create regular expressions. Nonetheless, we'll give a brief introduction to the topic here for those not familiar with the subject.

Regular expressions are made up of *patterns*, and these patterns can be used to match text in your data. Each character matches itself by default, so if you have the pattern

Hello

you can match the text "Hello". You can also use regular expression special characters and assertions, which start with a backslash, \, in your patterns. For example, to match the beginning or ending of a word, called a *word boundary*, you use \b. That means that the regular expression pattern shown here will match the *word* "Hello":

\bHello\b

Here are the special characters, called *metacharacters*, that you can use in regular expressions:

- \077   Octal char
- \d   Match a digit character
- \D   Match a non-digit character
- \E   End case modification
- \e   Escape
- \f   Form feed
- \l   Lowercase next char
- \L   Lowercase until \E found
- \n   Newline
- \Q   Quote (that is, disable) pattern metacharacters until \E found
- \r   Return
- \S   Match a non-whitespace character

- \s   Match a whitespace character

- \t   Tab

- \u   Uppercase next char

- \U   Uppercase until \E found

- \w   Match a word character (alphanumeric characters and "_")

- \W   Match a non-word character

- \x1A   Hex char

And here are the available assertions, which assert that a particular condition is true:

- ^   Match the beginning of the line

- $ Match the end of the line (or before newline at the end)

- \b   Match a word boundary

- \B   Match a non–(word boundary)

- \A   Match only at beginning of string

- \Z   Match only at end of string, or before newline at the end

- \z   Match only at end of string

For example, if you wanted to match a three-digit number, you can use the pattern \d\d\d. To match U.S. social security numbers, therefore, you can use this pattern:

\d\d\d-\d\d-\d\d\d\d

Here's another example, this time using *character classes*. For example, the character class [abc] matches only the characters "a", "b", or "c". You can use a dash in a character class as a shortcut to indicate a range, as in the character class that would match any uppercase letter, [A-Z].This regular expression will match any word made up of lower- or uppercase characters using a *character class*, [A-Za-z], which matches any single lower- or uppercase character, and a plus sign, +, which means "one or more of" in regular expressions:

\b([A-Za-z]+)\b

The + sign is a regular expression *quantifier*. You can use these quantifiers in regular expressions:

- *   Match zero or more times

- +   Match one or more times

- ? Match one or zero times

- {*n*} Match *n* times

- {*n*,} Match at least *n* times

- {*n*,*m*} Match at least *n*—but not more than *m*—times

This regular expression matches any word (even if it includes digits):

`\b\w+\b`

You can also group subexpressions in regular expressions using parentheses. For example, see if you can figure out how this regular expression works—it matches valid email addresses:

`\w+([-+.]\w+)*@\w+([-.]\w+)*\.\w+([-.]\w+)*`

The matches to the parenthesized subexpressions in a regular expression are preserved. The matched text can be accessed after the regular expression has been evaluated if you use the `fn:replace` function, as we'll see when we cover that function.

XPath 2.0 Versus XML Schema Difference

The regular expressions in XPath 2.0 are actually more powerful than those in XML schema. XML Schema uses regular expressions only for validity checking, which means it doesn't support some powerful text-handling techniques.

In particular, two *modes* are defined in XPath 2.0 regular expressions: string mode and multi-line mode (just as in Perl regular expressions). You specify which mode you want with flags, coming up in a page or two.

In addition, two special characters, ^ and $, are also supported in XPath 2.0 regular expressions. As in standard regular expressions, in string mode, the character ^ matches the start of the string, and $ matches the end of the string. In multiline mode, ^ matches the start of any line (lines are broken up with newline, \n, characters, which is #x0A in Unicode), and $ matches the end of any line.

As in standard regular expressions, when you're in string mode, the character . matches any character. In multiline mode, the metacharacter . matches any character except a newline character. For example, the regular expression `^J.*d$` will match this text:

`James Bond`

Minimal matching is also supported in XPath 2.0 regular expressions. For example, suppose you have the text, "That is some book, isn't it?" and you want to match the regular expression `.*is` to this string. In the default case, this expression will match as much as it can, so instead of matching "That is", this regular expression will match "That is some book, is". To indicate that you want to match as little as possible, you can use an additional question mark, so the regular expression `.*?is` would match "That is". Here is how minimal matching works in XPath 2.0 regular expressions:

- *X??* matches *X*, once or not at all.

- *X*?* matches *X*, zero or more times.

- *X+?* matches *X*, one or more times.

- *X{n}?* matches *X*, exactly *n* times.

- *X(n,}?* matches *X*, at least *n* times.

- *X{n,m}?* matches *X*, at least *n* times, and not more than *m* times total.

The three regular expression functions support an optional parameter, `$flags`, that you use to set options. This parameter is a string, and individual letters are used to set the corresponding options. The presence of a letter in the string indicates that the option is on; if it's not present, the option is off. Letters may appear in any order and may be repeated. Here are the current options:

- m   Makes a match operate in multiline mode. Otherwise, the match operates in string mode (the default).

- i   Makes a match operate in case-insensitive mode. Otherwise, the match operates in case-sensitive mode (the default) .

The `fn:matches` Function

The `fn:matches` function returns `true` if a regular expression matches the text in a string, and `false` otherwise. Here are the two ways to use this function:

```
fn:matches($srcval as xs:string?, $pattern as xs:string) as xs:boolean?
```

```
fn:matches($srcval as xs:string?, $pattern as xs:string,
    $flags as xs:string) as xs:boolean?
```

Here's an example; we'll check whether we can find the word "bananas" in a string like this: `fn:matches('Want some bananas today?', '\bbananas\b')`. You can see how this works in `ch10_15.xsl` in Listing 10.15.

LISTING 10.15 An XSLT Example Using the XPath Function fn:matches (ch10_15.xsl)

```
<xsl:stylesheet version="2.0"
    xmlns:xsl="http://www.w3.org/1999/XSL/Transform"
    xmlns:xs="http://www.w3.org/2001/XMLSchema">

    <xsl:template match="/">
        <xsl:value-of select="if(matches('Want some bananas today?',
            '\bbananas\b'))
            then 'Yes, we have some bananas.'
            else 'No, we have no bananas.'"/>
    </xsl:template>

</xsl:stylesheet>
```

And here's the result, where we matched the word "bananas":

```
<?xml version="1.0" encoding="UTF-8"?>
Yes, we have some bananas.
```

Using this function, then, you can perform regular expression matching.

The fn:replace Function

This function replaces matched text with other text. Here are the two ways to use it:

```
fn:replace($srcval as xs:string?, $pattern as xs:string,
    $replacement as xs:string) as xs:string?
```

```
fn:replace($srcval as xs:string?, $pattern as xs:string,
    $replacement as xs:string, $flags  as xs:string) as xs:string?
```

In this case, the function replaces matches to *$pattern* in *$srcval* with *$replacement*.

For example, say that you wanted to replace "bananas" in our text "Want some bananas today?" with "oranges". You can do that with the fn:replace function, as you see in ch10_16.xsl (Listing 10.16).

LISTING 10.16 An XSLT Example Using the XPath Function fn:replace (ch10_16.xsl)

```
<xsl:stylesheet version="2.0"
    xmlns:xsl="http://www.w3.org/1999/XSL/Transform"
    xmlns:xs="http://www.w3.org/2001/XMLSchema">
```

LISTING 10.16 Continued

```
<xsl:template match="/">
    <xsl:value-of select="replace('Want some bananas today?',
        '\bbananas\b', 'oranges')"/>
</xsl:template>

</xsl:stylesheet>
```

And here is the result:

```
<?xml version="1.0" encoding="UTF-8"?>
Want some oranges today?
```

If you enclose subexpressions in parentheses, you can refer to matches to those subexpressions as $1, $2, and so on up to $9 in the $replacement string. For example, say that you want to extract the two words from the string "Bananas, Apples". To do that, you can use the regular expression (\w+), (\w+), and refer to the text that matched the first \w+ subexpression as $1 in the replacement text, and the text that matched the second \w+ subexpression as $2 in the replacement text. You can see how this works in `ch10_17.xsl` (Listing 10.17) .

LISTING 10.17 Matching Subexpressions with `fn:replace` (ch10_17.xsl)

```
<xsl:stylesheet version="2.0"
    xmlns:xsl="http://www.w3.org/1999/XSL/Transform"
    xmlns:xs="http://www.w3.org/2001/XMLSchema">

    <xsl:template match="/">
        <xsl:value-of select="replace('Bananas, Apples',
            '(\w+), (\w+)', 'Item 1:$1 Item 2:$2')"/>
    </xsl:template>

</xsl:stylesheet>
```

And here are the results you get from Saxon:

```
<?xml version="1.0" encoding="UTF-8"?>
Item 1:Bananas Item 2:Apples
```

As you can see, using the `fn:replace` function, you can perform replacements using regular expressions.

The `fn:tokenize` Function

This function is designed to break up text into smaller parts, or *tokens*. Specifically, it breaks the string you pass it into a sequence of strings, using substrings that match a given pattern as separators. Here's how you use this function:

```
fn:tokenize($srcval as xs:string?, $pattern as xs:string) as xs:string*
```

```
fn:tokenize($srcval as xs:string?, $pattern as xs:string,
    $flags as xs:string) as xs:string*
```

You use this function to split up the text in $srcval into pieces separated by text matching the pattern in $pattern. For example, say that you want to break up the text "Now is the time" into the words "Now", "is", "the", "time". You can do that if you instruct the `fn:tokenize` function to break on space characters, `\s`.

You can see how this works in `ch10_18.xsl` (Listing 10.18).

LISTING 10.18 An XSLT Example Using the XPath Function `fn:tokenize` (`ch10_18.xsl`)

```
<xsl:stylesheet version="2.0"
    xmlns:xsl="http://www.w3.org/1999/XSL/Transform"
    xmlns:xs="http://www.w3.org/2001/XMLSchema">

    <xsl:template match="/">
        <xsl:value-of select="tokenize('Now is the time', '\s+')"
            separator=", "/>
    </xsl:template>

</xsl:stylesheet>
```

And here are the results you get from Saxon:

```
<?xml version="1.0" encoding="UTF-8"?>
Now, is, the, time
```

In Brief

In this chapter, we took a look at the XPath string functions. There are quite a number of these functions:

- `fn:compare`
- `fn:concat`

- `fn:string-join`
- `fn:starts-with`
- `fn:ends-with`
- `fn:contains`
- `fn:substring`
- `fn:string-length`
- `fn:substring-before`
- `fn:substring-after`
- `fn:normalize-space`
- `fn:normalize-unicode`
- `fn:upper-case`
- `fn:lower-case`
- `fn:translate`
- `fn:string-pad`
- `fn:escape-uri`
- `fn:codepoints-to-string`
- `fn:string-to-codepoints`
- `fn:matches`
- `fn:replace`
- `fn:tokenize`

XPath 2.0 Boolean, QName, and Date Functions

11

Boolean Functions

As you know, there are no explicit values named true and false that you can embed in XPath 2.0 expressions. Instead, if you need a true or false value, you use the Boolean constructor functions fn:true and fn:false. In addition, the fn:not function flips the logical value of its argument. Here are the Boolean functions in overview:

- fn:true returns the xs:boolean value true.

- fn:false returns the xs:boolean value false.

- fn:not flips the Boolean value of its argument, that is, if passed true it returns false; if passed false it returns true.

We'll take a brief look at all three functions.

The fn:true Function

The fn:true() function has no other purpose than to return a xs:boolean value of true. Here's its signature:

```
fn:true() as xs:boolean
```

Having a function that can return the xs:boolean value true can be useful at times because some XPath 2.0 functions require you to pass Boolean values of true or false.

The `fn:false` Function

This function simply returns the `xs:boolean` value `false`. Here's its signature:

```
fn:false() as xs:boolean
```

We've already used this function in Chapter 10, when we used the `fn:escape-uri` function to escape a URI. In that example (Listing 10.12), we didn't want to escape every possible character, so we passed the `fn:escape-uri` function a value of `false` using `fn:false`:

```
<xsl:stylesheet version="2.0"
    xmlns:xsl="http://www.w3.org/1999/XSL/Transform"
    xmlns:xs="http://www.w3.org/2001/XMLSchema">

    <xsl:template match="/">
        <xsl:value-of select="escape-uri(
            'http://www.XPathCorp/My Web Page.html', false())"/>
    </xsl:template>

</xsl:stylesheet>
```

The `fn:not` Function

This function just flips the Boolean value of its argument. Here's how you use it:

```
fn:not($srcval as item*) as xs:boolean
```

The sequence *$srcval* is first converted to a `xs:boolean` value by passing it to the `fn:boolean`. We're going to see this function in Chapter 12—it returns true *unless* you pass to it any of the following:

- The singleton `xs:boolean` value `false`.

- The singleton `xs:string` value "".

- A singleton numeric value that is numerically equal to zero.

- The singleton `xs:double` or `xs:float` value `NaN` ("Not a Number").

Otherwise, this function returns `true`. The result of `xs:boolean` is passed to the `fn:not` function, which flips `true` to `false` and `false` to `true` to yield the final value.

Here's an example; in this case, we'll check to make sure the temperature is not over 100 degrees Fahrenheit with this expression: `if(not($temperature > 100)) then...`. You can see this at work in `ch11_01.xsl` (Listing 11.1) .

LISTING 11.1   Using the `fn:not` Function (ch11_01.xsl)

```
<xsl:stylesheet version="2.0"
    xmlns:xsl="http://www.w3.org/1999/XSL/Transform"
    xmlns:xs="http://www.w3.org/2001/XMLSchema">
    <xsl:variable name="temperature" select="65" />

    <xsl:template match="/">
        <xsl:value-of select="if(not($temperature > 100))
            then 'Temperature is OK.'
            else 'Too hot.'"/>
    </xsl:template>

</xsl:stylesheet>
```

And here's the result, where we see that the handy `fn:not` function has indeed flipped the Boolean value of its argument:

```
<?xml version="1.0" encoding="UTF-8"?>
Temperature is OK.
```

This function is particularly useful when you're dealing with `true`/`false` values already stored in variables and you need to handle the reverse Boolean sense. For example, if a variable is named `$mortgageApproved` and you need to create a letter for those cases where the mortgage was not approved, you can use the expression `fn:not($mortgageApproved)`.

Functions That Work with Dates and Times

There is a very large emphasis in XPath 2.0 on functions that work with times and dates. The date and time functions that are designed to work on these XML schema types are as follows:

- `xs:dateTime` accepts representations of the form "CCYY-MM-DDThh:mm:ss" where "CC" represents the century, "YY" the year, "MM" the month, and "DD" the day, preceded by an optional leading "–" sign to indicate a negative number (if the sign is omitted, "+" is assumed). The letter "T" is the date/time separator and "hh", "mm", "ss" represent hour, minute, and second respectively. This may be immediately followed by a "Z" to indicate Coordinated Universal Time (UTC) or, to indicate the timezone (that is, the difference between the local time and Coordinated Universal Time, immediately followed by a sign, + or –, followed by the difference from UTC represented as hh:mm). For example, 2004-08-31T14:30:00-05:00 represents 2:30 p.m. on August the 31st, 2004 for Eastern Standard Time, which is 5 hours behind Coordinated Universal Time.

- `xs:date` accepts representations of the form "CCYY-MM-DD". An optional following timezone qualifier is permitted as for `xs:dateTime`.

- `xs:time` accepts representations of the form "hh:mm:ss.sss" with an optional following timezone indicator.

- `xs:gYearMonth` accepts representations that are reduced (right-truncated) from those allowed for `xs:dateTime`: "CCYY-MM". An optional following timezone qualifier is permitted.

- `xs:gYear` accepts representations that are reduced (right-truncated) from those allowed for `xs:dateTime`: "CCYY". An optional following timezone qualifier is permitted as for `xs:dateTime`.

- `xs:gMonthDay` accepts representations that are left-truncated from those accepted by `xs:date`: "--MM-DD". An optional following timezone qualifier is permitted as for `xs:date`.

- `xs:gMonth` The lexical representation for gMonth is the left- and right-truncated lexical representation for `xs:date`: --MM--. An optional following timezone qualifier is permitted as for `xs:date`.

- `xs:gDay` accepts representations that are left-truncated from those accepted by `xs:date`: "---DD". An optional following timezone qualifier is permitted as for `xs:date`.

MORE ON THE XML SCHEMA DATE-TIME TYPES

You can find more information on the standard XML schema date/time types at `http://www.w3.org/TR/xmlschema-2/#built-in-datatypes`.

Two other data types that are also defined in XPath 2.0 in the xdt namespace, which corresponds to `http://www.w3.org/2003/05/xpath-datatypes`: `xdt:yearMonthDuration` and `xdt:dayTimeDuration`, both of which are types derived from `xs:duration`. Here's how you use them:

- `xdt:yearMonthDuration` is derived from `xs:duration` by restricting it to contain only the year and month components. The reduced format looks like "PnYnM", where nY represents the number of years and nM the number of months. An optional preceding minus sign ("–") is permitted to indicate a negative duration. If the sign is omitted a positive duration is indicated. For example, to indicate an `xdt:yearMonthDuration` of 2 years and 3 months, you would write: P2Y3M.

- `xdt:dayTimeDuration` is derived from `xs:duration` by restricting it to contain only the day, hour, minute, and second components. That looks like "PnDTnHnMnS", where nD represents the number of days, T is the date/time separator, nH the number of hours, nM the number of minutes, and nS the number of seconds. An optional minus sign ("–") is permitted to precede the "P", indicating a negative duration. For example, to indicate a duration of 5 days, 12 hours, and 22 minutes, you would write: P5DT12H22M.

SHOP TALK

THE TWO XDT DATA TYPES

When working with XPath, I sometimes feel that the two types derived from the `xs:duration` types, `xdt:yearMonthDuration` and `xdt:dayTimeDuration`, stick out rather awkwardly as add-on types to the XML-schema-defined types.

That makes me wonder what the story is here. Does the XPath 2.0 committee really want to keep these types separate from the XML schema specification?

It turns out that the answer may be no—the XML Query Working Group has recently requested the W3C XML Schema Working Group to include these two types, `xdt:yearMonthDuration` and `xdt:dayTimeDuration`, in the XML schema built-in data types.

It's not clear yet what the XML Schema Working Group will say to this request, but it's likely to be granted. In that case, these two data types will be removed from the `xdt` namespace and moved into the XML Schema namespace (`http://www.w3.org/2001/XMLSchema`) instead. Watch the XPath specifications for further details.

In XPath 2.0, you can use operators like =, >, <, and so on, on date/time values. For example, suppose that you wanted to determine whether an `xs:dateTime` was earlier or later than some other `xs:dateTime`. You could start by creating two variables, say $now and $then, and assigning $now the date 8/30/2004 and $then the date 8/31/2004:

```
<xsl:stylesheet version="2.0"
    xmlns:xsl="http://www.w3.org/1999/XSL/Transform"
    xmlns:xs="http://www.w3.org/2001/XMLSchema">
    <xsl:variable name="now" select="xs:dateTime('2004-08-30T10:20:00-05:00')" />
    <xsl:variable name="then" select="xs:dateTime('2004-08-31T10:20:00-05:00')" />
```

.
.
.

Now all you have to do is to compare the two `xs:dateTime` values using the > operator, as you see in ch11_02.xsl (Listing 11.2).

USING TIMEZONES

XML Schema date/time values may or may not include a timezone. This can create problems when you try to compare two values of the same type one of which has a timezone and the other does not. Such comparisons can in some cases be indeterminate. To avoid these problems, for comparisons and for some arithmetic functions, XPath 2.0 adds an implicit timezone from the evaluation context to date/time values that do not have a timezone. Note that the timezone is added only for the operator or function. The value itself is not changed.

LISTING 11.2   Comparing Date-Time Values (ch11_02.xsl)

```
<xsl:stylesheet version="2.0"
    xmlns:xsl="http://www.w3.org/1999/XSL/Transform"
    xmlns:xs="http://www.w3.org/2001/XMLSchema">
    <xsl:variable name="now" select="xs:dateTime('2004-08-30T10:20:00-05:00')" />
    <xsl:variable name="then" select="xs:dateTime('2004-08-31T10:20:00-05:00')" />

    <xsl:template match="/">
        <xsl:value-of select="if($now > $then)
            then 'Now is later than then.'
            else 'Then is later than now.'"/>
    </xsl:template>

</xsl:stylesheet>
```

And here's the result you get when you run this through Saxon:

```
<?xml version="1.0" encoding="UTF-8"?>
Then is later than now.
```

You can also add and subtract time/date values using the + and - operators. Here is the list of op functions that show how + and - work on the various date/time data types (recall that op functions are not callable in XPath 2.0—they just show what the behavior of the + and - operators is supposed to be):

- op:subtract-dates returns the difference between two xs:date values as an xdt:dayTimeDuration value.

- op:subtract-times returns the difference between two xs:time values as an xdt:dayTimeDuration value.

- op:add-yearMonthDuration-to-dateTime adds an xdt:yearMonthDuration value to an xs:dateTime value.

- op:add-dayTimeDuration-to-dateTime adds an xdt:dayTimeDuration value to an xs:dateTime value.

- op:subtract-yearMonthDuration-from-dateTime subtracts an xdt:yearMonthDuration value from an xs:dateTime value.

- op:subtract-dayTimeDuration-from-dateTime subtracts an xdt:dayTimeDuration value from an xs:dateTime value.

- op:add-yearMonthDuration-to-date adds an xdt:yearMonthDuration value to an xs:date value.

- op:add-dayTimeDuration-to-date adds an xdt:dayTimeDuration value to an xs:date value.

- op:subtract-yearMonthDuration-from-date subtracts an xdt:yearMonthDuration value from an xs:date value.

- op:subtract-dayTimeDuration-from-date subtracts an xdt:dayTimeDuration value from an xs:date value.

- op:add-dayTimeDuration-to-time adds the value of the hour, minute, and second components of an xdt:dayTimeDuration value to an xs:time value.

- op:subtract-dayTimeDuration-from-time subtracts the value of the hour, minute, and second components of an xdt:dayTimeDuration value from an xs:time value.

For example, when you subtract one xs:date time from another, you get an xdt:dayTimeDuration value. Here's an example—in this case, we're subtracting xs:date('2003-11-12') from xs:date('2004-10-06') to get an xdt:dayTimeDuration value corresponding to 325 days (this one's not in the code that accompanies the book, because Saxon doesn't support subtracting date/time values yet) :

```
<xsl:stylesheet version="2.0"
    xmlns:xsl="http://www.w3.org/1999/XSL/Transform"
    xmlns:xs="http://www.w3.org/2001/XMLSchema">

    <xsl:template match="/">
        <xsl:value-of select="xs:date('2004-10-06') - xs:date('2003-11-12')"/>
    </xsl:template>

</xsl:stylesheet>
```

Besides these operators, there are many functions designed to work on dates and times. We'll take a look at them now, starting with functions designed to extract values like hours or minutes from date/time values.

Functions That Extract Data from Date/Time Values

There is an entire set of functions designed to let you work with date/time values by extracting data from those values:

- fn:get-years-from-yearMonthDuration returns the year component of an xdt:yearMonthDuration value.

- fn:get-months-from-yearMonthDuration returns the month component of an xdt:yearMonthDuration value.

- fn:get-days-from-dayTimeDuration returns the day component of an xdt:dayTimeDuration value.

- `fn:get-hours-from-dayTimeDuration` returns the hour component of an `xdt:dayTimeDuration` value.

- `fn:get-minutes-from-dayTimeDuration` returns the minute component of an `xdt:dayTimeDuration` value.

- `fn:get-seconds-from-dayTimeDuration` returns the second component of an `xdt:dayTimeDuration` value.

- `fn:get-year-from-dateTime` returns the year component of an `xs:dateTime` value.

- `fn:get-month-from-dateTime` returns the month component of an `xs:dateTime` value.

- `fn:get-day-from-dateTime` returns the day component of an `xs:dateTime` value.

- `fn:get-hours-from-dateTime` returns the hour component of an `xs:dateTime` value.

- `fn:get-minutes-from-dateTime` returns the minute component of an `xs:dateTime` value.

- `fn:get-seconds-from-dateTime` returns the second component of an `xs:dateTime` value.

- `fn:get-timezone-from-dateTime` returns the timezone of an `xs:dateTime` value.

- `fn:get-year-from-date` returns the year component of an `xs:date` value.

- `fn:get-month-from-date` returns the month component of an `xs:date` value.

- `fn:get-day-from-date` returns the day component of an `xs:date` value.

- `fn:get-timezone-from-date` returns the timezone of an `xs:date` value.

- `fn:get-hours-from-time` returns the hour component of an `xs:time` value.

- `fn:get-minutes-from-time` returns the minute component of an `xs:time` value.

- `fn:get-seconds-from-time` returns the second component of an `xs:time` value.

- `fn:get-timezone-from-time` returns the timezone of an `xs:time` value.

Each of these functions has its own syntax and usage, so we'll take a look at them briefly.

The `fn:get-years-from-yearMonthDuration` Function

This function lets you extract the year component of an `xdt:yearMonthDuration` value. Here's how it works:

```
fn:get-years-from-yearMonthDuration($srcval as xdt:yearMonthDuration?)
    as xs:integer?
```

This function returns an `xs:integer` representing the value of the year component of *$srcval*, which may be negative.

You can see an example in `ch11_03.xsl` (Listing 11.3), where we're extracting the years from the duration "P20Y03M" (20 years, 3 months). Note that to use `xdt:yearMonthDuration` values, we have to add an `xmlns:xdt` attribute to declare the `xdt` namespace: "http://www.w3.org/2003/05/xpath-datatypes".

LISTING 11.3   Using `fn:get-years-from-yearMonthDuration` (`ch11_03.xsl`)

```
<xsl:stylesheet version="2.0"
    xmlns:xsl="http://www.w3.org/1999/XSL/Transform"
    xmlns:xdt="http://www.w3.org/2003/05/xpath-datatypes"
    xmlns:xs="http://www.w3.org/2001/XMLSchema">

    <xsl:template match="/">
        <xsl:value-of select="get-years-from-yearMonthDuration(
            xdt:yearMonthDuration('P20Y03M'))"/>
    </xsl:template>

</xsl:stylesheet>
```

As you'd expect, this is the result when you use this example in Saxon:

```
<?xml version="1.0" encoding="UTF-8"?>
20
```

The `fn:get-months-from-yearMonthDuration` Function

This function just lets you extract the value of the month component of an `xdt:yearMonthDuration` value. Here's how you use it:

```
fn:get-months-from-yearMonthDuration($srcval as xdt:yearMonthDuration?)
as xs:integer?
```

This function returns an `xs:integer` representing the month component of `$srcval`, which may be negative. For example, `fn:get-months-from-yearMonthDuration(xdt:yearMonthDuration("P20Y03M"))` returns 3.

The `fn:get-days-from-dayTimeDuration` Function

The `fn:get-days-from-dayTimeDuration` function lets you extract the value of the day component from an `xdt:dayTimeDuration` value. Here's how you use it:

```
fn:get-days-from-dayTimeDuration($srcval as xdt:dayTimeDuration?)
    as xs:integer?
```

This function returns an xs:integer representing the value of the day component of *$srcval*, which may be negative. You can see an example in ch11_04.xsl (Listing 11.4), where we're extracting the number of days from the xs:dayTimeDuration value "P5DT11H" (5 days, 11 hours).

LISTING 11.4   Using fn:get-days-from-dayTimeDuration (ch11_04.xsl)

```
<xsl:stylesheet version="2.0"
    xmlns:xsl="http://www.w3.org/1999/XSL/Transform"
    xmlns:xdt="http://www.w3.org/2003/05/xpath-datatypes"
    xmlns:xs="http://www.w3.org/2001/XMLSchema">

    <xsl:template match="/">
        <xsl:value-of select="get-days-from-dayTimeDuration(
            xdt:dayTimeDuration('P5DT11H'))"/>
    </xsl:template>

</xsl:stylesheet>
```

And here's the result—5 days:

```
<?xml version="1.0" encoding="UTF-8"?>
5
```

The fn:get-hours-from-dayTimeDuration Function

The fn:get-hours-from-dayTimeDuration function lets you extract the value of the hour component of an xdt:dayTimeDuration value. Here's how you use it:

```
fn:get-hours-from-dayTimeDuration($srcval as xdt:dayTimeDuration?)
    as xs:integer?
```

This function returns an xs:integer containing the value of the hour component of *$srcval*, which may be negative. Here's an example:

```
fn:get-hours-from-dayTimeDuration(xdt:dayTimeDuration("P5DT11H")) returns 11.
```

The fn:get-minutes-from-dayTimeDuration Function

This function lets you extract the value of the minute component from an xdt:dayTimeDuration value. Here's how you use it:

```
fn:get-minutes-from-dayTimeDuration($srcval as xdt:dayTimeDuration?)
    as xs:integer?
```

This function returns an xs:integer representing the minute component of *$srcval*, which may be negative. You can see an example in ch11_05.xsl (Listing 11.5), where we're extracting the minutes from the xdt:dayTimeDuration value "P3DT11H22M".

LISTING 11.5   Using fn:get-minutes-from-dayTimeDuration (ch11_05.xsl)

```
<xsl:stylesheet version="2.0"
    xmlns:xsl="http://www.w3.org/1999/XSL/Transform"
    xmlns:xdt="http://www.w3.org/2003/05/xpath-datatypes"
    xmlns:xs="http://www.w3.org/2001/XMLSchema">

    <xsl:template match="/">
        <xsl:value-of select="get-minutes-from-dayTimeDuration(
            xdt:dayTimeDuration('P3DT11H22M'))"/>
    </xsl:template>

</xsl:stylesheet>
```

And here's the result when you use Saxon—22 minutes:

```
<?xml version="1.0" encoding="UTF-8"?>
22
```

The fn:get-seconds-from-dayTimeDuration Function

As you can guess from its name, this function extracts the value of the second component from an xdt:dayTimeDuration value. Here's the signature for this function:

```
fn:get-seconds-from-dayTimeDuration( $srcval  as xdt:dayTimeDuration?)
    as xs:decimal?
```

This function just returns an xs:decimal value representing the value of the second component of *$srcval*, which may be negative. Here's an example:

```
fn:get-seconds-from-dayTimeDuration(xdt:dayTimeDuration("P5DT11H23.4S"))
returns 23.4.
```

The fn:get-year-from-dateTime Function

This function extracts the year from xs:dateTime values. Here's its signature:

```
fn:get-year-from-dateTime($srcval as xs:dateTime?) as xs:integer?
```

This function returns an xs:integer representing the value of the year component of *$srcval*, which may be negative.

Here's an example where we're checking the year of someone's birthday. In this case, we'll check if that year is before or after 1900, as you can see in ch11_06.xsl (Listing 11.6).

LISTING 11.6   Using fn:get-year-from-dateTime (ch11_06.xsl)

```
<xsl:stylesheet version="2.0"
    xmlns:xsl="http://www.w3.org/1999/XSL/Transform"
    xmlns:xs="http://www.w3.org/2001/XMLSchema">
    <xsl:variable name="birthday"
        select="xs:dateTime('1899-07-04T19:21:00-05:00')" />

    <xsl:template match="/">
        <xsl:value-of select="if (get-year-from-dateTime($birthday) lt 1900)
            then 'Getting kind of old, eh?'
            else 'Happy Birthday!'"/>
    </xsl:template>

</xsl:stylesheet>
```

And here's the result:

```
<?xml version="1.0" encoding="UTF-8"?>
Getting kind of old, eh?
```

The fn:get-month-from-dateTime Function

This function just extracts the month from xs:dateTime values, and here's how you use it:

```
fn:get-month-from-dateTime($srcval as xs:dateTime?) as xs:integer?
```

This function returns an xs:integer between 1 and 12, inclusive, representing the value of the month component of *$srcval*.

Here's an example:

```
fn:get-month-from-dateTime(xs:dateTime("2004-07-11T19:21:00-05:00")) returns 7.
```

The fn:get-day-from-dateTime Function

This function returns the value of the day component from an xs:dateTime value, like this:

```
fn:get-day-from-dateTime($srcval as xs:dateTime?) as xs:integer?
```

When called, this function returns an xs:integer between 1 and 31, inclusive, representing the value of the day component of $srcval. Here's an example:

```
fn:get-day-from-dateTime(xs:dateTime("2004-05-31T13:20:00-05:00")) returns 31.
```

The fn:get-hours-from-dateTime Function

The fn:get-hours-from-dateTime function extracts the value of the hour component from xs:dateTime values, and here's what this function looks like:

```
fn:get-hours-from-dateTime($srcval as xs:dateTime?) as xs:integer?
```

Here, this function returns an xs:integer between 0 and 23, inclusive, representing the value of the hour component of $srcval. And here's an example:

```
fn:get-hours-from-dateTime(xs:dateTime("2004-11-09T12:00:00")) returns 12.
```

The fn:get-minutes-from-dateTime Function

As you can guess from its name, the fn:get-minutes-from-dateTime function extracts the value of the minute component from an xs:dateTime value, like this:

```
fn:get-minutes-from-dateTime($srcval as xs:dateTime?) as xs:integer?
```

This function returns an xs:integer value between 0 and 59, inclusive, containing the value of the minute component of $srcval.

The fn:get-seconds-from-dateTime Function

The fn:get-seconds-from-dateTime function extracts the value of the second component from xs:dateTime values, like this:

```
fn:get-seconds-from-dateTime($srcval as xs:dateTime?) as xs:decimal?
```

When called, this function returns an xs:decimal value between 0 and 60.999..., inclusive, corresponding to the value of the second component in $srcval (the value can be greater than 60 seconds to allow for leap seconds). Here's an example:

```
fn:get-seconds-from-dateTime(xs:dateTime("2004-08-19T11:30:29-05:00")) returns 29.
```

The fn:get-timezone-from-dateTime Function

This function lets you determine the timezone of an xs:dateTime value, and here's how you use it:

```
fn:get-timezone-from-dateTime($srcval as xs:dateTime?) as xdt:dayTimeDuration?
```

The `fn:get-timezone-from-dateTime` function returns the timezone component of *$srcval* as an `xdt:dayTimeDuration` value indicating the difference from UTC (its value may range from +14:00 to –14:00 hours, inclusive).

For example, this expression returns an `xdt:dayTimeDuration` value of "-PT5H":

```
fn:get-timezone-from-dateTime(xs:dateTime("2004-08-19T11:30:29-05:00"))
```

The `fn:get-year-from-date` Function

As you can gather from this function's name, it extracts the year from an `xs:date` value. Here's how you use this function:

```
fn:get-year-from-date($srcval as xs:date?) as xs:integer?
```

This function returns an `xs:integer` value containing the value of the year component of *$srcval*, which may be negative. For example, `fn:get-year-from-date(xs:date("2004-09-01"))` returns 2004.

The `fn:get-month-from-date` Function

The `fn:get-month-from-date` function just gets the month from `xs:date` values, and here's how you use it:

```
fn:get-month-from-date($srcval as xs:date?) as xs:integer?
```

This function returns an `xs:integer` between 1 and 12, inclusive, containing the value of the month component of *$srcval*. For example, `fn:get-month-from-date(xs:date("2004-03-11+05:00"))` returns 3.

The `fn:get-day-from-date` Function

This function returns the day component of `xs:date` values:

```
fn:get-day-from-date($srcval as xs:date?) as xs:integer?
```

The value returned is an `xs:integer` between 1 and 31, inclusive, containing the day component of *$srcval*. For example, `fn:get-day-from-date(xs:date("2004-03-11+05:00"))` returns 11.

The `fn:get-timezone-from-date` Function

This function extracts the timezone from `xs:date` values:

```
fn:get-timezone-from-date($srcval as xs:date?) as xdt:dayTimeDuration?
```

The value returned is the timezone component of *$srcval* as an xdt:dayTimeDuration value that indicates the difference from UTC (its value may range from +14:00 to –14:00 hours, inclusive). For example, `fn:get-timezone-from-date(xs:date("2004-03-11+05:00"))` returns an xdt:dayTimeDuration value of "-PT5H". The expression `fn:get-timezone-from-date(xs:date("2004-09-12Z"))` returns the xdt:dayTimeDuration value of PT0H.

The `fn:get-hours-from-time` Function

This function retrieves the value of the hour component of an xs:time value:

```
fn:get-hours-from-time($srcval as xs:time?) as xs:integer?
```

The returned value is an xs:integer between 0 and 23, inclusive, representing the value of the hour component of *$srcval*. For example, `fn:get-hours-from-time(xs:time("10:37:00"))` returns 10 and `fn:get-hours-from-time(xs:time("02:19:27+05:00"))` returns 21.

The `fn:get-minutes-from-time` Function

The `fn:get-minutes-from-time` function returns the minute component from an xs:time value:

```
fn:get-minutes-from-time($srcval as xs:time?) as xs:integer?
```

The return value is an xs:integer value between 0 to 59, inclusive, containing the value of the minute component of *$srcval*. For example, `fn:get-minutes-from-time(xs:time("14:23:19"))` returns 23.

The `fn:get-seconds-from-time` Function

This function returns the second component from an xs:time value:

```
fn:get-seconds-from-time($srcval as xs:time?) as xs:decimal?
```

The returned value is an xs:decimal value between 0 and 60.999..., inclusive. For example, `fn:get-seconds-from-time(xs:time("13:20:10.5"))` returns 10.5.

The `fn:get-timezone-from-time` Function

The `fn:get-timezone-from-time` function is the last of the date/time extraction functions, and it extracts the timezone from an xs:time value. Here's how you use it:

```
fn:get-timezone-from-time($srcval as xs:time?) as xdt:dayTimeDuration?
```

When called, this function returns an xdt:dayTimeDuration value containing the timezone component of *$srcval* as an xdt:dayTimeDuration value. The returned value indicates the difference of the timezone of *$srcval* from UTC (this value may range from +14:00 to –14:00 hours, inclusive).

For example, fn:get-timezone-from-time(xs:time("19:48:00-05:00")) returns an xdt:dayTimeDuration value of "-PT5H".

Functions That Adjust Time Zones

There's also a set of functions designed to adjust the timezone of xs:dateTime, xs:date, and xs:time values:

- fn:adjust-dateTime-to-timezone adjusts an xs:dateTime value to a specific timezone, or to no timezone at all.

- fn:adjust-date-to-timezone adjusts an xs:date value to a specific timezone, or to no timezone at all.

- fn:adjust-time-to-timezone adjusts an xs:time value to a specific timezone, or to no timezone at all.

The fn:adjust-dateTime-to-timezone Function

This function adjusts timezones for xs:dateTime values:

```
fn:adjust-dateTime-to-timezone($srcval as xs:dateTime?) as xs:dateTime?
```

```
fn:adjust-dateTime-to-timezone($srcval as xs:dateTime?, $timezone
    as xdt:dayTimeDuration?) as xs:dateTime?
```

When you call this function, it returns an xs:dateTime value with a new timezone as specified in *$timezone*. If you don't specify *$timezone*, *$timezone* is set to the value of the implicit timezone in the evaluation context. And if *$srcval* has a timezone component but *$timezone* is an empty sequence, *$srcval* is returned without a timezone component.

Here's an example:

```
fn:adjust-dateTime-to-timezone(xs:dateTime("2004-07-09T19:48:00"),
    xdt:dayTimeDuration("-PT02H"))
```

This example returns an xs:dateTime with the time "2004-07-09T19:48:00-02:00".

The `fn:adjust-date-to-timezone` Function

The `fn:adjust-date-to-timezone` function adjusts the timezone in `xs:date` values:

```
fn:adjust-date-to-timezone($srcval as xs:date?) as xs:date?
fn:adjust-date-to-timezone($srcval as xs:date?,
$timezone as xdt:dayTimeDuration?) as xs:date?
```

This function returns an `xs:date` value with the given timezone, or with no timezone at all. If *$srcval* does not have a timezone and *$timezone* is not the empty sequence, the result returned is *$srcval* with *$timezone* as the timezone component. If *$srcval* does have a time-zone component and *$timezone* is the empty sequence, the result is *$srcval* without a time-zone component. On the other hand, if you don't specify *$timezone*, *$timezone* is set to the value of the implicit timezone in the evaluation context.

For example, this expression returns an `xs:date` value with the date "2004-03-01-03:00":

```
fn:adjust-date-to-timezone(xs:date("2004-03-01"), xdt:dayTimeDuration("-PT03H"))
```

The `fn:adjust-time-to-timezone` Function

This is the last of the timezone-adjusting functions, and you use it on `xs:time` values:

```
fn:adjust-time-to-timezone($srcval as xs:time?) as xs:dateTime?

fn:adjust-time-to-timezone( $srcval  as xs:time?,
$timezone  as xdt:dayTimeDuration?) as xs:time?
```

This function returns an `xs:time` value with the given timezone, or with no timezone at all. If *$srcval* does not have a timezone and you pass a *$timezone* value, the result is *$srcval* with the timezone *$timezone*. If *$srcval* has a timezone component and *$timezone* is an empty sequence, you get *$srcval* back without a timezone component. As with the other timezone-adjusting functions, if you don't specify *$timezone*, *$timezone* is set to the value of the implicit timezone in the evaluation context.

For instance, this example returns an `xs:time` value set to "19:48:00-05:00":

```
fn:adjust-time-to-timezone(xs:time("19:48:00"), xdt:dayTimeDuration("-PT05H"))
```

Subtracting `xs:dateTime` Values

The final date/time functions in this chapter involve subtracting `xs:dateTime` values. We saw earlier that there are various operators that take care of subtraction for the date/time types, but with these functions you can specify if you want the result as an xdt:yearMonthDuration value or an xdt:dayTimeDuration value:

- fn:subtract-dateTimes-yielding-yearMonthDuration returns the difference between two xs:dateTime values as an xdt:yearMonthDuration value.

- fn:subtract-dateTimes-yielding-dayTimeDuration returns the difference between two xs:dateTime values as an xdt:dayTimeDuration value.

The fn:subtract-dateTimes-yielding-yearMonthDuration Function

As you can gather from its name, this function returns an xdt:yearMonthDuration value when you subtract two xs:dateTime values. Here's how you use it:

```
fn:subtract-dateTimes-yielding-yearMonthDuration($srcval1 as xs:dateTime,
    $srcval2 as xs:dateTime) as xdt:yearMonthDuration
```

The return value is an xdt:yearMonthDuration value containing the difference between $srcval1 and $srcval2.

For example, this expression returns an xdt:yearMonthDuration value holding the value 11 months:

```
fn:subtract-dateTimes-yielding-yearMonthDuration(xs:dateTime("2004-01-30T19:48:00"),
    xs:dateTime("2003-02-28T12:00:00"))
```

The fn:subtract-dateTimes-yielding-dayTimeDuration Function

This function returns the difference between two xs:dateTime values as an xdt:dayTimeDuration value:

```
fn:subtract-dateTimes-yielding-dayTimeDuration($srcval1 as xs:dateTime,
    $srcval2 as xs:dateTime) as xdt:dayTimeDuration
```

The return value is an xdt:dayTimeDuration value that contains the difference between $srcval1 and $srcval2 as an xdt:dayTimeDuration value.

For example, this expression returns an xdt:dayTimeDuration value corresponding to 1 day, 3 hours, 22 minutes, and 2 seconds:

```
fn:subtract-dateTimes-yielding-dayTimeDuration(xs:dateTime("2004-04-09T04:22:07"),
    xs:dateTime("2004-04-08T01:00:05"))
```

Functions That Work with QNames

There are two XPath 2.0 functions designed to create expanded QName values—xs:QName values:

- fn:resolve-QName returns an xs:QName following the form given in the first argument. The prefix is resolved using the namespace nodes for a given element.

- fn:expanded-QName returns an xs:QName with the namespace URI as given in the first argument and the local name as given in the second argument.

There is also a set of XPath 2.0 functions that are designed to work on xs:QName values:

- fn:get-local-name-from-QName returns an xs:string value containing the local part of the xs:QName you pass to this function.

- fn:get-namespace-uri-from-QName returns the namespace URI for the xs:QName value you pass.

- fn:get-namespace-uri-for-prefix returns the namespace URI of the in-scope namespace for the given element, that is associated with the passed prefix.

- fn:get-in-scope-prefixes returns a sequence of the prefixes of the in-scope namespaces for the given element.

We'll take a quick look at these functions here.

The fn:resolve-QName Function

This function creates an xs:QName value when you pass it a string, using the namespaces for a given element:

```
fn:resolve-QName($qname as xs:string, $element as element) as xs:QName
```

The return value is an xs:QName value that depends on the form of the string you pass to it— either *prefix:local-name* or *local-name*. The prefix you pass to this function is resolved using the in-scope namespaces of the element you pass it.

Here's an example. Say that the element node in *$element* has one namespace node, which is bound to the prefix xdata. In that case, this expression returns an xs:QName with local name "data" that is not in any namespace:

```
fn:resolve-QName("data", $element)
```

On the other hand, the following expression returns an xs:QName value whose namespace URI is given by the URI of the namespace node matching the prefix xdata and whose local name is data:

```
fn:resolve-QName("xdata:data", $element)
```

The `fn:expanded-QName` Function

This function creates an xs:QName value when you pass it a namespace URI and a local name:

```
fn:expanded-QName($URI as xs:string, $Local as xs:string) as xs:QName
```

The return value is an xs:QName that has the namespace URI given in $URI and the local name given in $Local. If $URI is an empty string, the return value has no namespace.

For example, this expression returns an xs:QName value with the namespace URI http://www.XPathCorp.com/actors and the local name carygrant:

```
fn:expanded-QName("http://www.XPathCorp.com/actors", "carygrant")
```

The `fn:get-local-name-from-QName` Function

The fn:get-local-name-from-QName function lets you retrieve the local name from an xs:QName value:

```
fn:get-local-name-from-QName($srcval as xs:QName?) as xs:string?
```

The return value is an xs:string representing the local part of $srcval.

Here's an example—in this case, we're creating an xs:QName value with fn:expanded-QName("http://www.XPathCorp.com/actors", "carygrant"), and then extracting its local name. You can see how this works in ch11_07.xsl (Listing 11.7).

LISTING 11.7   Using fn:get-local-name-from-QName (ch11_07.xsl)

```
<xsl:stylesheet version="2.0"
    xmlns:xsl="http://www.w3.org/1999/XSL/Transform"
    xmlns:xdt="http://www.w3.org/2003/05/xpath-datatypes"
    xmlns:xs="http://www.w3.org/2001/XMLSchema">

    <xsl:template match="/">
        <xsl:value-of select="get-local-name-from-QName(
            expanded-QName('http://www.XPathCorp.com/actors', 'carygrant'))"/>
    </xsl:template>

</xsl:stylesheet>
```

And here is the result, showing that we have indeed been able to extract the local name of this xs:QName value:

```
<?xml version="1.0" encoding="UTF-8"?>
carygrant
```

The `fn:get-namespace-uri-from-QName` Function

This function retrieves the namespace URI from an xs:QName value:

```
fn:get-namespace-uri-from-QName($srcval as xs:QName?) as xs:string?
```

The return value is the namespace URI for *$srcval* as an xs:string.

You can see an example in ch11_08.xsl (Listing 11.8), where we're extracting the namespace URI from the xs:QName we created in the preceding example: fn:expanded-QName("http://www.XPathCorp.com/actors", "carygrant"). (Note that get-namespace-uri-from-QName was previously named get-namespace-from-QName, which is the way it's implemented in Saxon, so we'll call it that in this example's code.)

LISTING 11.8   Using fn:get-namespace-from-QName (ch11_08.xsl)

```
<xsl:stylesheet version="2.0"
    xmlns:xsl="http://www.w3.org/1999/XSL/Transform"
    xmlns:xdt="http://www.w3.org/2003/05/xpath-datatypes"
    xmlns:xs="http://www.w3.org/2001/XMLSchema">

    <xsl:template match="/">
        <xsl:value-of select="get-namespace-from-QName(
            expanded-QName('http://www.XPathCorp.com/actors', 'carygrant'))"/>
    </xsl:template>

</xsl:stylesheet>
```

And here is the result, showing the namespace URI we want:

```
<?xml version="1.0" encoding="UTF-8"?>
http://www.XPathCorp.com/actors
```

The `fn:get-namespace-uri-for-prefix` Function

This function returns the namespace URI for a given prefix:

```
fn:get-namespace-uri-for-prefix($element as element,
    $prefix as xs:string) as xs:string?
```

The return value is an xs:string that is the namespace URI of the in-scope namespace for $element that matches the namespace prefix in $prefix.

For example, if the element node in $element has an in-scope prefix xdata that corresponds to http://www.XPathCorp.com, the following would return "http://www.XPathCorp.com".

```
fn:get-namespace-uri-for-prefix($element, "xdata")
```

The fn:get-in-scope-prefixes Function

This function returns a sequence of the in-scope prefixes for an element. Here's how you use this function:

```
fn:get-in-scope-namespaces($element as element) as xs:string*
```

To put this to work, we might add a new prefix, xdata, to our planetary data document like this:

```
<?xml version="1.0"?>
<planets xmlns:xdata="http://www.XPathCorp.com">

    <planet>
        <name>Mercury</name>
        <mass units="(Earth = 1)">.0553</mass>
        <day units="days">58.65</day>
        <radius units="miles">1516</radius>
        <density units="(Earth = 1)">.983</density>
        <distance units="million miles">43.4</distance>
        <!--At perihelion-->
    </planet>
        .
        .
        .
```

Now you can find the in-scope prefixes for the <planets> element as you see in ch11_09.xsl (Listing 11.9). (Saxon knows this function by its previous name, get-in-scope-namespaces, so we'll leave it like that for this example's code.)

LISTING 11.9   Using fn:get-in-scope-namespaces (ch11_09.xsl)

```
<xsl:stylesheet version="2.0"
    xmlns:xsl="http://www.w3.org/1999/XSL/Transform"
    xmlns:xdt="http://www.w3.org/2003/05/xpath-datatypes"
    xmlns:xs="http://www.w3.org/2001/XMLSchema">
```

LISTING 11.9 Continued

```
<xsl:template match="/planets">
    <xsl:value-of select="get-in-scope-namespaces(.)" separator=", "/>
</xsl:template>

</xsl:stylesheet>
```

Here are the results, showing the in-scope prefixes for the `<planets>` element, which are the xdata and the default xml prefixes:

```
<?xml version="1.0" encoding="UTF-8"?>
xdata, xml
```

In Brief

- XPath 2.0 supports these Boolean functions: `fn:true`, `fn:false`, and `fn:not`.

- XPath 2.0 also supports a large number of functions to work with times and dates, including: `fn:get-years-from-yearMonthDuration`, `fn:get-months-from-yearMonthDuration`, `fn:get-days-from-dayTimeDuration`, `fn:get-hours-from-dayTimeDuration`, `fn:get-minutes-from-dayTimeDuration`, `fn:get-seconds-from-dayTimeDuration`, `fn:get-year-from-dateTime`, `fn:get-month-from-dateTime`, `fn:get-day-from-dateTime`, `fn:get-hours-from-dateTime`, `fn:get-minutes-from-dateTime`, `fn:get-seconds-from-dateTime`, `fn:get-timezone-from-dateTime`, `fn:get-year-from-date`, `fn:get-month-from-date`, `fn:get-day-from-date`, `fn:get-timezone-from-date`, `fn:get-hours-from-time`, `fn:get-minutes-from-time`, `fn:get-seconds-from-time`, and `fn:get-timezone-from-time`.

- You can adjust the timezone of time/date values with these functions: `fn:adjust-dateTime-to-timezone`, `fn:adjust-date-to-timezone`, and `fn:adjust-time-to-timezone`.

- You can subtract `xs:dateTime` values to yield `xdt:yearMonthDuration` values or `xdt:dayTimeDuration` values with the `fn:subtract-dateTimes-yielding-yearMonthDuration` and `fn:subtract-dateTimes-yielding-dayTimeDuration` functions.

- There are two XPath 2.0 functions designed to create expanded QName values: `fn:resolve-QName` and `fn:expanded-QName`.

- There are also a set of XPath 2.0 functions that are designed to work on `xs:QName` values, and these functions are: `fn:get-local-name-from-QName`, `fn:get-namespace-uri-from-QName`, `fn:get-namespace-uri-for-prefix`, and `fn:get-in-scope-prefixes`.

XPath 2.0 Node and Sequence Functions

Using Node Functions

The XPath 2.0 node functions let you handle nodes, and here's an overview of these functions:

- `fn:name` returns the name of the specified node as an `xs:string` value.

- `fn:local-name` returns the local name of the specified node as an `xs:NCName` value.

- `fn:namespace-uri` returns the namespace URI as an `xs:string` value for a given node.

- `fn:number` returns the value of the specified item converted to an `xs:double` value.

- `fn:lang` returns a Boolean value, depending on whether the language of the context node (defined with the `xml:lang` attribute) matches the language passed to this function.

- `fn:root` returns the root of the tree to which the node argument belongs.

There's also a set of `op` functions (corresponding to operators we already know about) that we won't cover in detail:

- `op:is-same-node` returns `true` if the two arguments have the same identity. Backs up the `is` operator.

- `op:node-before` indicates whether one node appears before another node in document order. Backs up the `<<` operator.

■ op:node-after indicates whether one node appears after another node in document order. Backs up the >> operator.

We'll start covering the XPath 2.0 node functions in depth now.

The fn:name Function

This function returns the name of a node as an xs:string value, which satisfies the restrictions on xs:QName values:

```
fn:name() as xs:string
fn:name($srcval as node?) as xs:string
```

If you don't pass any argument to this function, it uses the context node. Also, if the node has no name (as is the case for a document node, a comment, a text node, or a namespace node having no name), you get an empty string return. If the node you're working with has a namespace prefix, you'll get the node's name in the form *prefix:local-name*.

You can see an example using this function in ch12_01.xsl (Listing 12.1), where we use this function to determine the name of a <planet> node in our planetary data document.

LISTING 12.1   Using fn:name (ch12_01.xsl)

```
<xsl:stylesheet version="2.0"
    xmlns:xsl="http://www.w3.org/1999/XSL/Transform"
    xmlns:xs="http://www.w3.org/2001/XMLSchema">

    <xsl:template match="/planets/planet[1]">
        <xsl:value-of select="name()"/>
    </xsl:template>

    <xsl:template match="/planets/planet[2] ¦ /planets/planet[3]">
    </xsl:template>

</xsl:stylesheet>
```

And here's the result:

```
<?xml version="1.0" encoding="UTF-8"?>
planet
```

The fn:local-name Function

This function is just the same as fn:name, except that it returns the node's local name only. Here's how you use it:

```
fn:local-name() as xs:string
fn:local-name($srcval as node?) as xs:string
```

If you don't supply an argument, this function uses the context node.

The `fn:namespace-uri` Function

This function returns the namespace URI of a node as an `xs:string` value:

```
fn:namespace-uri() as xs:string
fn:namespace-uri($srcval as node?) as xs:string
```

If you don't pass it any arguments, this function uses the context node. If the node has no namespace URI, you'll get an empty string return value.

The `fn:number` Function

The `fn:number` function treats the value of a node as a number and returns that number as an `xs:double` value. Here's how you use this function:

```
fn:number() as xs:double
fn:number($srcval as item?) as xs:double
```

Note that if the value of the node cannot be converted to an `xs:double` value (see the XPath specification for the exact details on how this conversion is made), the NaN (Not a Number) value is returned.

The `fn:lang` Function

This function lets you check the language of the context node—given by the `xml:lang` attribute:

```
fn:lang($testlang as xs:string) as xs:boolean
```

The `fn:lang` function returns `true` if the language of the context node is the same as—or a sublanguage of—the language given by `$testlang`, and `false` otherwise. Note that if there is no context node, this function returns `false`.

For example, say that we add an `xml:lang` attribute to our planetary data document:

```
<?xml version="1.0" encoding="UTF-8"?>
<planets>

    <planet xml:lang="en-us">
        <name>Mercury</name>
        <mass units="(Earth = 1)">.0553</mass>
```

```
        <day units="days">58.65</day>
        <radius units="miles">1516</radius>
        <density units="(Earth = 1)">.983</density>
        <distance units="million miles">43.4</distance>
        <!--At perihelion-->
    </planet>
          .
          .
          .
```

Now we can check the language used in this example as you see in `ch12_02.xsl` (Listing 12.2)
.

LISTING 12.2   Using `fn:lang` (`ch12_02.xsl`)

```
<xsl:stylesheet version="2.0"
    xmlns:xsl="http://www.w3.org/1999/XSL/Transform"
    xmlns:xs="http://www.w3.org/2001/XMLSchema">

    <xsl:template match="/planets/planet[1]">
        <xsl:value-of select="if(lang('en-us'))
            then 'Correct.'
            else 'Richtig.'"/>
    </xsl:template>

    <xsl:template match="/planets/planet[2] ¦ /planets/planet[3]">
    </xsl:template>

</xsl:stylesheet>
```

And here's the result:

```
<?xml version="1.0" encoding="UTF-8"?>
Correct.
```

The `fn:root` Function

The `fn:root` function returns the root of the tree to which the context node, or the node you pass, belongs. Here's how you use this function:

```
fn:root() as node
fn:root($srcval as node) as node
```

Note that the root node that this function returns is usually, but doesn't have to be, a document node. If you don't pass a node at all, the context node is used.

Here's an example—in this case, we'll select the first planet in our planetary data document, Mercury, and then access the name of the second planet using the expression root()/planets/planet[2]/name, as you see in ch12_03.xsl (Listing 12.3).

LISTING 12.3   Using fn:root (ch12_03.xsl)

```
<xsl:stylesheet version="2.0"
    xmlns:xsl="http://www.w3.org/1999/XSL/Transform"
    xmlns:xs="http://www.w3.org/2001/XMLSchema">

    <xsl:template match="/planets/planet[1]">
        <xsl:value-of select="root()/planets/planet[2]/name"/>
    </xsl:template>

    <xsl:template match="/planets/planet[2] | /planets/planet[3]">
    </xsl:template>

</xsl:stylesheet>
```

And here's the result—as you can see, we were indeed able to extract the name of the second planet this way:

```
<?xml version="1.0" encoding="UTF-8"?>
Venus
```

That takes care of the XPath 2.0 node functions; we're going to turn to the functions that handle sequences next.

The XPath 2.0 Sequence Functions

There are plenty of functions that work with sequences; here's an overview:

- fn:zero-or-one returns the sequence you pass to it if it contains zero or one items. Otherwise it raises an error.

- fn:one-or-more returns the sequence you pass to it if it contains one or more items. Otherwise it raises an error.

- fn:exactly-one returns the sequence you pass to it if it contains exactly one item. Otherwise it raises an error.

- `fn:boolean` casts a sequence to an `xs:boolean` value.

- `fn:index-of` returns a sequence of `xs:integer` values, each of which is the index of a item in the sequence given as the first argument that is equal to the value of the second argument.

- `fn:empty` indicates whether the passed sequence is empty.

- `fn:exists` indicates whether the passed sequence is not empty.

- `fn:distinct-values` returns a sequence from which duplicate values have been removed.

- `fn:insert-before` inserts an item or sequence of items into a sequence at a specified position.

- `fn:remove` removes an item from the given position in a sequence.

- `fn:subsequence` returns the subsequence of a given sequence. You pass the location at which to start the subsequence and, optionally, the length of the sequence.

- `fn:unordered` indicates that the given sequence may be returned in any order.

- `fn:deep-equal` returns `true` if the two passed sequences have items that compare equal in corresponding positions.

- `fn:count` returns the number of items in the passed sequence.

- `fn:avg` returns the average value of a sequence of values.

- `fn:max` returns the maximum value from a sequence of comparable items.

- `fn:min` returns the minimum value from a sequence of comparable items.

- `fn:sum` returns the sum of a sequence of values.

- `fn:id` returns the sequence of nodes having IDs that match IDREF values in the passed sequence.

- `fn:idref` returns the sequence of nodes with IDREF values matching the ID values in the argument sequence.

- `fn:doc` returns a document node retrieved from the given URI.

- `fn:collection` returns a sequence of document nodes retrieved from the given URI.

Sequences are new in XPath 2.0, and as you can see here, there's a rich set of functions to work with them. We'll take this list apart, function by function, in the remainder of this chapter, starting with the `fn:zero-or-one` function.

The `fn:zero-or-one` Function

This function returns *$srcval* if it is a sequence that holds zero or one items only. Here's how it works:

```
fn:zero-or-one($srcval as item*) as item?
```

This function does not handle the case where you've passed a sequence with more than zero or one items gracefully. Instead, it causes an error with this text: "fn:zero-or-one called with a sequence containing more than one item".

The `fn:one-or-more` Function

This function returns *$srcval* if it is a sequence that holds one or more items only. Here's how you use this function:

```
fn:one-or-more($srcval as item*) as item+
```

This function does not handle the case where you've passed a sequence with zero items well; in this case, it causes an error with this text: "fn:one-or-more called with a sequence containing zero items".

The `fn:exactly-one` Function

This function returns *$srcval* if it contains exactly one item:

```
fn:exactly-one($srcval as item*) as item
```

If you call this function with a sequence containing zero or more than one item, you'll get an error with the text "fn:exactly-one called with a sequence containing zero or more than one item".

SHOP TALK

EXCEPTIONS WITHOUT ERRORS

At this point in the development of the XPath 2.0 specification, it's a little difficult to see how the `fn:zero-or-one`, `fn:one-or-more`, and `fn:exactly-one` functions are intended to be used. No examples are provided in the XQuery 1.0 and XPath 2.0 Functions and Operators document.

If these functions are intended as simple tests, they'd probably be better implemented to return a Boolean value—something like this, where we're testing to avoid returning the empty sequences:

```
if(fn:one-or-more($seq)) then $seq else (1, 2, 3)
```

Instead, these functions either return simply the sequence you pass them, or cause an error. And the way these functions are written makes it look as though causing that error may be considered standard procedure.

Ever since the (very useful) introduction of try/catch blocks in languages like C++ and Java, programming language developers have become somewhat lax about the use of errors. This laxness has gotten to the point where runtime errors are being treated as a programming device rather than a recovery mechanism—instead of handling runtime errors as exceptions and trying to recover from them, language elements now routinely throw exceptions during normal processing as part of their standard operation.

However, there's considerable backlash against this kind of practice now, which abuses the exception-handling mechanisms built into programming languages. We'll see how these functions develop as XPath 2.0 develops, and whether they stay as they are or become more standard test functions instead.

The `fn:boolean` Function

This function returns the effective Boolean value of a sequence:

```
fn:boolean($srcval as item*) as xs:boolean
```

This function returns `false` if $srcval is the empty sequence. If $srcval is an atomic value, it returns `false` if $srcval is the singleton xs:boolean value `false`, "", a numeric value equal to zero, a singleton xs:double, or an xs:float value that is NaN.

Otherwise, this function returns a value of `true`.

The `fn:index-of` Function

This function returns a sequence of positive integers giving the position(s) in a sequence of an item. Here's how you can use `fn:index-of`:

```
fn:index-of($seq as xs:anyAtomicType*,
$srchParam as xs:anyAtomicType) as xs:integer*
```

```
fn:index-of($seq as xs:anyAtomicType*,
$srchParam as xs:anyAtomicType,
$collation as xs:string) as xs:integer*
```

In this case, $seq is a sequence to search, $srchParam is the item you're searching for, and $collation represents an (optional) collation.

This function lets you search sequences for multiple matches—here are a few examples:

```
fn:index-of((2, 3, 4), 2) returns 1.
fn:index-of((2, 3, 4), 3) returns 2.
fn:index-of((2, 3, 4), 5) returns ().
fn:index-of((2, 3, 3, 4), 3) returns (2, 3).
fn:index-of((2, 3, 3, 3, 4), 3) returns (2, 3, 4).
```

The fn:empty Function

This function tests for the empty sequence:

```
fn:empty($srcval as item*) as xs:boolean
```

If $srcval is the empty sequence, this function returns true; otherwise, this function returns false.

For example, fn:empty(()) returns true.

The fn:exists Function

The fn:exists function returns true if you pass it a sequence that is *not* the empty sequence, and false otherwise. Here's how you use it:

```
fn:exists($srcval as item*) as xs:boolean
```

Here are a few examples:

```
fn:exists(()) returns false.
fn:exists(1) returns true.
fn:exists((1, 2, 3)) returns true.
```

This function is a useful and quick one to make sure you're not dealing with an empty sequence.

The fn:distinct-values Function

You use fn:distinct-values to strip duplicate values from a general sequence:

```
fn:distinct-values($srcval as xs:anyAtomicType*) as xs:anyAtomicType*
```

```
fn:distinct-values($srcval as xs:anyAtomicType*,
$collation as xs:string) as xs:anyAtomicType*
```

Note that you can specify a collation with this function if you want to.

Here's an example; in this case, we're going to extract the distinct values from the sequence (1, 2, 2, 3) using fn:distinct-values, as you can see in ch12_04.xsl (Listing 12.4) .

LISTING 12.4   Using fn:distinct-values (ch12_04.xsl)

```
<xsl:stylesheet version="2.0"
    xmlns:xsl="http://www.w3.org/1999/XSL/Transform"
    xmlns:xs="http://www.w3.org/2001/XMLSchema">

    <xsl:template match="/">
        Here are the distinct values:
        <xsl:value-of select="distinct-values((1, 2, 2, 3))"
        separator=", "/>
    </xsl:template>

</xsl:stylesheet>
```

And here's the result—as you can see, we've been able to get the distinct values from the sequence:

```
<?xml version="1.0" encoding="UTF-8"?>
Here are the distinct values: 1, 2, 3
```

The fn:insert-before Function

As you can guess from its name, the fn:insert-before function lets you insert one sequence into another. Here's how you use this function:

```
fn:insert-before($target as item*,
$position as xs:integer,
$inserts as item*) as item*
```

This is the first of the sequence-editing functions that we'll cover. In this case, this function inserts the sequence $inserts into the $target sequence, starting at $position, and returns the results.

Note that there is no "fn:insert-after" function.

Here are a few examples:

```
fn:insert-before((1, 2, 3), 1, 4) returns (4, 1, 2, 3)
fn:insert-before((1, 2, 3), 2, 4) returns (1, 4, 2, 3)
fn:insert-before((1, 2, 3), 3, 4) returns (1, 2, 4, 3)
fn:insert-before((1, 2, 3), 4, 4) returns (1, 2, 3, 4)
fn:insert-before((1, 2, 3), 4, (4, 5, 6)) returns (1, 2, 3, 4, 5, 6)
fn:insert-before((1, 2, 3), 2, (4, 5, 6)) returns (1, 4, 5, 6, 2, 3)
```

As you can see, this powerful function lets you put your own sequences together from other sequences.

The fn:remove Function

This function simply removes an item from a sequence and returns the resulting sequence:

```
fn:remove($srcval as item*, $position as xs:integer) as item*
```

The fn:remove function removes the item in *$srcval* at position *$position* and returns the resulting sequence. There's no provision here for removing more than one item.

For example, we can convert the sequence (1, 2, 2, 3) to (1, 2, 3) using fn:remove, as you see in ch12_05.xsl (Listing 12.5).

LISTING 12.5   Using fn:remove (ch12_05.xsl)

```
<xsl:stylesheet version="2.0"
    xmlns:xsl="http://www.w3.org/1999/XSL/Transform"
    xmlns:xs="http://www.w3.org/2001/XMLSchema">

    <xsl:template match="/">
        Here is the result:
        <xsl:value-of select="remove((1, 2, 2, 3), 3)"
        separator=", "/>
    </xsl:template>

</xsl:stylesheet>
```

And here's the result:

```
<?xml version="1.0" encoding="UTF-8"?>
Here is the result: 1, 2, 3
```

The fn:subsequence Function

The fn:subsequence function lets you extract a subsequence from a sequence. Here's how you use this function:

```
fn:subsequence($srcval as item*, $start as xs:double) as item*

fn:subsequence($srcval as item*,
$start as xs:double,
$length as xs:double) as item*
```

This function is great when you want to carve a subsequence out of a sequence. Here are a few examples:

```
fn:subsequence((1, 2, 3, 4), 2) returns (2, 3, 4)
fn:subsequence((1, 2, 3, 4), 3) returns (3, 4)
fn:subsequence((1, 2, 3, 4), 2, 2) returns (2, 3)
```

The `fn:unordered` Function

You pass this function a sequence—or an expression that yields a sequence—and this function indicates that the resulting sequence may be returned in any order. Here's how you use this function:

```
fn:unordered($srcval as item*) as item*
```

The `fn:deep-equal` Function

This function compares two sequences and returns a Boolean value:

```
fn:deep-equal($parameter1 as item*, $parameter2 as item*) as xs:boolean
```

```
fn:deep-equal($parameter1 as item*,
$parameter2 as item*,
$collationLiteral as string) as xs:boolean
```

For this function to return a value of true, the two sequences must have the same values, which means that they have the same number of items and that items in corresponding positions in the two sequences must compare equal. Otherwise, the function returns false.

Here are some examples:

```
fn:deep-equal((1, 2, 3), (1, 2, 3, 4)) returns false.
fn:deep-equal((1, 2, 3), (1, 2, 3)) returns true .
```

The `fn:count` Function

The `fn:count` function works much the same way as the XPath 1.0 aggregate function count. In XPath 2.0, `fn:count` returns the number of items in a sequence. Here's how you use it:

```
fn:count($srcval as item*) as xs:integer
```

For example, `fn:count((1, 2, 3, 4))` returns 4, `fn:count(())` returns 0, and `fn:count((1, 2), (3, 4, 5))` returns 5.

The `fn:avg` Function

This function averages the numeric values (as well as `yearMonthDuration` and `dayTimeDuration` values) you pass to it and returns the result:

```
fn:avg($srcval as xdt:anyAtomicType*) as xdt:anyAtomicType?
```

This function just evaluates `sum($srcval)` `div` `count($srcval))` and returns the result.

You can see an example in `ch12_06.xsl` (Listing 12.6), where we're averging the values 1, 2, 3, and 4.

LISTING 12.6   Using `fn:avg` (ch12_06.xsl)

```
<xsl:stylesheet version="2.0"
    xmlns:xsl="http://www.w3.org/1999/XSL/Transform"
    xmlns:xs="http://www.w3.org/2001/XMLSchema">

    <xsl:template match="/">
        The average value is <xsl:value-of select="avg((1, 2, 3, 4))"/>.
    </xsl:template>

</xsl:stylesheet>
```

And here's the result:

```
<?xml version="1.0" encoding="UTF-8"?>
The average value is 2.5.
```

The `fn:max` Function

The `fn:max` function returns the maximum value of a sequence of values:

```
fn:max($srcval as xdt:anyAtomicType*) as xdt:anyAtomicType?
```

```
fn:max($srcval as xdt:anyAtomicType*,
$collation as string) as xdt:anyAtomicType?
```

Note that you can also include a collation when calling this function.

This function works as you'd expect—here are a few examples:

```
fn:max((1, 2, 3)) returns 3.
fn:max((1, 2, 1)) returns 2.
fn:max((6, 5, 4, 3, 2, 1)) returns 6.
```

The `fn:min` Function

As you can tell from this function's name, `fn:min` returns the minimum value from a sequence of values. Here are the signatures for this function:

```
fn:min($srcval as xdt:anyAtomicType*) as xdt:anyAtomicType?
```

```
fn:min($srcval as xdt:anyAtomicType*,
$collation as string) as xdt:anyAtomicType?
```

Here are some examples:

```
fn:min((1, 2, 3)) returns 1.
fn:min((7, 2, 1)) returns 1.
fn:min((6, 5, 4, 3, 2)) returns 2.
```

The `fn:sum` Function

This function returns a sum of the values that you pass it in a sequence:

```
fn:sum($srcval as xdt:anyAtomicType*) as xdt:anyAtomicType?
```

You can see an example in `ch12_07.xsl` (Listing 12.7), where we're using this function to add up the total masses in our planetary data document.

LISTING 12.7   Using `fn:sum` (ch12_07.xsl)

```
<xsl:stylesheet version="2.0"
    xmlns:xsl="http://www.w3.org/1999/XSL/Transform"
    xmlns:xs="http://www.w3.org/2001/XMLSchema">

    <xsl:template match="/">
        The total mass is <xsl:value-of select="sum(//planet/mass)"/>.
    </xsl:template>

</xsl:stylesheet>
```

And here's the result:

```
<?xml version="1.0" encoding="UTF-8"?>
The total mass is 1.8703.
```

The fn:id Function

This function lets you retrieve element nodes with specified ids; here's how you use it:

fn:id(*$srcval* as xs:string*) as element*

In this case, *$srcval* is of type xs:string and is treated as if it were of type xs:IDREFS, that is, as a space-separated sequence of tokens, each of which is interpreted as an xs:IDREF. The function returns a sequence of those elements that have an ID value equal to one or more of the IDREFs in the list of IDREFs (the ID values are set using attributes of type xs:ID) .

The fn:idref Function

This function works in much the opposite way as the fn:id function—it returns all the nodes with IDREF values that reference one or more of the IDs you pass to this function. Here's how it works:

fn:idref(*$srcval* as xs:string*) as node*

In this case, *$srcval* is treated as if it were a space-separated sequence of tokens, each interpreted as an ID.

The fn:doc Function

The fn:doc function is an interesting function that lets you read in entire documents. You just supply the URI of the document:

fn:doc(*$uri* as xs:string?) as document?

Note that *$uri* here must be an xs:string that obeys the restrictions for xs:anyURI. When you use this function, it will return a valid document node from the new document you're reading in, unless the URI cannot be resolved.

Say that you wanted to work with an entirely new document in the middle of processing another document—for example, you may want to fetch some crucial data from that new document that will aid in processing the current document. Being able to work with multiple documents in this way is powerful.

Here's an example; in this case, we'll read in our planetary data document and extract data from it. In this case, that document will be in the same directory as we're already working in, so we can load in that document using the fn:doc function this way in Saxon:

```
<xsl:template match="/">
    That planet is <xsl:value-of select="doc('ch02_01.xml')..."/>.
</xsl:template>
```

Now we have a document node for the target document, and can apply XPath expressions to it as you see in ch12_08.xsl (Listing 12.8), where we're extracting the name of the first planet in the document, which is Mercury.

LISTING 12.8   Using fn:doc (ch12_08.xsl)

```
<xsl:stylesheet version="2.0"
    xmlns:xsl="http://www.w3.org/1999/XSL/Transform"
    xmlns:xs="http://www.w3.org/2001/XMLSchema">

    <xsl:template match="/">
        That planet is <xsl:value-of select="doc('ch02_01.xml')//planet[1]/name"/>.
    </xsl:template>

</xsl:stylesheet>
```

And here's the result you get when you run this through Saxon:

```
<?xml version="1.0" encoding="UTF-8"?>
That planet is Mercury.
```

It's often more useful to load a new document into its own variable and work with that variable, which will be accessible throughout an XSLT document. For example, here's how that might look in this case, where we're assigning the planetary data document to a variable named $document:

```
<xsl:stylesheet version="2.0"
    xmlns:xsl="http://www.w3.org/1999/XSL/Transform"
    xmlns:xs="http://www.w3.org/2001/XMLSchema">
    <xsl:variable name="document" select="doc('ch02_01.xml')"/>

            .
            .
            .
```

Now we're free to use that variable in our XPath 2.0 expressions, like this:

```
<xsl:stylesheet version="2.0"
    xmlns:xsl="http://www.w3.org/1999/XSL/Transform"
    xmlns:xs="http://www.w3.org/2001/XMLSchema">
    <xsl:variable name="document" select="doc('ch02_01.xml')"/>

    <xsl:template match="/">
        That planet is <xsl:value-of select="$document//planet[1]/name"/>.
    </xsl:template>

</xsl:stylesheet>
```

You can also use the `fn:doc` function to compare two documents, using the `is` operator. You can see a simple example of this in `ch12_09.xsl` (Listing 12.9), where we're just comparing a document to itself.

LISTING 12.9 Using `fn:doc` to Compare Documents (`ch12_09.xsl`)

```
<xsl:stylesheet version="2.0"
    xmlns:xsl="http://www.w3.org/1999/XSL/Transform"
    xmlns:xs="http://www.w3.org/2001/XMLSchema">

    <xsl:template match="/">
        <xsl:value-of select="if(doc('ch02_01.xml') is doc('ch02_01.xml'))
            then 'The documents are the same.'
            else 'The documents are not the same.'"/>
    </xsl:template>

</xsl:stylesheet>
```

Here's the result—not surprisingly, when you compare a document to itself, the comparison reveals that the compared documents are the same:

```
<?xml version="1.0" encoding="UTF-8"?>
The documents are the same.
```

The `fn:collection` Function

This function is designed to let you work with collections of nodes, and here's how you use it:

```
fn:collection($srcval as xs:string) as node*
```

You pass it an `xs:string` value that is restricted to legal values for `xs:anyURI` and this function will return a document node from that URI, unless there's been an error. This function is not implemented in Saxon yet.

That completes our look at the node and sequence functions—and that completes our book on XPath 1.0 and 2.0.

We've come far in this book and covered a great deal, from the most basic up through many advanced topics. All that's left is to put all this technology to work for yourself!

In Brief

- XPath 2.0 contains a number of built-in functions to work with nodes—`fn:name`, `fn:local-name`, `fn:namespace-uri`, `fn:number`, `fn:lang`, and `fn:root`.

- XPath 2.0 also contains many built-in functions to work with sequences—`fn:zero-or-one`, `fn:one-or-more`, `fn:exactly-one`, `fn:boolean`, `fn:item-at`, `fn:index-of`, `fn:empty`, `fn:exists`, , `fn:distinct-values`, `fn:insert-before`, `fn:remove`, `fn:subsequence`, `fn:unordered`, `fn:deep-equal`, , `fn:count`, `fn:avg`, `fn:max`, `fn:min`, `fn:sum`, `fn:id`, `fn:idref`, `fn:doc`, and `fn:collection`.

Index

SYMBOLS

How can we make this index more useful? Email us at indexes@samspublishing.com

G

How can we make this index more useful? Email us at indexes@samspublishing.com

H - I

J - K - L

How can we make this index more useful? Email us at indexes@samspublishing.com

How can we make this index more useful? Email us at indexes@samspublishing.com

P

S

T

How can we make this index more useful? Email us at indexes@samspublishing.com

X

Y - Z

KICK START

< QUICK >
< CONCISE >
< PRACTICAL >

XSLT 2.0 Kick Start
by Andrew H. Watt
0-672-32437-7
$34.99

XQuery Kick Start
by James McGovern, et al
0-672-32479-2
$34.99

Struts Kick Start
by James Turner and Kevin Bedell
0-672-32472-5
$34.99

ASP.NET Kick Start
by Stephen Walther
0-672-32476-8
$34.99

Microsoft Visual C# .NET Kick Start
by Steven Holzner
0-672-32547-0
$34.99

ASP.NET Data Web Controls Kick Start
by Scott Mitchell
0-672-32501-2
$34.99

Mono Kick Start
by Hans-Juergen Schoenig and Ewald Geschwinde
0-672-32579-9
$34.99

Radio UserLand Kick Start
by Rogers Cadenhead
0-672-32563-2
$34.99